GOOD CHARTS

GOOD CHARTS

SCOTT BERINATO

The HBR Guide to Making Smarter, More Persuasive Data Visualizations

HARVARD BUSINESS REVIEW PRESS
Boston, Massachusetts

Printed in the United States of America

10 9 8 7 6 5 4 3

Library of Congress Cataloging-in-Publication Data

Names: Berinato, Scott, author.
Title: Good charts : the HBR guide to making smarter, more persuasive data visualizations / by Scott Berinato.
Description: Boston, Massachusetts : Harvard Business Review Press, [2016]
Identifiers: LCCN 2015046676 (print) | LCCN 2016002607 (ebook) | ISBN 9781633690707 (paperback) | ISBN 9781633690714 ( )
Subjects: LCSH: Business presentations—Charts, diagrams, etc. | Visual communication. | Communication in management. | BISAC: BUSINESS & ECONOMICS / Business Communication / Meetings & Presentations. | BUSINESS & ECONOMICS / Business Communication / General. | BUSINESS & ECONOMICS / Strategic Planning.
Classification: LCC HF5718.22 .B475 2016 (print) | LCC HF5718.22 (ebook) | DDC 658.4/52—dc23
LC record available at http://lccn.loc.gov/2015046676

The paper used in this publication meets the requirements of the American National Standard for Permanence of Paper for Publications and Documents in Libraries and Archives Z39.48-1992

ISBN: 978-1-63369-070-7
eISBN: 978-1-63369-071-4

M S
E

CONTENTS

INTRODUCTION

A NEW LANGUAGE AND A NECESSARY CRAFT

". . . for there is nothing either good or bad, but thinking makes it so."

—*Shakespeare*

IN A WORLD governed by data, in knowledge economies where ideas are currency, visualization has emerged as our shared language. Charts, graphs, maps, diagrams—even animated GIFs and emojis—all transcend text, spoken languages, and cultures to help people understand one another and connect. This visual language is used everywhere in the world, every day.

Dashboard maps in cars help commuters avoid the thick red lines of heavy traffic and find the kelly green routes where traffic is light. Weather apps use iconography and rolling trend lines to make forecasts accessible at a glance. Fitness-tracking apps default to simple charts that show steps taken, sleep patterns, eating habits, and more. Utility company bills include charts so consumers can see how their energy use compares with their neighbors'. Newspapers, magazines, and websites all use visualization to attract audiences and tell complex stories. The social web teems with data visualizations—some practical, some terrible, some rich with insight, some simply fun to look at—all vying to go viral. Sports broadcasts superimpose visual data on live action, from first-down lines on a football field to more sophisticated pitch-sequence diagrams and spray charts that show a baseball's trajectory and expose pitching and hitting trends.

You may not notice all the ways in which dataviz has seeped into your daily life, but you have come to expect it. Even if you think you can't *speak* this language, you hear it and understand it every day.

It's time to learn to speak it, too. Just as the consumerization of technology adoption and the widespread use of social media changed business, the ubiquity of dataviz in our lives is driving demand for good charts in unit meetings, sales presentations, customer research reports, performance reviews, entrepreneurs' pitches, and all the way up to the boardroom.[1] Increasingly, when an executive sees a line chart that's been spit out of Excel and pasted into a presentation, she wonders why it doesn't look more like the simple, beautiful charts on her fitness-tracker app. When a manager spends time trying to parse pie charts and donut charts and multiple trend lines on a company dashboard, he wonders why they don't look as nice or *feel* as easily understood as his weather app.

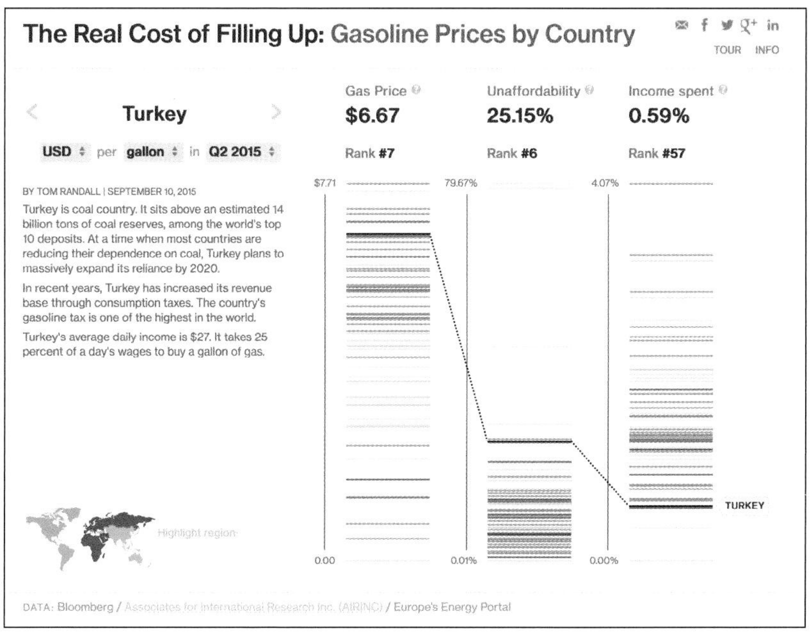

The Real Cost of Filling Up: Gasoline Prices by Country
TOUR INFO
Turkey
USD per gallon in Q2 2015
Gas Price
$6.67
Rank #7
Unaffordability
25.15%
Rank #6
Income spent
0.59%
Rank #57
BY TOM RANDALL | SEPTEMBER 10, 2015
Turkey is coal country. It sits above an estimated 14 billion tons of coal reserves, among the world's top 10 deposits. At a time when most countries are reducing their dependence on coal, Turkey plans to massively expand its reliance by 2020.
In recent years, Turkey has increased its revenue base through consumption taxes. The country's gasoline tax is one of the highest in the world.
Turkey's average daily income is $27. It takes 25 percent of a day's wages to buy a gallon of gas.
$7.71
79.67%
4.07%
0.00
0.01%
0.00%
TURKEY
DATA: Bloomberg / Associates for International Research Inc. (AIRINC) / Europe's Energy Portal

Data visualization is everywhere, from live sports to the news to fitness apps.

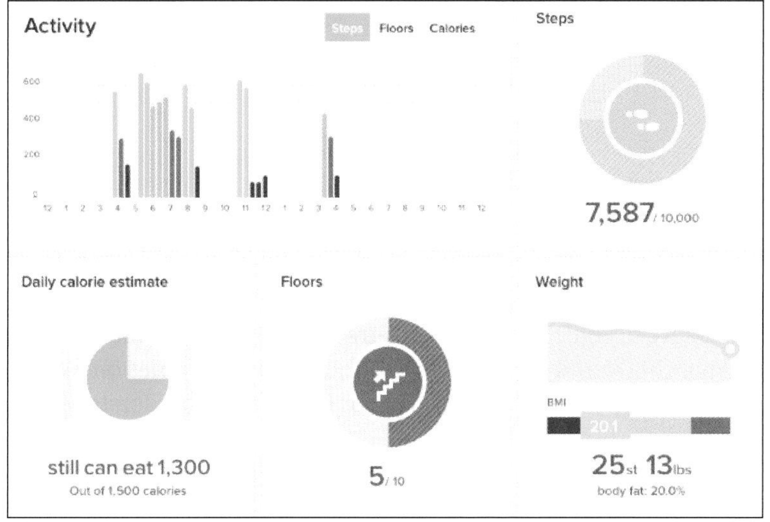

BUSINESS'S NEW LINGUA FRANCA

Speaking this new language requires us to adopt a new way of thinking—*visual thinking*—that is evolving quickly in business. Making good charts isn't a special or a nice-to-have skill anymore; it's a must-have skill. If all you ever do is click a button in Excel or Google Charts to generate a basic chart from some data set, you can be sure that some of your colleagues are doing more and getting noticed for it. No company today would hire a manager who can't negotiate the basics of a spreadsheet; no company tomorrow will hire one who can't think visually and produce good charts.

Dataviz has become an imperative for competitive companies. Those that don't have a critical mass of managers capable of thinking visually will lag behind the ones that do. Vincent Lebunetel is the vice president of innovation at Carlson Wagonlit Travel, which invests in hiring and training information designers. He says that business managers and leaders who can't create clear visualizations are just less valuable: "If you're not able to make your message simple and accessible, you probably don't own your topic well enough. And visualization is probably the best way to help people grasp information efficiently."

After a group at Accenture Technology Labs produced visualizations of NBA team shooting patterns that went viral, its consultants started asking the group for help producing charts that would produce a similar visceral reaction in their own clients.[2] So Accenture built an online and in-person "visual literacy curriculum" for them. The VLC has been so effective internally that Accenture is making the curriculum a client service and developing a visualization career track for its consultants.

Daryl Morey, the general manager of the NBA's Houston Rockets, puts it plainly: "Everyone in our business knows they need to visualize data, but it's easy to do it poorly. We invest in it. We're excited if we can use it right while they use it wrong."

So what's "right," and what's "wrong"?

WHAT'S A GOOD CHART?

The rise of visualization has generated numerous opinions about how to do it right—and harsh judgment of charts that get it wrong. Missing from most attempts to establish rules are an overarching view of what it means to think visually and a framework and repeatable process for constructing good charts.

To build fluency in this new language, to tap into this vehicle for professional growth, and to give organizations a competitive edge, you first need to recognize a good chart when you see one.

How about this Global Revenue chart? Is it a good chart?

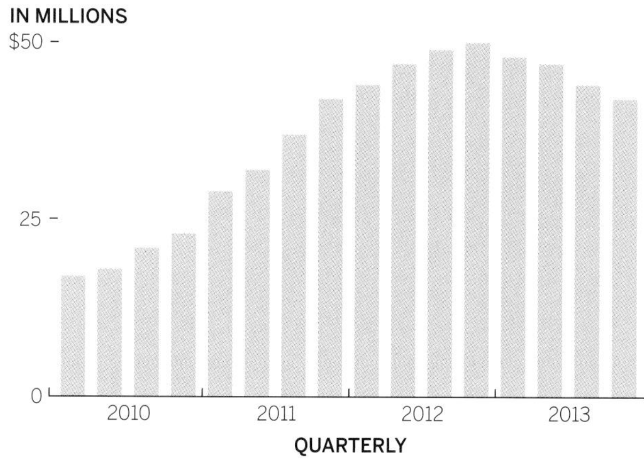

Ultimately, when you create a visualization, that's what you need to know. Is it good? Is it effective? Are you helping people see and learn? Are you making your case? Maybe even is it impressing your boss?

So, is this one good?

It certainly looks smart. It's labeled well. It eschews needless ornamentation. It uses color judiciously. And it tells a clear, simple story: After years of healthy growth, revenue peaked and then started to taper. If we held this chart up to the rules and principles proffered by data visualization experts and authors such as Edward Tufte, Stephen Few, and Dona Wong, it would probably pass most of their tests.[3]

But does that mean it's good?

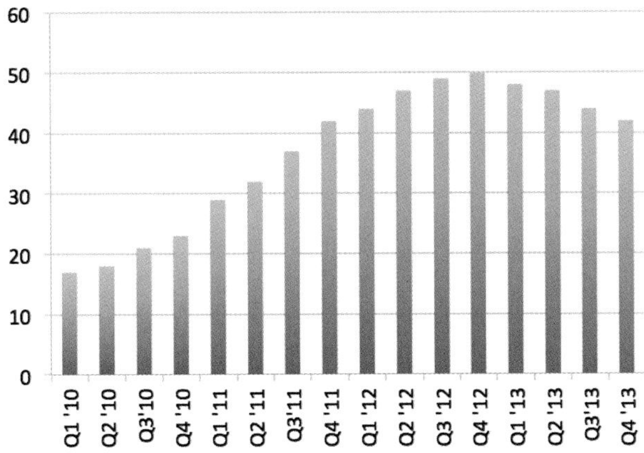

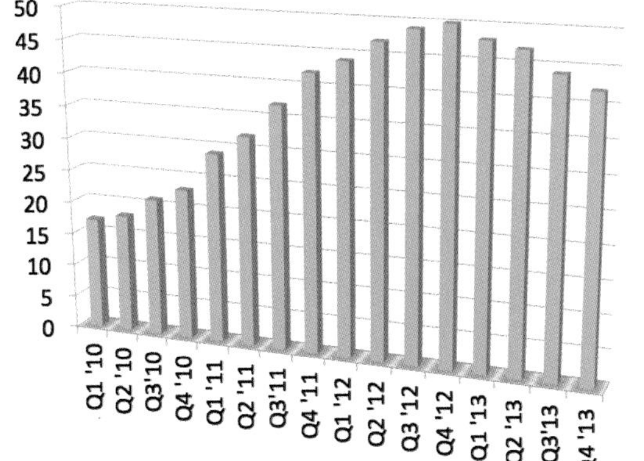

Data tools such as Excel can create charts almost instantly, but does that mean they're good charts?

It's probably better than what you could produce quickly in an Excel doc or a Google Sheet—most managers' go-to dataviz tools. You could turn a row of data into a chart there with a single click. And if you needed to present to the CEO, or to shareholders, you might play with some of Excel's preset options to make it look fancier and more dynamic. Many people love the 3-D option; it seems to draw the eye.

These tools are right there with our data, and they're very easy to use. But as dataviz becomes a *thing*, and we constantly encounter more well-designed, thoughtful, persuasive, and inspiring charts and graphs, we recognize that charts like these fall short, even if we can't say exactly why. As most managers use it, Excel visualizes data cells automatically, unthinkingly. The result beats looking at a spreadsheet—but that's a low bar.

So these charts aren't as good as the first one, but the question remains: Is that first chart good?

We don't know. Without context, no one—not me, not you, not a professional designer or data scientist, not Tufte or Few or Wong—can say whether that chart is *good*. In the absence of context, a chart is neither good nor bad. It's only well built or poorly built. To judge a chart's value, you need to know more—much more—than whether you used the right chart type, picked good colors, or labeled axes correctly. Those things can help make charts good, but in the absence of context they're academic considerations. It's far more important to know *Who will see this? What do they want? What do they need? What idea do I want to convey? What could I show? What should I show?* Then, after all that, *How will I show it?*

If you're presenting to the board, it may not be a good chart. The directors know the quarterly revenues; they're going to tune you out, check their phones, or, worse, get annoyed that you've wasted their time. Maybe they're looking for markets to invest in to reverse the revenue trend. In that case, a breakdown of changes in the global distribution of revenue might make a good chart:

REGIONAL REVENUE TRENDS, Q1 '10–Q4 '13

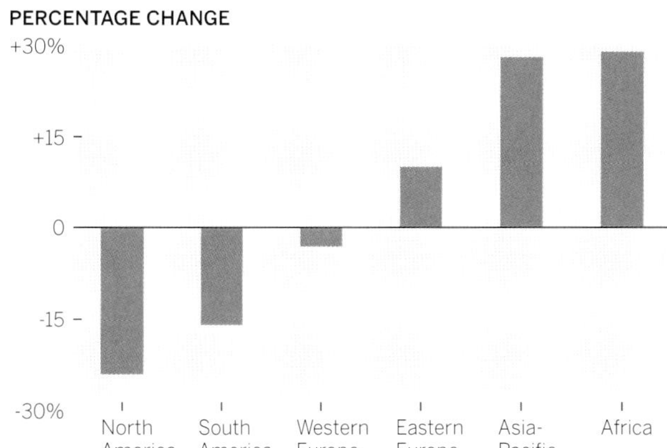

SOURCE: COMPANY RESEARCH

Same data set. Completely different chart.

If the boss has said, "Let's talk about revenue trends in our next one-on-one," this isn't a bad chart per se, but it may be overkill. In that scenario, the time spent refining the chart might be better used exploring ideas around the revenue data on a white-board, which has the advantage of being an interactive space, ready to be marked up:

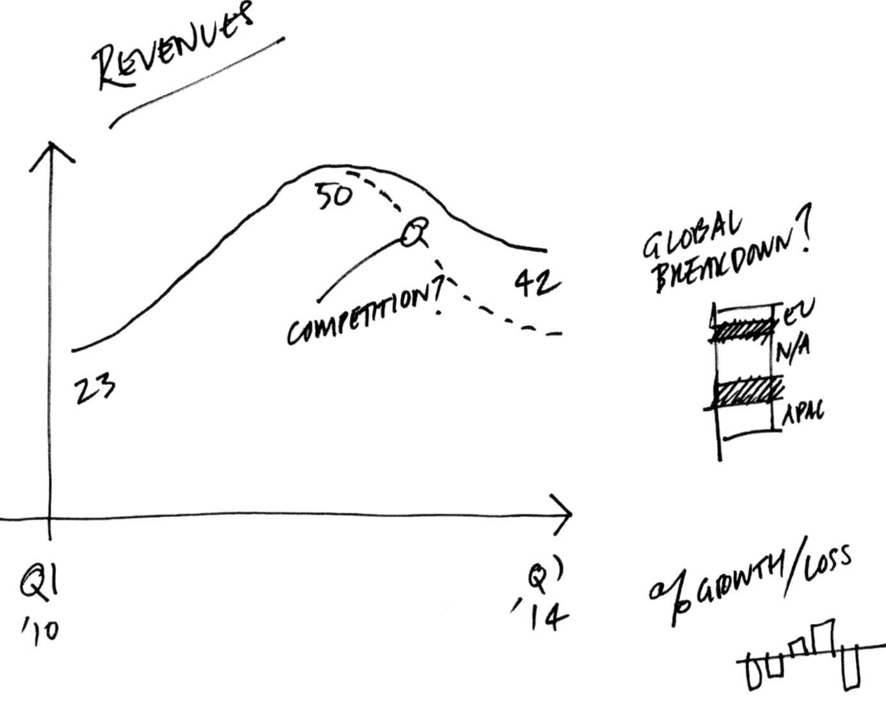

But if it's for a strategy off-site with the executive committee where future scenarios will be played out, it's probably not a good chart. How can you talk about the future with a chart that only shows the past? A good chart in that context would reflect multiple future scenarios, as seen on the Revenue Projections chart on the following page.

Then again, if you're meeting with a new manager who needs to understand basic facts about the company, then yes, the original chart is a good chart.

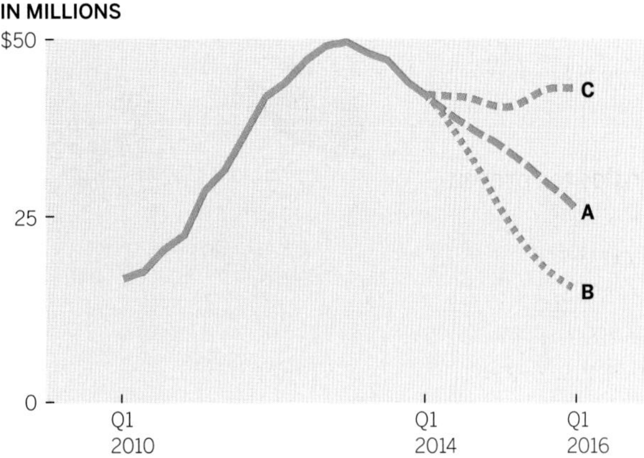

BEYOND RULES AND PLATITUDES

This simple example should liberate you from the idea that the value of a chart comes primarily from its execution (it doesn't) and that its quality can be measured by how well it follows the rules of presentation (it can't). Just as reading Strunk and White's *The Elements of Style* doesn't ensure you'll write well, learning visual grammar doesn't guarantee that you'll create good charts.

In his excellent *Style: Toward Clarity and Grace*, Joseph M. Williams explains why grammar rule books fall short:

Telling me to "Be clear" is like telling me to "Hit the ball squarely." I know that. What I don't know is how to do it. To explain how to write clearly, I have to go beyond platitudes.

I want you to understand this matter—to understand why some prose seems clear, other prose not, and why two readers might disagree about it; why a passive verb can be a better choice than an active verb; why so many truisms about style are either incomplete or wrong. More important, I want that understanding to consist not of anecdotal bits and pieces, but of a coherent system of principles more useful than "Write short sentences."[4]

What Williams says about writing is just as true for dataviz. You need to get beyond rules and understand what's happening when you encounter visualization. Why do you like some charts and not others? Why do some seem clear and others muddled?

How do you know, say, when to use a map instead of a line chart? One rule book for building charts states unequivocally, "No mapping unless geography is relevant."[5] That's like telling you to "hit the ball squarely." How do you know whether geography is relevant? What does *relevant* mean? Geography could be considered the most relevant factor in your chart showing regional revenue growth for the board. Should you map it instead?

Does a map make the point about regional revenues better than a chart does? Would it help you persuade the board that regional revenues matter? Are you even trying to do that? Would mapping this data geographically be worth the extra effort?

These questions seek the context that rules for presentations can't address. My point here is not to suggest that rules for crafting good visualizations aren't necessary or useful. They're both. But rules are open to interpretation, and sometimes arbitrary or even counterproductive when it comes to producing good visualizations. They're for responding to context, not setting it.

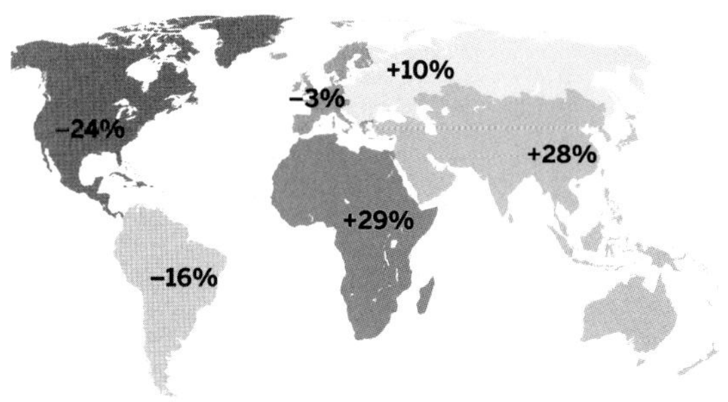

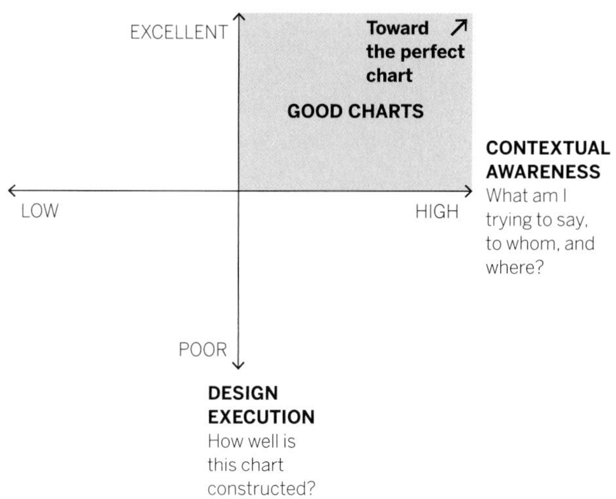

Instead of worrying about whether a chart is "right" or "wrong," focus on whether it's *good*. You need, as Williams says, principles that help you understand *why* you'd choose a bar chart or a line chart or no chart at all. A perfectly relevant visualization that breaks a few presentation rules is far more valuable—it's *better*—than a perfectly executed, beautiful chart that contains the wrong data, communicates the wrong message, or fails to engage its audience. The more relevant a data visualization is, the more forgiving, to a point, we can be about its execution.

The charts you make should fall into the top-right zone in the Good Charts Matrix, shown at the left. Learning to think visually in order to produce good charts is the subject of this book.

THE VISUAL THINKING IMPERATIVE

Three interrelated trends are driving the need to learn and practice visual thinking. The first is the massive increase of visualization, mentioned above. The more sophisticated, higher-quality dataviz in products and media we see now has raised expectations for the charts that others provide us, both in our consumer lives and in our business lives.

The second trend is data: both its sheer volume and the velocity with which it comes at us. So much information hitting us so fast demands a new way of communicating that abstracts, simplifies, and helps us cope.

At Boeing, for example, engineers want to increase the operational efficiency of the Osprey—a plane that takes off and lands like a helicopter. The plane's sensors produce a terabyte of data to analyze on each takeoff and landing. Ten Osprey flights produce as much data as the entire print collection of the Library of Congress.[6] The idea of scouring that data in any raw format borders on absurd, but they tried—a team of five worked on it for seven months, looking without success for ways to improve efficiency.

Then Boeing switched to visual analysis to find signals in the noise. Within two weeks a pair of data scientists had identified inefficiencies and maintenance failures. But it wasn't enough to find the signals; they had to communicate them to the decision makers. Their complex visualizations were translated into simpler ones for the management team, which approved changes to the Osprey's maintenance code. Operations improved. "It's hard to tell this kind of story," says David Kasik, a technical fellow at Boeing who worked on the Osprey project. "Ultimately we have to provide a form for telling our story in a way that others can in fact comprehend." That form is visual.

And it's not limited only to such specialized data. Even common data such as financials and marketing analytics, which companies generate as a matter of course, is so deep and complex now that they can't effectively deal with it in raw form.

The third trend: Everybody's doing it. Historically, some technologies have enjoyed a democratizing moment, when the innovation becomes cheap enough to buy and easy enough to use that anyone can try it. Examples of this shift are legion. Aldus PageMaker, the first word processor, and Hypertext Markup Language (HTML) each in its own way made everyone a potential publisher. Dan Bricklin, a cocreator of VisiCalc, the first spreadsheet, once said that his democratizing software "took 20 hours of work per week for some people and turned it out in 15 minutes and let them become much more creative."[7]

When ownership of the technology suddenly shifts from a small group of experts to the masses, experimentation flourishes, for better and worse. (HTML led to garish GeoCities websites, but also to Google.)

Dataviz is no different. What was once a niche discipline owned by a few highly skilled cartographers, data scientists, designers, programmers, and academics is now enjoying a noisy experimentation phase with the rest of us. For the first time, the tools used to visualize data are both affordable (sometimes free) and easy to use (sometimes drag-and-drop). Scores of websites have emerged that allow you to upload a data set and get bespoke visualizations kicked out in seconds. Tableau Software, currently a darling of visualization programming, aims to become no less than the word processor of data visualization, guiding your "visual grammar" and design for you.

Meanwhile, vast reserves of the fuel that feeds visualization—data—have been made freely or cheaply available through the internet. It costs virtually nothing to try to visualize data, so millions are trying. But drag-and-drop software can't ensure good charts any more than rule books can. Learning to think visually now will help managers use these burgeoning tools to their full potential when this adolescence ends, as it naturally will.

A SIMPLE APPROACH TO AN ACCESSIBLE CRAFT

The best news of all is that this is not a hard language to learn, even if it seems intimidating. Mastering a simple process will have an outsized impact on the quality and effectiveness of your visual communication. You may have heard people refer to the "art" of visualization, or the "science" of it. A better term for what this book presents is *craft,* a word that suggests both art and science. Think of a cabinetmaker, who may understand some art and some science but who ultimately builds something functional.

An apprentice cabinetmaker might start learning his craft by understanding cabinets—their history, how people use them, the materials and tools needed to make them. Then he'd learn a system for building good cabinets, and he'd probably build a hell of a lot of them. He'd also install them, and learn how cabinets work in different types of spaces and with different types of customers. Eventually his skills would be deep enough to add his own artistic and clever functional details.

Learning how to build good charts isn't unlike learning how to build good cabinets, so this book will proceed in the same way. Part one—**Understand**—provides a brief history of visualization and a high-level summary of the art and science behind charts. It leans on (and sometimes also challenges) the wisdom of experts and academics in visual perception science, design thinking, and other fields to illuminate what visualization is and what happens when a chart hits our eyes. In addition to providing an intellectual foundation, this brief section should assuage your fears about learning a whole new discipline. You don't have to become a professional designer or data scientist to reach a new level in your chart making.

With a foundation of knowledge in place, you can start making better charts. Part two—**Create**—is the practical core of the book. It lays out a simple framework for improving your charts. You'll learn what tools and skills you must develop (or hire) to succeed with each of four basic types of visualization. You'll learn how to think through what you want to show and then draft an approach. The process requires less effort than you might suspect. In as little as an hour you can vastly improve those basic charts you're used to spitting out of Excel. You may protest that because you're not a visual learner by nature, this will be harder for you. That's probably not true. Research suggests that although we clearly identify ourselves as either visual or verbal thinkers, that distinction may not exist.[8] Research also shows that anyone can improve basic visual fluency, just as anyone can learn enough fundamentals to communicate in a new language without mastering it.

Part three—**Refine**—turns to the important skill of rendering a soundly structured chart as a polished and artful visual, both impressive and persuasive. Rather than present a list of design dos and don'ts, it connects design techniques to the feelings they create. What techniques can you employ to make a chart feel *clean*, or so simple that viewers get it instantly? This section shows how to craft charts that don't just convey some facts clearly but change minds and impel people to action. It also explores the limits of persuasion and why certain techniques can drift across a blurry line into dishonest manipulation.

Finally, part four—**Present and Practice**—shows how to make charts even more effective by controlling how they're presented and using storytelling to get them beyond eyes and into minds. It also offers a framework for using self-directed "crit sessions" on your own charts and others' to help you find core ideas and learn how you like to craft them. It's also meant to provide an antidote to the burgeoning and frankly intimidating chart criticism that's carried out daily online and in Twitter feeds, wherein a community of dataviz enthusiasts takes it upon itself to judge visualizations publicly.[9]

Good Charts is structured as a single argument, but each of its four parts can also stand alone as a reference for information and inspiration, depending on your specific need, and a brief recap of key concepts is included at the end of each chapter. When your challenge is an upcoming presentation that will include charts, dive right into the **Present and Practice** section. If you're looking to think through some visual challenges with your team, use the **Create** section. I hope this book will become a well-worn, dog-eared companion.

Finally, a few points of relevant data: First, I use many words to describe visual communication, including *visualization, data visualization, dataviz, information visualization, infoviz, charts, graphs, information graphics,* and *infographics.* I recognize that some people assign specific definitions to these words. I'm staying out of that. Throughout this book, these words are general descriptors and I will vary use for readability and grace.

Second, the subject of data—finding it, collecting it, structuring it, cleaning it, messing with it—itself fills entire books. In order to focus on the process of visualizing, I begin after the data has been collected and assume that readers understand and use spreadsheets and other data manipulation tools regularly. For more-complicated data analysis and manipulation, I recommend working with experts using a *paired analysis* approach, discussed at length in chapter 4.

Finally, most of the charts in this book, and their narrative context, are based on real-life situations and real data. In some cases the data, the subject of a chart, names, or other attributes have been altered to protect identities and proprietary information.

A GOOD CHART

Before we get started, take inspiration from Catalin Ciobanu. Not long ago he was a physics PhD brand-new to the business world, hired as a manager at Carlson Wagonlit Travel. As a physicist, Ciobanu had learned to think visually; analyzing the massive data sets physicists use demanded it. "I had used many visual tools for analysis in science," he says, "and when I moved to business, I found everything based in Excel. I felt very, very limited in the amount of insights I could convey from this. Greatly limited."

Ciobanu was preparing for an event in Paris at which he'd present data to clients regarding what Carlson Wagonlit was learning about business travel and stress. The clients, he knew, were well versed in the aggregate figures on travel spending and the stress of business travel. But Ciobanu wanted them to see more. "What I wanted to convey wasn't in the Excel file," he says. "I wanted to convey this idea that travel stress is personal. It's about people."

After thinking through his challenge, Ciobanu produced this scatter plot:

WHO SUFFERS MOST FROM TRAVEL STRESS?

TRAVEL STRESS INDEX
70% –

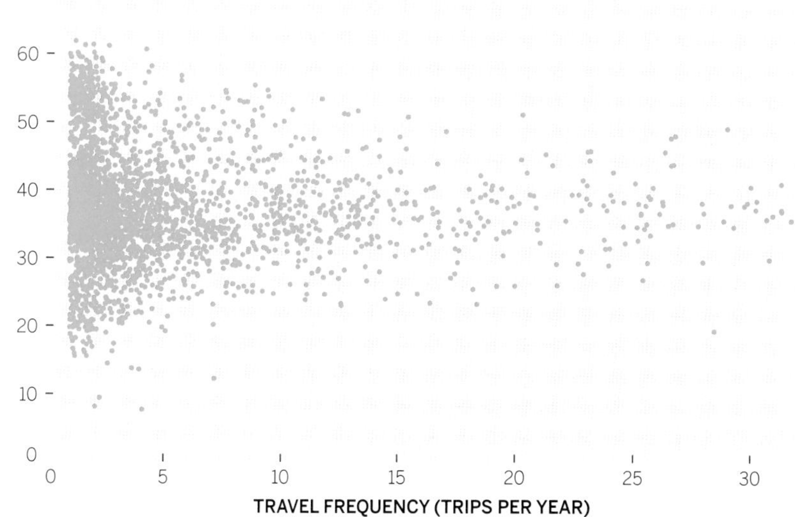

SOURCE: CARLSON WAGONLIT TRAVEL (CWT) SOLUTIONS GROUP, TRAVEL STRESS INDEX RESEARCH (2013)

When he put this chart up during his presentation, its effect was immediate and visceral. The dots created a sense of individuality that a table of percentages or trend lines couldn't. Ciobanu focused on individuality by plotting *everyone*, not categories of people combined in bars representing some aggregate level of travel frequency. "Every point here is somebody," Ciobanu says. "We found ourselves talking about people, not chunks of data." Even the title, with its use of *who*, stressed the humanness of the challenge.

On the spot, clients began forming new insights from this visualization. They had assumed that stress rose with frequency of travel along a steady slope—a positive correlation that goes up and to the right: as trips increase, stress increases. This chart, though, shows that stress can either increase or decrease with more-frequent travel. It *normalizes*. Infrequent travelers show wild variability in the amount of stress they experience.

The client group eagerly discussed why that might be. Maybe some people who rarely travel view any trip as a treat and don't let delays or cramped economy-class seating bother them. Or some travelers may have to coordinate home and work schedules while they're away without executive assistance, creating the greater stress of holding down the fort while hitting the road. (Both these hypotheses were borne out by further research.) The clients discussed how programs and services could be adjusted on the basis of this graph's shape alone.

"The conversation got passionate," Ciobanu remembers. "There were powerful outcomes in terms of re-sign rates and engagement." His colleagues and bosses were impressed, too; he gained respect for his visualization. "Following this," he says, "executives were coming to me asking me how we could show some data set of theirs, or asking if I could help them make their charts better. Personally, this was one of those moments where I hit the mark."

It was a good chart.

PART ONE

UNDERSTAND

CHAPTER 1

A BRIEF HISTORY OF DATAVIZ

THE ART AND SCIENCE THAT BUILT A NEW LANGUAGE

HERE'S A BREAKNECK SYNOPSIS of data visualization's development from simple communication tool to burgeoning cross-disciplinary science.

ANTECEDENTS

The first data visualization was probably drawn in the dirt with a stick, when one hunter-gatherer scratched out a map for another hunter-gatherer to show where they could find food. If data is information about the world, and if communication is conveying information from one person to another, and if people use five senses to communicate, and if, of those five senses, sight accounts for more than half our brain activity, then visualization must have been a survival tactic.[1] Far from being a new trend, it's primal.

For a long time, visualization was probably limited to cave paintings; eventually maps, calendars, trees (for example, genealogies), musical notation, and structural diagrams followed. In a sense, an abacus provides a visualization of data. No matter, I'm flying forward: Tables arrived in the late 17th or early 18th century and created spatial regularity that made reading many data points much less taxing. Ledgers were born. For two centuries, tables dominated.

What we think of as data visualization today—charts and graphs—dates to the late 1700s and a man named William Playfair, who in 1786 published *The Commercial and Political Atlas*, which was full of line charts and bar charts. He later added pie charts. Histories of infographics often start with a celebrated 1861 diagram by Charles Minard that shows the decimation of Napoleon's army during his doomed Russian campaign. Praise also goes to Florence Nightingale's "coxcomb diagrams" of British casualties in the Crimean War, published about the same time as Minard's famous chart. Nightingale's work is credited with improving sanitation in hospitals because it showed how disease, above all, was what killed soldiers.

BRINTON TO BERTIN TO TUKEY TO TUFTE

It's no accident that charting began to take off with the Industrial Revolution. Visualization is an abstraction, a way to reduce complexity, and industrialization brought unprecedented complexity to human life. The railroad companies were charting pioneers. They created some of the first organizational charts and plotted operational

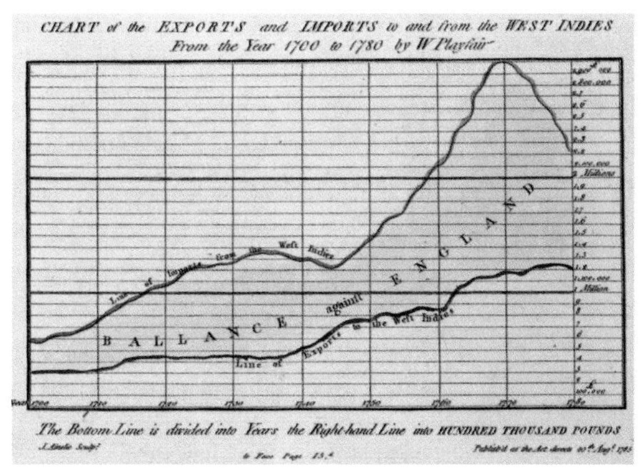

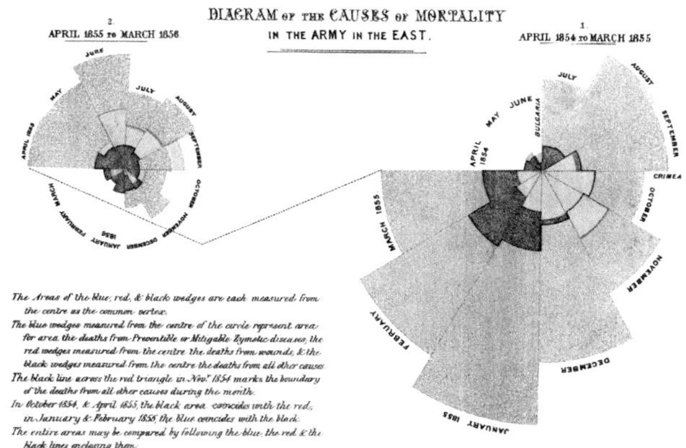

William Playfair, Florence Nightingale, and Charles Minard, the big three of early modern charting.

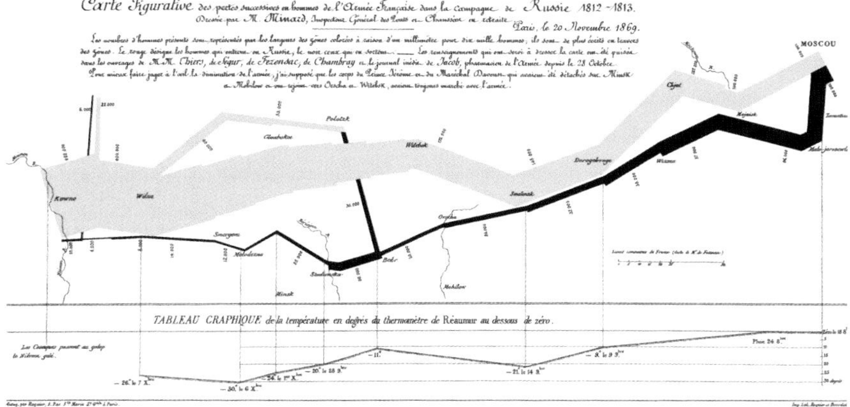

Willard Brinton's *Graphic Methods for Presenting Facts* provided advice to chart makers and critiques of charts in the early 20th century.

Fig. 3. **Disposition of a Family Income of from $900 to $1000**

This cut shows an attempt to put figures in popular form. The eye is likely to judge by the size of the pictures rather than by the angles of the sectors

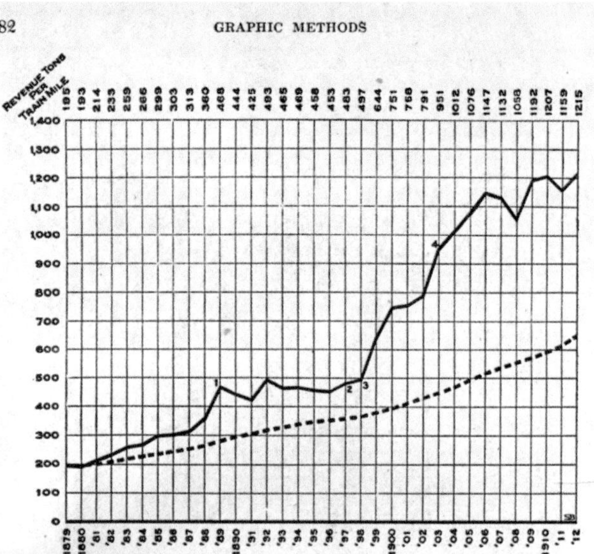

Fig. 80. **Yearly Average of Revenue Tons per Train Mile on the Pittsburgh and Lake Erie Railroad. The Slanting Line Shows a Progressive Average**

Here we have the data of Fig. 79 plotted in a curve which can be interpreted easily and accurately This chart may be considered a model of good practice in curve plotting. All of the work, including the lettering, has been done by hand, thus insuring better results than can usually be obtained from printing

data such as "revenue-tons per train mile" (line chart) and "freight car-floats at a railroad terminal" (dual-axis timeline).[2] The work of their skilled draftsmen was a prime inspiration for what can be considered the first business book about data visualization: *Graphic Methods for Presenting Facts*, by Willard C. Brinton, published in 1914.

Brinton parses railroad companies' charts (and many others) and suggests improvements. He documents some rules for presenting data and gives examples of chart types to use and types to avoid. Some of his work is delightfully archaic—he expounds, for example, on the best kind of pushpin for maps and how to prepare piano wire for use as a pin connector ("heated in a gas flame so as to remove some of the spring temper").

Then again, many of his ideas were in the vanguard. Brinton lays out the case for using small multiples (he doesn't call them that), currently a popular way to show a series of simple graphs with the same axes, rather than piling lines on top of one another in a single graph. He shows examples of bump charts and slope graphs, styles many people assume are more modern inventions. He looks askance at spider graphs (they should be "banished to the scrap heap"), and he questions the efficacy of pie charts a century ahead of today's gurus.

Eventually, Brinton lays out a system for creating "curves for the executive" which can "tell the complete story [of the business] in every detail if placed in proper graphic form."

By mid-century, the US government had become a complex and data-driven enterprise that demanded abstraction in unprecedented volume. Fortunately for the feds, they employed Mary Eleanor Spear, a charting pioneer who worked for dozens of government agencies and taught at American University. She produced two books in the spare, directive prose of someone who has a lot of work to do and not a lot of time to explain. *Charting Statistics* (1952) arose as a response to "problems encountered during years of analyzing and presenting data" in government. *Practical Charting Techniques* (1969) was an update and expansion on the previous. Spear's books, like Brinton's, are filled with commonsensical advice, along with some now-obsolete passages of her own (she expertly lays out how to apply various crosshatching patterns to distinguish variables on black-and-white charts). And she engaged in some ahead-of-her-time thinking—in 1952 she included tips and techniques for presenting charts on color TV.

Jacques Bertin, a cartographer, wanted to ground all this practical advice about chart making in some kind of theoretical foundation. So he formed a theory of information visualization in his watershed 1967 book, *Sémiologie graphique*. Rather than focus on which chart types to use and how to use them, Bertin describes an elemental system that still frames and provides the vocabulary for contemporary dataviz theory. He broadly defines seven "visual variables" with which we "encode" data: position, size, shape, color, brightness, orientation, and texture.[3]

Bertin also established two ideas that remain deeply influential to this day. The first is the *principle of expressiveness*: Say everything you want to say—no more, no less—and don't mislead. This is a reasonably universal idea: It's editing. Writers, composers, directors, cooks, people in any creative pursuit, strive (okay, struggle) to pare down their work to the essential.

The second is the *principle of effectiveness*: Use the best method available for showing your data. That is, choose the visual form that will most efficiently and most accurately convey the data's meaning. If position is the best way to show your data, use that. If color is more effective, use that. This second principle is obviously trickier, because even today, determining the "best" or "most appropriate" method isn't easy. Often, what's best comes down to convention, or taste, or what's readily available. We're still learning, scientifically, what's best, and the process is complicated by the fact that in a world of digital interactivity and animation, what's best may change from page to screen, or even from screen to screen.

Bertin was followed in the 1970s by John Tukey, a statistician and scientist who was making 3-D scatter plots way back in the mainframe era. Tukey can be credited with popularizing the concepts of *exploratory* and *confirmatory* visualization—terms I'll borrow to use later in this book.

Jock Mackinlay built on Bertin's work in his influential 1986 PhD thesis.[4] Mackinlay focused on automatically encoding data with software so that people could spend more time exploring what emerged in the visuals and less time thinking about how to create them. He also added an eighth variable to Bertin's list: motion. Working in computer science at the dawn of the PC era, he could see animation's powerful application for communicating data.

If Brinton is modern data visualization's first apostle, and Spear and Bertin its early disciples, Edward Tufte is its current pope. With disciplined design principles and a persuasive voice, Tufte created an enduring theory of information design in *The Visual Display of Quantitative Information* (1983) and ensuing tomes. For some, *Display* is visualization gospel, its famous commandments oft repeated. For example: "Above all else show the data" and "Chartjunk can turn bores into disasters, but it can never rescue a thin data set." Even though his work was rooted in scientific precision, Tufte is to the design-driven tradition what Bertin was to the scientific. A generation of designers and data-driven journalists grew up under the influence of Tufte's minimalist approach.[5]

ANDRIS ZOLTNERS

THE VISUALIZATIONS THAT LAUNCHED A COMPANY

"ZS exists because of visualizations that solved a tough problem."

The ZS Zoltners is referring to is ZS Associates, a global sales consultancy he founded, which now employs more than 3,500 people. The visualizations were maps and some simple line charts. The tough problem was assigning sales territories.

That may seem like a small thing, but in the late 1970s, it wasn't. "You have two problems you have to solve," says Zoltners. "Where do I put the salesperson? And then what customers, accounts, and prospects do I assign to him?" Companies would spend three to six months sketching out sales territories on paper maps by hand. It was a major challenge to get it right.

The territory problem became a chapter in Zoltners's dissertation. For a time it went no further than that, but he never stopped thinking about the problem. While teaching at the University of Massachusetts, he decided to take it up again; this time he worked with a Springfield, Massachusetts, company with 57 salespeople to see if he could solve its territory problem.

"I was messing around with optimization and discovered you could get math to solve the problem," he says. "You could create some search algorithms that did a good job aligning the sales force." Problem solved, right? Actually, no. "When I proposed the results, they didn't like it. We had good criteria for alignment. We created roughly the same workload for all the salespeople. But when I presented them with the results, it was a table. Names on paper that listed what counties the salespeople would call on."

The company didn't buy in.

Zoltners moved on to Northwestern and ended up in the B-school's marketing department. While he was searching for some tenure-track research, the alignment issue popped up again. This time, Eli Lilly was trying to solve the riddle. It was a tremendous challenge, because the pharma company relied on thousands of salespeople calling on hundreds of thousands of doctors in more than 40,000 zip codes.

By this time, the early 1980s, computers had arrived. Zoltners saw an opportunity. He and his colleagues—and a small army of grad students—built a massive (at the time) geographic database of state, county, and road maps of the entire United States. Then they wrote software that would allow them to trace out sales territories with a light pen. "We could just change the boundaries, right there on the map, with this light pen," he says.

In addition to the map, Zoltners created charts. "Our algorithms could predict for any sales force size what sales and profitability would be. When we hit the optimizer button, we'd generate this very simple chart. On the x-axis was the size of the sales force, and on the y was some measure like sales or profits. And we'd just show where they were now and where the alignment would put them. There was nothing like this at the time."

Reaction to the visualizations was immediate and visceral. "One man came up to me after we demonstrated it, and he just said, so earnestly, 'I've been waiting my whole life for this.'

"It was a bonanza. It started the company."

What had previously taken companies months now took a few weeks. (Part of Zoltners's business was providing a change process to implement the realignment.) Zoltners never advertised, but, he says, the phone never stopped ringing. One executive called and said, "I heard what you got. I have to see it." Zoltners apologized and said he was all booked. The executive said, "Make time for me. I'll come on Sunday." He did. And he bought in.

Another time, Zoltners flew from Chicago to Syracuse for a demo late in the week. He remembers fondly lugging his Apple II and a monitor on the plane as carry-on. When he arrived, a blizzard hit. Dozens of executives were expected, but only two people showed up. Back in Chicago that weekend, he told people in his growing office that there was no way they'd get business from the trip.

Both people who had shown up called that Monday, ready to buy. Since those early days, ZS has done more than 10,000 sales force alignments in 50 countries.

As he recalls the company's rocket trajectory, Zoltners is by turns excited and reverential. "Look, no one can get the kick we got in those days," he says. "You couldn't believe it. Every time we showed someone the maps and charts, they signed up."

Zoltners points out that the visuals didn't actually change the alignment algorithms he had worked out and used in Springfield, where he presented tables and lists of counties and zip codes. But they affected people in a way the raw information couldn't. "Without the visualizations," he says, "I could have optimized till the cows came home and we couldn't have done this. We'd get zero buy-in. Visuals helped with buy-in. It put them in control over choosing a solution, by *seeing* it. We were able to do what no one else could: we showed them what their options *looked like*."

EARLY EVIDENCE

While Tufte was declaring the best ways to create beautiful, effective charts, researchers were learning how people read them. In 1984 William S. Cleveland and Robert McGill took on "graphic perception" by testing how well people could decipher simple charts.[6] Pie charts have seemingly been under assault as long as they've existed, but Cleveland and McGill provided the first evidence that people find the curved area of pie slices more difficult to parse than other proportional forms. The two instigated a decade-plus of research aimed at understanding how we read charts and applying the results to a burgeoning visual grammar.[7] They felt duty-bound to challenge accepted wisdom: "If progress is to be made in graphics," they concluded, "we must be prepared to set aside old procedures when better ones are developed, just as is done in other areas of science." A few old procedures were set aside; a few new ones were developed.[8] This research deeply influenced the rapidly developing computer science community. Foundational texts that emerged from this era were Cleveland's *The Elements of Graphing Data* (1985) and *The Grammar of Graphics* (1999) by Leland Wilkinson.

Viz communities grew apart. Computer scientists increasingly focused on automation and new ways to see complex data, scientific visualization using 3-D modeling, and other highly specialized techniques. They were comfortable with visualizations that didn't look great. (In some ways this was unavoidable; computers weren't very good at graphics yet.) Meanwhile, designers and journalists focused on capturing the mass market with eye-catching, dramatic visuals and infographics.

Then the internet happened and messed up everything.

REFORMATION

Tufte couldn't have anticipated when he published *Display* that the PC, which debuted about the same time as his book, would, along with the internet that runs through it, ultimately overwhelm his restrained, efficient approach to dataviz. This century has brought broad access to digital visualization tools, mass experimentation, and ubiquitous publishing and sharing.[9]

The early twenty-first century's explosion of infoviz—good and bad—has spurred a kind of reformation. The two traditions have dozens of offshoots. The followers of Tufte are just one sect now, Catholics surrounded by so many Protestant denominations, each practicing in its own way, sometimes flouting what they consider stale principles from an academic, paper-and-ink world.

Some offshoots have mastered design-driven visualization in which delight and attractiveness are as valuable as precision.[10] Others view dataviz as an art form in which embellishment and aesthetics create

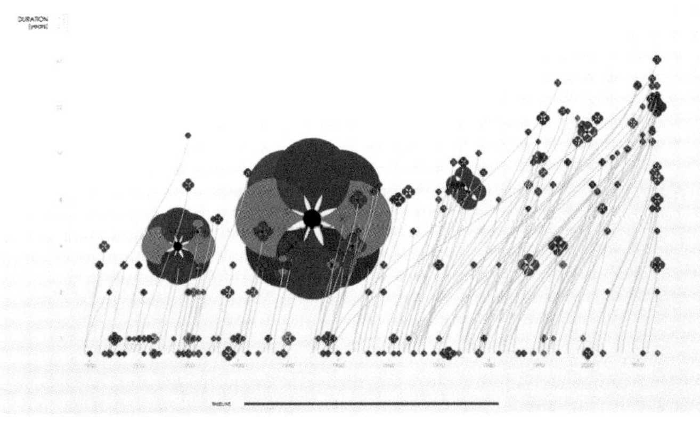

Once the province of a few experts and specialists, visualization now belongs to everyone, including designers, artists, journalists, and scientists.

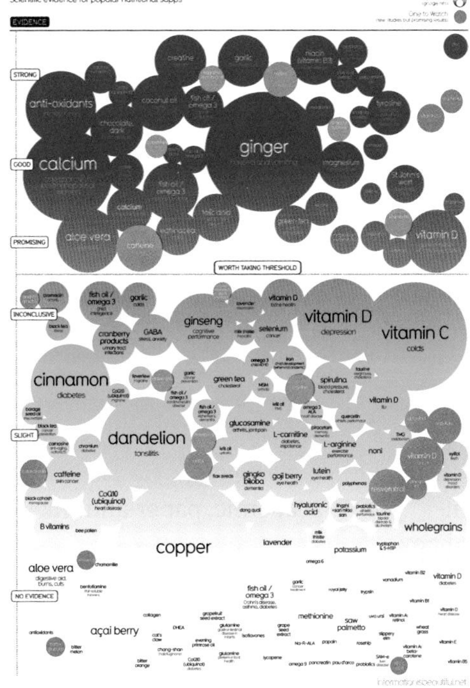

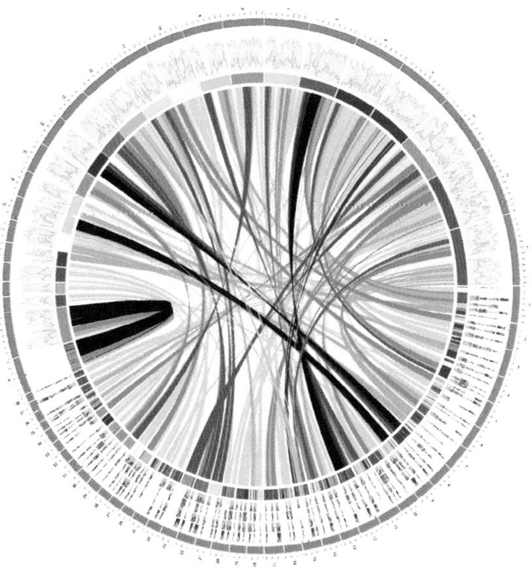

Beijing, like all of the Chinese cities analyzed here, has air pollution that maxes out in the winter. But unlike the other cities, its pollution bottoms out in spring and peaks around midnight.

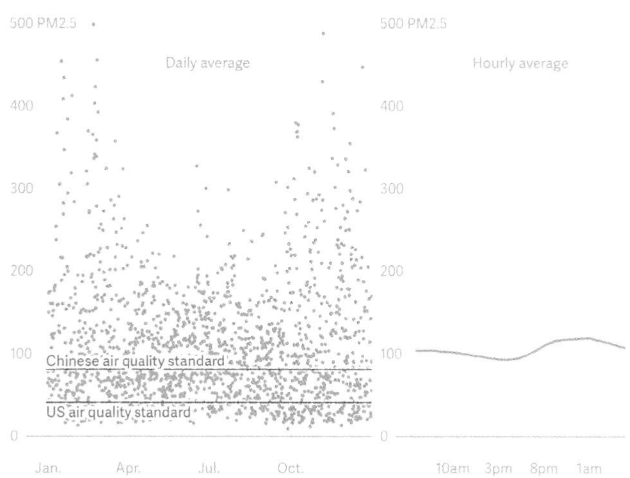

an emotional response that supersedes numerical understanding.[11] There are new storytellers and journalists who use visualization to bolster reporting and to lure and engage audiences.[12] Some use it as a means of persuasion, in which accuracy or restraint may be counterproductive.[13]

The point is, no one owns the idea of what data visualization is or *should be* anymore, because everyone does.

This transfer of ownership from experts to everyone has diminished the influence of scientific research from the 1980s and 1990s. Cleveland and McGill's results are sound, but most of their work focused on learning how people see static, mostly black-and-white charts, and it was limited to simple tasks such as identifying larger and smaller values. In a full-color, digital, interactive world, new research is needed.

Additionally, two assumptions were embedded in that early research: The first is that chart makers already have the undivided attention of the person decoding the chart. They don't. You need only look at a Twitter feed, or at all the faces staring down at smartphones during presentations, to know that every chart must fight to be seen. Early research didn't test how charts gain attention in the first place, which requires different and possibly conflicting techniques from the ones that show data most effectively. For example, complexity and color catch the eye; they're captivating. They can also make it harder to extract meaning from a chart.

The second assumption is that the most efficient and effective transfer of the encoded data is always our primary goal when creating a visualization. It's not. Our judgments may not be as precise with pie charts as they are with bar charts, but they may be *accurate enough*. If one chart type is *most* effective, that doesn't mean others are *in*effective. Managers know they must make trade-offs: Maybe the resources required to use the *best* chart type aren't worth the time or effort. Maybe a colleague just seems to respond more positively to pie charts. Context matters.

AN EMERGING SCIENCE

The next key moment in the history of dataviz is now. This disruptive, democratizing moment has fractured data visualization into a thousand different ideas, with little agreed-upon science to help put it back together. But a group of active, mostly young researchers have flocked to the field to try. While honoring the work of the 1980s and 1990s, they're also moving past it, attempting to understand dataviz as a physiological and psychological phenomenon. They're borrowing from contemporary research in visual perception, neuroscience, cognitive psychology, and even behavioral economics.

Here are some important findings from this new school of researchers:

Chartjunk may not be so bad. *Chartjunk* is Tufte's term for embellishment or manipulation—such as 3-D bars, icons, and illustrations—that doesn't add to data's meaning or clarity. It has long been scoffed at, but new research suggests that it can make some charts more memorable.[14] Other studies are evaluating the role of aesthetics, persuasiveness, and memorability in chart effectiveness. The findings aren't yet definitive, but they won't all align with the long-held design principles of the past. Some research even suggests that if you have only a few categories of information, a pie chart is probably fine.[15]

A chart's effectiveness is not an absolute consideration. Of course, reality is turning out to be far more complicated than "Don't use pie charts" or "Line charts work best for trends." Personality type, gender, display media, even the mood you're in when you see the chart—all will change your perception of the visualization and its effectiveness.[16] There may even be times to forgo visualization altogether.[17] Research shows that charts help people see and correct their factual misperceptions when they're uncertain or lack strong opinions about a topic. But when we understand a topic well or feel deep opposition to the idea being presented, visuals don't persuade us. Charts that present ideas counter to our strongly held beliefs threaten our sense of identity; when that happens, simply presenting more and more visuals to prove a point seems to backfire. (The research goes on to suggest that what's more persuasive in those situations is affirmation—being reminded that we're good, thoughtful people.[18]) The takeaway here is that if you're looking for a key to tell you what chart to use when, it doesn't exist and won't exist for the foreseeable future.

Visualization literacy can be measured. Some researchers are attempting to create standard visual literacy levels. Early results suggest that most people test just below what could be considered "dataviz literate," but that they can be taught to become proficient or even fluent with charts and graphs.[19] This research also shows that we don't trust our judgments of charts as much as we should: even when we correctly identify the idea a chart conveys, we want to check whether we're right.

Our visual systems are quite good at math. In some cases we can process multiple cues simultaneously, and when we're looking at charts with multiple variables (say, color and size), our ability to identify average values and variability is more precise than when we're looking at numbers. This suggests that representation is sometimes a more intuitive and human way to understand values than statistics is.[20]

This idea that we sense values visually—that we do math with our eyes—is buttressed by breakthrough findings from Ronald Rensink of the University of British Columbia. Rensink has demonstrated that our ability to detect change in charts seems to follow a fundamental rule of sensory perception known as Weber's law.

Weber's law states that "a noticeable change in stimulus is a constant ratio of the original stimulus."[21] Imagine a perfectly black room. Light a match, and you'll notice a big change in how bright the room is. But if you start with three lamps turned on, lighting a single match won't make the room seem brighter. The more light that exists to begin with, the more light you need to add to notice any change in brightness.

A

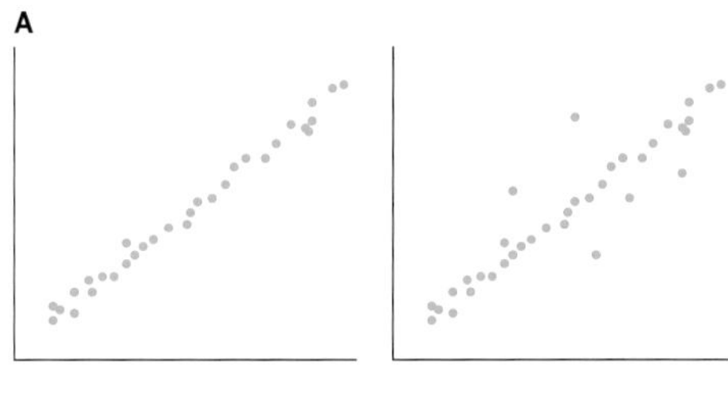

B

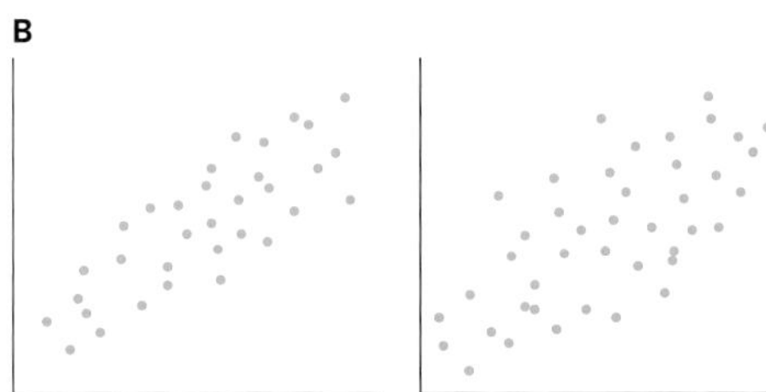

C

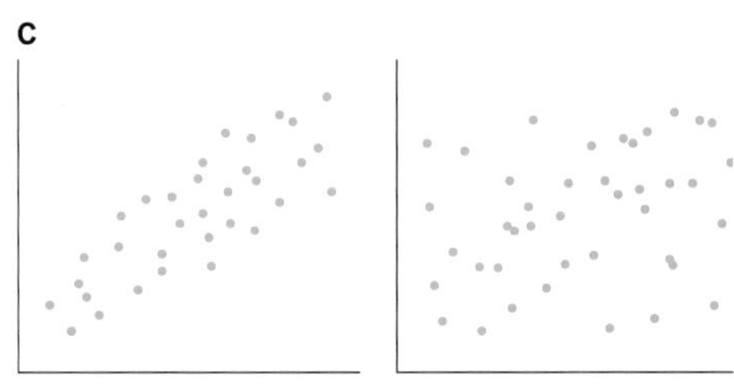

SOURCE: LANE HARRISON

The key to Weber's law is that the relationship between starting state and new state is predictable and linear—twice as much original light means you need to generate twice as much new light to create a "just noticeable difference" or JND. We perceive change in the world in this linear way with light and color, scent, weight, sound, even how salty something tastes.

Rensink has discovered that we perceive change in correlation in scatter plots the same way.[22] For example, in scatter plot pair A, with a correlation near 1, you notice a big change when just a few dots are moved.

But pair B has a correlation around 0.5, so you don't notice much change in correlation when the same number of dots as before are moved. Weber's law tells you how much change you'd need to show before someone noticed a difference: twice as much, as shown in pair C.

Rensink's breakthrough has been replicated and applied to other types of correlative (and negatively correlative) charts by Lane Harrison and a group at Tufts University. The implications of a predictable pattern to seeing correlation are profound, for two reasons. First, if Weber's law applies to an instance of higher-order thinking, not just fundamental physical stimuli like light, then maybe we're not reading data at all, but rather "encoding down," as Harrison puts it, to something much more fundamental, such as shape, angle, and space, which we then "calculate" visually to find correlation.

Second, although the relationship between perception and correlation is linear for all types of charts the researchers tested, the linear *rate* varies between chart types. As shown in the Perceiving Change chart set on the facing page, people see a difference between 0.3 and 0.8 correlations much more easily in a scatter plot than they do in a line chart.[23]

That means we can begin to measure and rank order the effectiveness of various chart types for showing correlation (and negative correlation)—which Harrison has done, and others have built on. The results of their work is shown in the Ranking Methods matrix on the facing page.[24]

PERCEIVING CHANGE

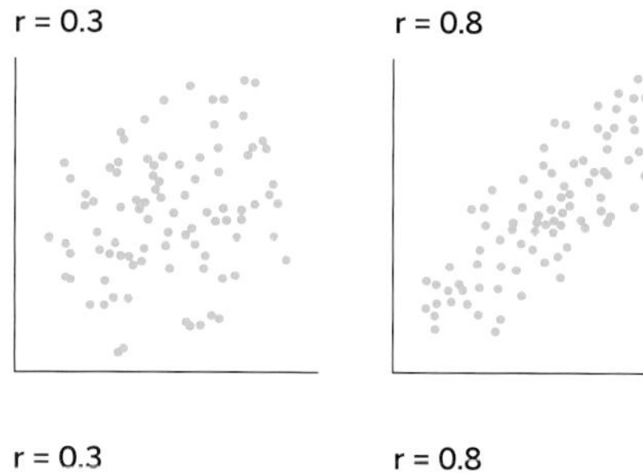

r = 0.3

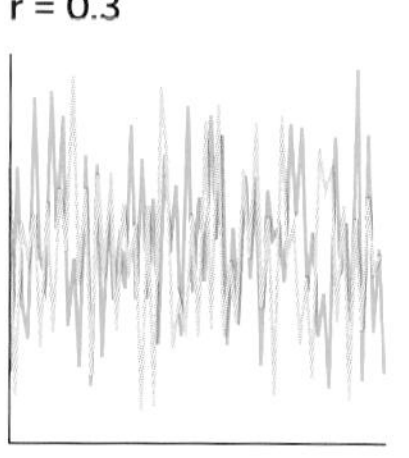

r = 0.8

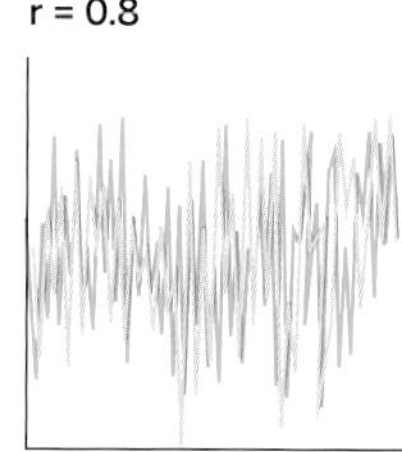

SOURCE: LANE HARRISON

Rensink, too, is using this discovery to test the effectiveness of chart forms. He has discovered that we see correlation changes in strip plots and color plots, shown on the next page, as well as or better than we do in scatter plots.

Many in the dataviz world believe in space *über alles*, the idea that spatial relationships are the best way to plot data. But these effective forms use space only on the x-axis, making them more compact than charts with traditional spatially oriented y-axes. Because we descry correlation here as well as or better than in scatter plots, these under-utilized chart types could be valuable. Perhaps,

RANKING METHODS TO SHOW CORRELATION

GOOD

Scatter plot (positive)

Ordered line (positive)

Stacked line (negative)

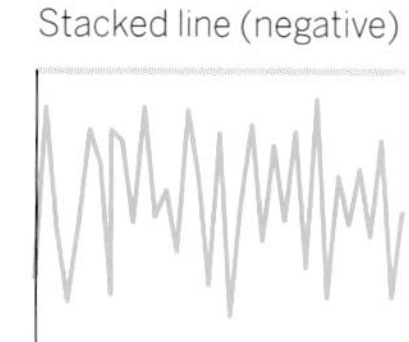

OKAY

Slope graph (negative)

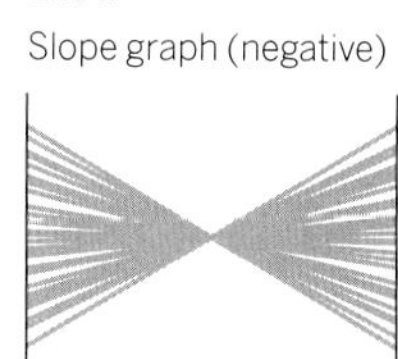

Donut (negative)

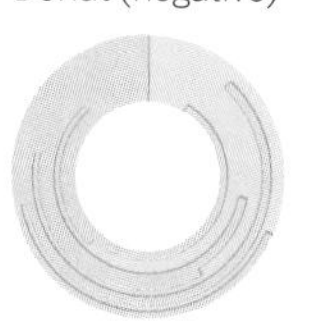

Parallel coordinate (positive)

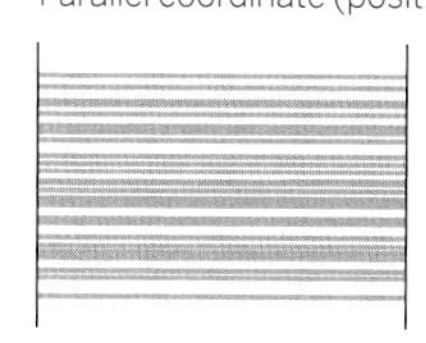

Scatter plot (negative)

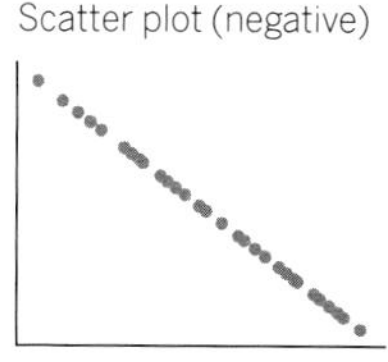

Stacked area (negative)

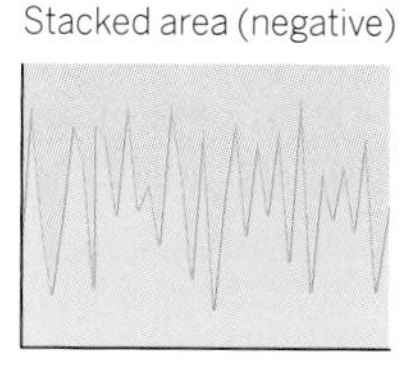

BAD

Stacked bar (negative)

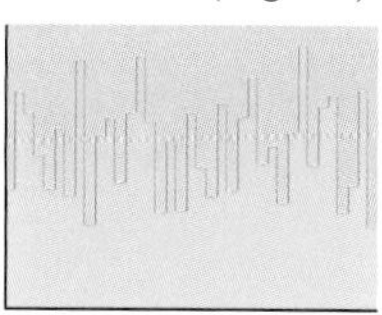

Ordered line (negative)

Line (positive)

Radar (positive)

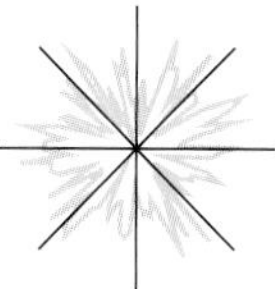

SOURCE: LANE HARRISON, MATTHEW KAY, AND JEFFREY HEER

Researchers have studied how readily we perceive change in both positive and negative correlation in a number of chart types and categorized them by their relative effectiveness.

STRIP PLOTS

r = 1

r = 0

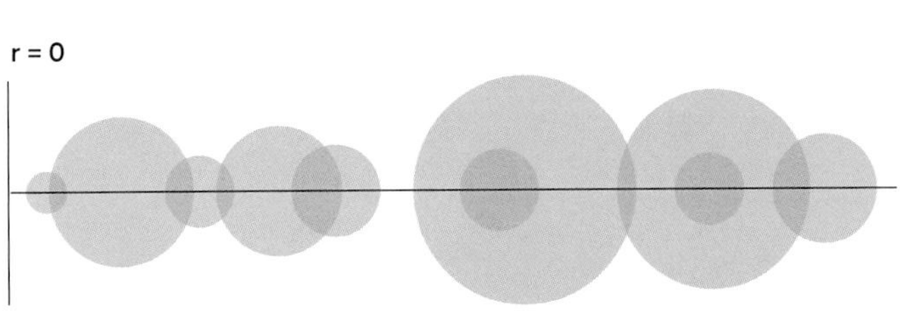

COLOR PLOTS

r = 1

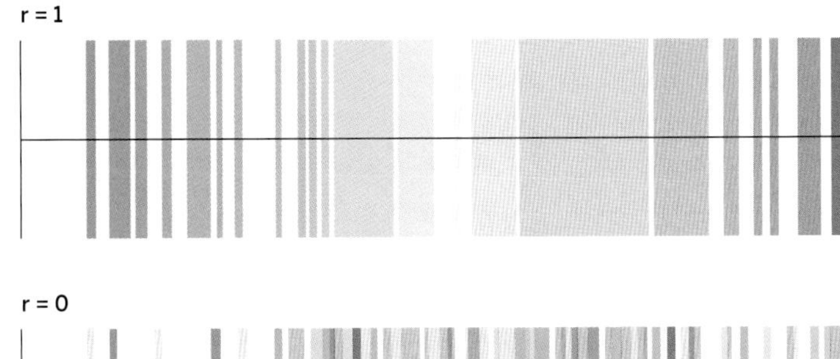

r = 0

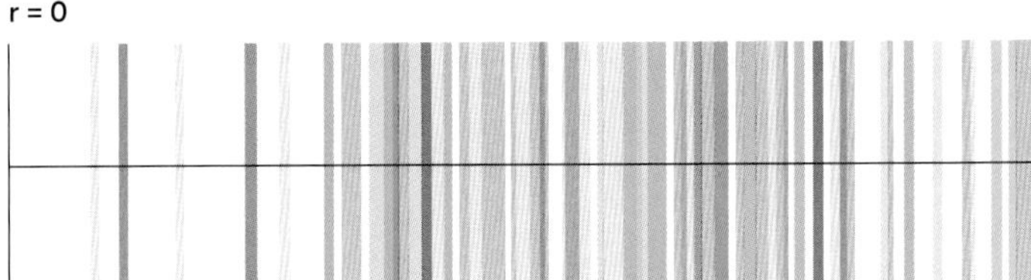

SOURCE: RONALD RENSINK

as Cleveland and McGill said, new procedures are being discovered, and old ones will be set aside.

Researchers next want to see whether other data representations such as outlier detection and cluster detection follow the same predictable scheme. If they do, Harrison can imagine being able to develop intelligent visualization systems in which we know, scientifically, which charts will be most effective for the task at hand.

As the grammar of graphics evolves (and it will continue to evolve, just as linguistic grammar does), visualization will remain what it always has been—an intermingling of the scientific and design traditions. It will be a mash-up of art and science, of taste and proof. But even if the grammar were already fully developed, understanding it alone wouldn't ensure good charts, just as knowing the rules for prepositions and the passive voice doesn't ensure good writing. The task at hand remains the same: We must learn to think visually, to understand the context, and to design charts that communicate ideas, not data sets.

And the best way to start learning how to produce good charts is to understand how people consume them. That starts by understanding some of the basics of visual perception.

RECAP

A BRIEF HISTORY OF DATAVIZ

Visual communication is primal, but what we now think of as data visualization started just two centuries ago. The history of visualization provides a foundation for learning and helps dispel several misconceptions about the practice. Above all, it allows us to dismiss the myth that dataviz is a fully formed science with rules that must be obeyed. In fact, dataviz is a craft that relies on both art and science, in which experimentation and innovation should be rewarded, not punished.

A TIMELINE OF SOME KEY MOMENTS:

Late 1700s
William Playfair produces what are often considered the first modern charts, including line charts, bar charts, pie charts, and timelines.

1858
Florence Nightingale produces "coxcomb diagrams" that show the devastating effect of disease on the British army.

1861
Charles Minard publishes a diagram showing the toll taken on Napoleon's army by his march on Russia.

1914
Willard Brinton publishes *Graphic Methods for Presenting Facts*, the first book about visualization for business.

1952
Mary Eleanor Spear publishes *Charting Statistics*, a book of chart-making best practices based on decades of work with many groups in the US government.

1967
Jacques Bertin publishes *Sémiologie graphique*, the first overarching theory of visualization, and one that remains deeply influential. Bertin describes seven "visual variables": position, size, shape, color, brightness, orientation, and texture. He also establishes two core principles: the *principle of expressiveness* (show what you need to; no more, no less) and the *principle of effectiveness* (use the most efficient method available to visualize your information).

1970s
John Tukey pioneers the use of visualization with computers and popularizes the concepts of *exploratory* and *confirmatory* visualization.

1983

Edward Tufte publishes *The Visual Display of Quantitative Information*, combining statistical rigor with clear, clean design principles and inspiring two generations of information designers and data journalists.

1984

William Cleveland and Robert McGill publish the first of several research papers that attempt to measure "graphic perception," setting off two decades of research into what makes visualizations effective.

1986

Jock Mackinlay publishes his highly influential PhD thesis, which carries Jacques Bertin's work into the digital age.

1990s–2000s

The computer-driven, scientific visualization community and the design-driven, journalistic visualization community diverge in their approaches to dataviz.

2010s

The social internet, cheap and easy-to-use software, and massive volumes of data democratize the practice of visualization, creating mass experimentation. Viz is no longer the province of a small community of experts; it's an internet phenomenon.

2010

Ronald Rensink publishes research suggesting that our perception of correlation in a scatter plot follows what's known as Weber's law and, for the first time, that a method for calculating a chart type's effectiveness may exist.

2014

Lane Harrison replicates Rensink's findings and applies them to additional chart types. He creates a ranking of chart-type effectiveness for showing correlation. Harrison's work is part of a new generation of research into establishing science around graphic perception, which draws on many other disciplines, including psychology, neuroscience, and economics.

Today

Experimentation continues across a broad spectrum of disciplines. Tools for visualizing increasingly improve. They create better charts faster and allow for interactivity and dynamic updating of visuals.

CHAPTER 2

WHEN A CHART HITS OUR EYES

SOME SCIENCE OF HOW WE SEE

I'VE COMPARED THE PROCESS of learning dataviz to learning how to write and to learning a new language. Maybe the best analog, though, is music. Everyone hears music and forms opinions about it without taking courses in music theory. We may sense *something* about the music we like—its "texture," or that it sounds "brooding," without knowing that we're actually describing syncopation or a minor key.

Similarly, everyone sees charts and decides whether they're good or bad without a degree in visual perception theory. You may sense *something* about a chart you like—you may even be able to describe it as "clear" or "revealing" without understanding that you're actually describing elementary encodings or perceptual salience.

If you wanted to compose, you might learn some music theory. Similarly, now that you've decided to make good charts, it's helpful to learn a little bit about how we see. Unlike music, though, infoviz theory is new and changing. It draws on multiple disciplines, including perception science, neuroscience, and psychology.[1] You don't need a degree in perception science here; you just need five broadly applicable ideas to understand what we see when we see a chart.

FIVE IDEAS TO KNOW

1. We don't go in order. In the tacit contract between a reader and a writer, the writer agrees to use words to communicate. The words will be strung together as sentences, the sentences as paragraphs, and the paragraphs as stories that will be presented "in order," which in the West means left to right and top to bottom on the page.

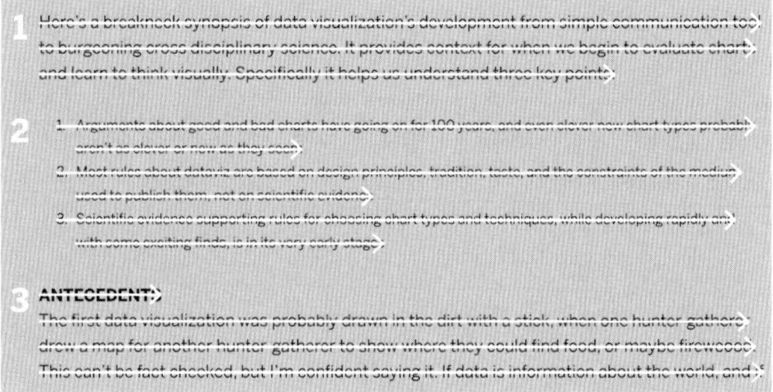

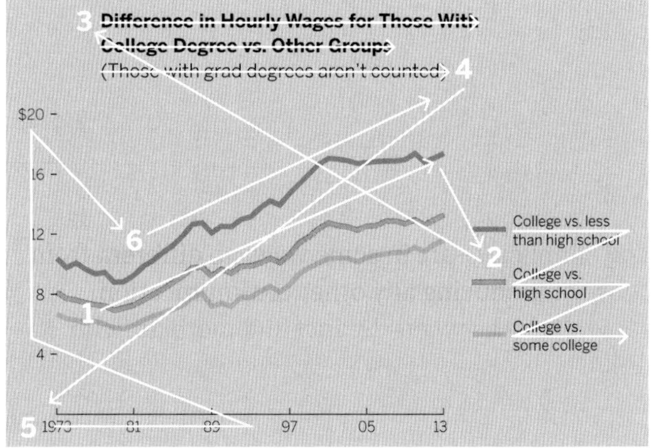

There's an unspoken contract between writer and reader about how readers will proceed through text. No such contract exists with visualizations.

Different cultures read in different orders.[2] In all cases, though, reading is done sequentially and at a reasonably even tempo.

With visualizations, no such contract exists between a producer and a consumer. A chart reader may not get to the title at the top until well after she has started scanning the visual middle. She may jump around. She may read halfway across an axis and then move on to something else—or skip some parts of the chart entirely.

Pacing, too, is completely different. Reading a book is like running a marathon, taking a steady pace along a linear path. Parsing a chart is more like playing hockey, with fast bursts across space interspersed with intense action in concentrated zones. We go where our eyes are stimulated to go. There's no agreed-upon convention.

The order in which people look at charts varies with chart type and with the person looking. Some research suggests that people with expertise in the subject matter of a chart or with practice using a certain type will read through it differently (and more efficiently) than others.[3] All of which is to say that although the challenges of producing good visual communication—to achieve clarity, focus, and simplicity—are in some ways no different from those of producing any other communication, they're in other ways distinct and more difficult.

2. We see first what stands out. Our eyes go right to change and difference—peaks, valleys, intersections, dominant colors, outliers. Many successful charts—often the ones that please us the most and are shared and talked about—exploit this inclination by showing a single salient point so clearly that we feel we understand the chart's meaning without even trying. Like this:

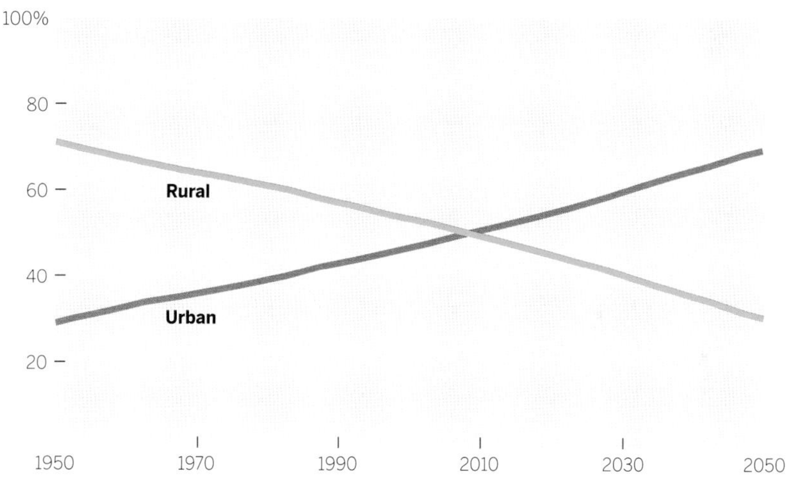

In this chart, the first thing we notice is the crossover. You probably didn't even read the axes. Most likely you saw the crossover, checked the labels, and glanced at the title, in that order, nearly instantaneously, and you got the point: People are flocking to cities.

But not every chart is so simple, or should be. What are the first three things you see here?

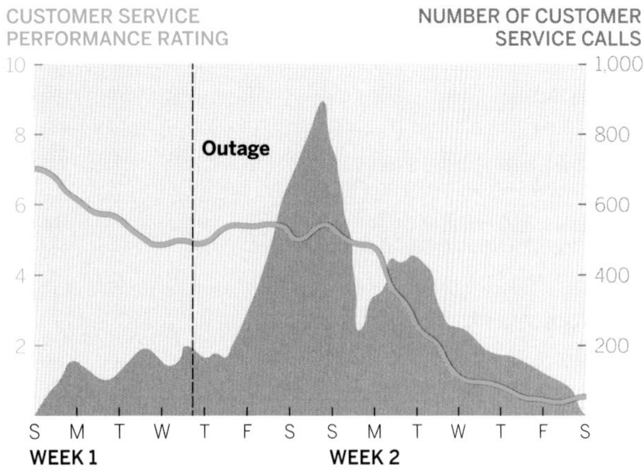

Without choosing to, most people will first see the blue line, the steep gray mountain area, and the "outage" line. If the manager who presents this chart wants to communicate the relationship between an outage, customer service calls, and customer service performance, this chart rightly calls attention to those three points.

But what if she's concerned that customer service's issues are systemic rather than a result of the outage? What if she wants to convey to her boss that even after customer-service calls returned to pre-outage levels, customer service performance continued to decline?

If we work at it, we can find that trend in the chart, but it's not what we notice first. It doesn't stand out. Our eyes have been drawn to something else. How might the manager make her idea what we see first?

Including the number of customer service calls in the first chart made our eyes go straight to data that this manager thinks is *not* the issue. Her new chart eliminates it, thereby removing a distracting message. The addition of the "service restored" marker provides important context that highlights the continuing downward trend even after that point. And we may not have noticed it before, but now we see that the downward trend started *before* the outage.

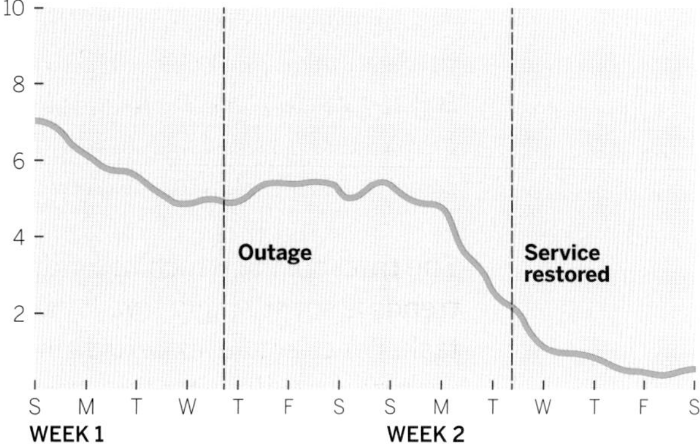

The capper is the new title: "Declining Call Center Performance." Despite their position, titles aren't usually the first thing a chart reader sees. Rather, they're clues to help us find the meaning that started to emerge when we looked at the picture. Here, the word *declining* confirms the chart's message and purpose.

If this manager had given her boss the first chart, she'd have to fight his inclination to focus on what stands out in it—that peak in customer service calls—and get him to see the trend she cares about. Now she can start a conversation about performance overall.

3. We see only a few things at once. The more data that's plotted in a visualization, the more singular the chart's meaning becomes. For example, if her boss wanted to see a simple before-and-after representation of call center employees' performance, the manager might produce a slope graph. Here she has plotted January and June ratings for a few dozen employees. But she can't expect her boss to process dozens of connected data points. It's impossible to have a conversation about individuals or even subsets of this group with this chart. The boss is seeing only generally rising performance, in a thick band.

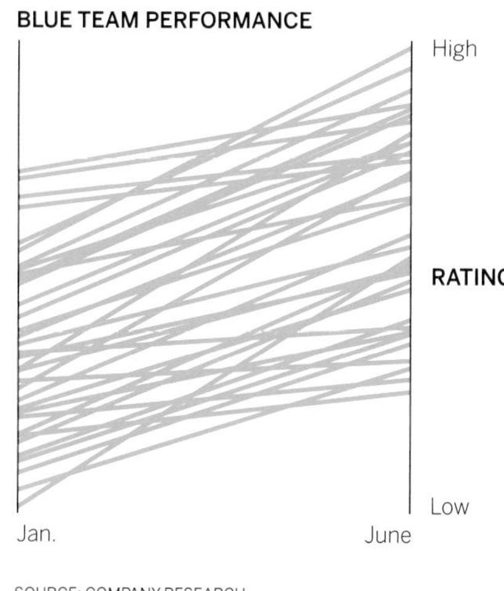

If the manager wanted to give her boss a big-picture view of how the team is performing, such a chart would be supremely effective. But she knows that he'll be making decisions about individual employees' performance. How few points of data should she present so that he can do that?

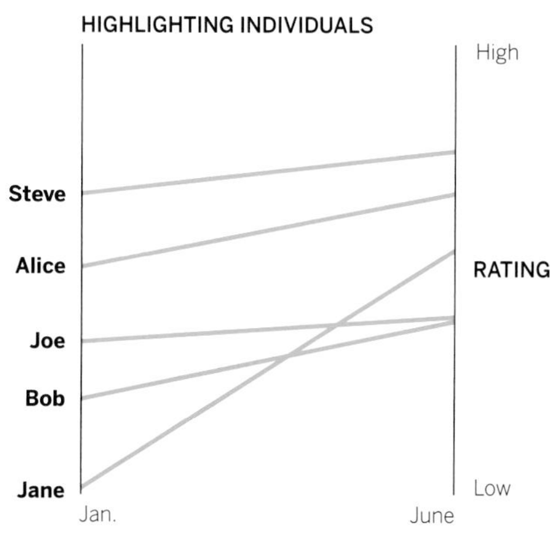

The threshold at which individual data points melt into aggregate trends is surprisingly low. It varies according to chart type and task. For example, experts think that we can't distinguish more than about eight colors at a time.[4] A good guide is that with more than five to ten variables or elements, individual meaning begins to fade.

The manager's boss can judge individuals' work here, but even this chart hints at the limits of showing multiple individual data points together. It still takes a moment to separate the pick-up sticks before we can start to see a singular pattern in their performance. If the manager needs to convey the individual performance of hundreds of employees, she has a challenge ahead of her.

A bar chart is more effective than a slope or a trend in a line chart at getting us to focus on each discrete category of data—each bar. But even bars create singular shapes when enough of them are plotted and they're snug against each other. What's the first thing you see in the Plug-In Vehicles chart—20 separate values or a steep slope?

We don't always find simpler meaning in complex charts. Some charts use color, callouts, and other devices to draw our attention in too many directions at once, like the Most Common 311 Complaints chart. That chart plots 21 discrete categories across 24 tightly packed hours. What's more, some of the categories' values are so small as to become barely distinguishable slivers. Try following changes to "illegal parking" over the course of the day. Also, the color choices aren't systematic—in fact, different complaints share like colors. The lengthy legend disconnects the y-axis values from the bars. What stands out here? We might argue that a general middle bump is discernible, but if that's what needs to be shown, all those categories and colors are distracting from it.

PLUG-IN VEHICLES: THE FIRST THREE YEARS

CUMULATIVE NUMBER OF VEHICLES SOLD, IN THOUSANDS

160
120
80
40

March 2011 | Sept. | March 2012 | Sept. | March 2013 | Sept.

SOURCE: ADAPTED FROM PLOT.LY PLOT BASED ON DATA COMPILED BY BRETT WILLIAMS AND CHARTED AT FIGSHARE.COM

THE MOST COMMON 311 COMPLAINTS IN NYC

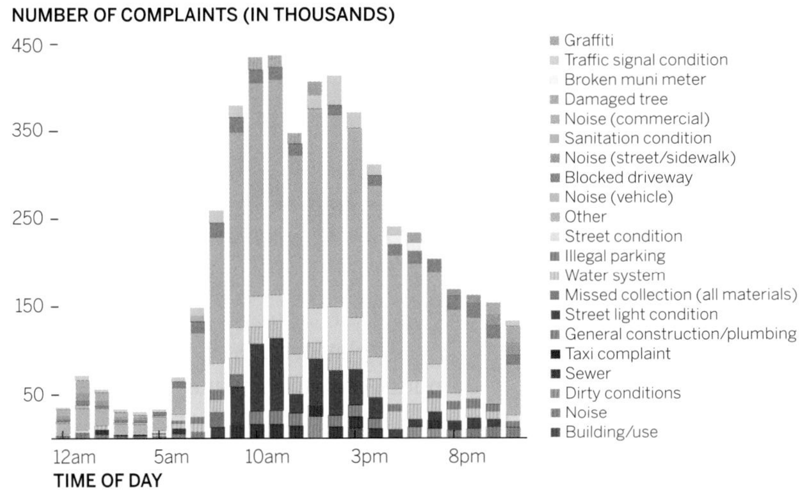

SOURCE: PLOT.LY

Bad complexity neither elucidates important salient points nor shows coherent broader trends. It will obfuscate, frustrate, and ultimate convey trendlessness and confusion to the viewer.

Good complexity, in contrast, emerges from visualizations that use more data than humans can reasonably process to form a few salient points. Here's an extreme example:

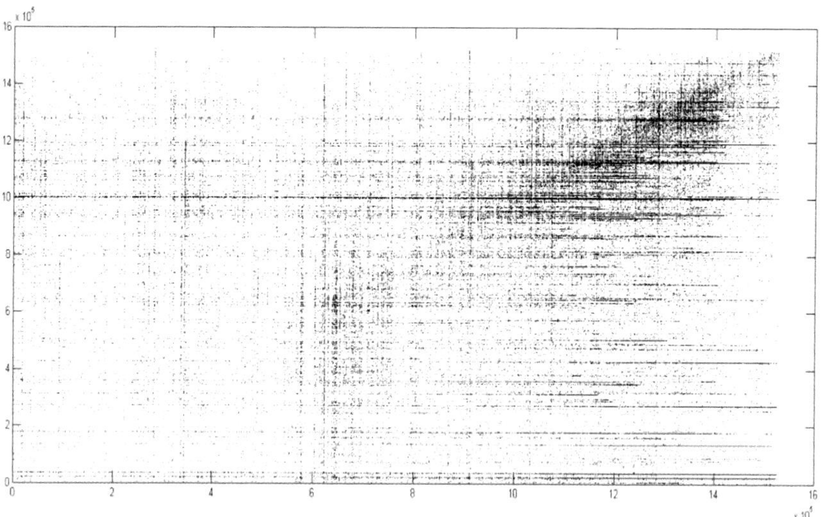

This is a scatter plot of *10 million* data points that charts the social connections between stock traders on a social trading platform. Despite the overwhelming amount of data displayed, we see just a few things to focus on: the dense black spot, an upward-right increase in density, and some striation, especially to the right.[5] That's all we can talk about here.

We can process these visualizations at the "blurry level," as one researcher puts it, and estimate the values they represent reasonably well.[6] When deeply complex charts work, we find them effective and beautiful, just as we find a symphony, which is another marvelously complex arrangement of data that we experience as a coherent whole.

4. We seek meaning and make connections.

Once we see what stands out, we try to make sense of it immediately and incessantly. When you looked at the complex scatter plot to the left, you may have thought, *Why is it smudged black in the top right?* Sometimes we even vocalize the impulse to make meaning, with a "Hmmm," or a "What's that about?"

Even as we ask ourselves such questions, we're generating a narrative. With the original Customer Service Calls chart, for example, it doesn't take long to string the first three points we see into a simple story: An *outage* led to a *spike in service calls* and then a *performance decline.* With the Team Performance slope chart, we quickly translate the angle and density of the lines as *Performance is improving in general, but most people are lower-performing to begin with.*

Seeking sense this way has obvious benefits. For one, we process visual information thousands of times more efficiently than we do text. Some of our processing is even "preconscious"—it happens before we're aware we've done it—so we can grasp visual information more clearly with less effort. For example, imagine your office building is on fire. As smoke fills the room, you rush to the door, where you see the emergency exit placard to the left.

In the room next to yours, someone rushes to the door and sees the Fire Escape Plan map instead. Who do you think makes it to the first exit faster?

Exit this room. Turn right and walk 10 feet to the end of the hallway, where you'll be facing a large conference room. Turn left and walk another 12 feet until you come to the end of that hallway. To your left is a fire alarm, near the elevator. To your right at the end of the hall is a stairwell. Do not go to the elevator. Turn right and walk another 12 feet to the end of the hall, turn left and enter the stairwell. Go down two flights of stairs and exit the building at the door at the bottom of the stairs.

FIRE ESCAPE PLAN

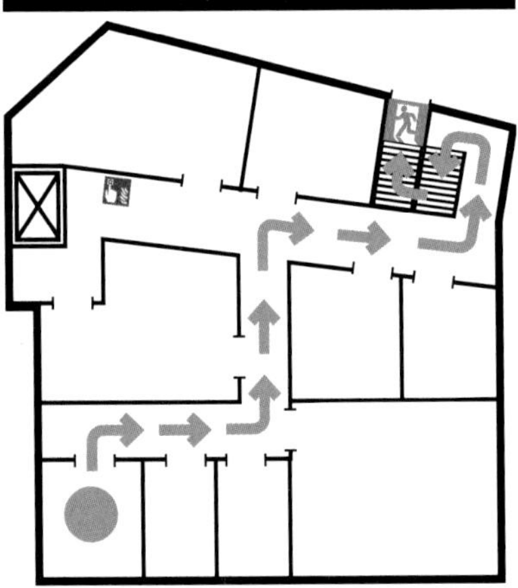

The ability to find meaning so efficiently may be a blessing in a fire, but it can also lead us to construct false narratives from data visualizations. What if the customer service manager showed her boss the chart to the right comparing customer service ratings to revenue when he asked for some data to review the effect of the outage?

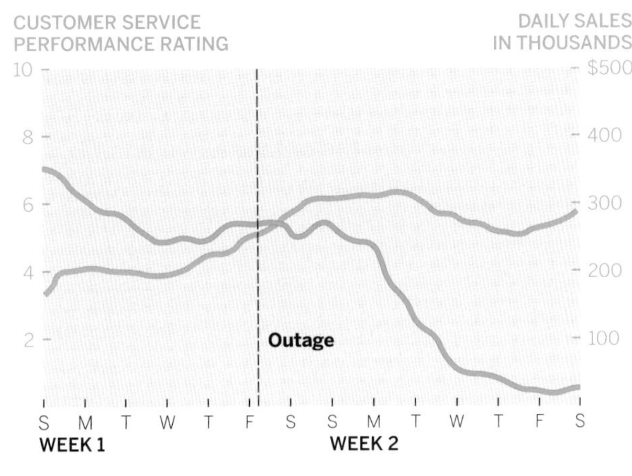

SOURCE: COMPANY RESEARCH

We can't help making connections in what we're presented with. Anything that stands out becomes part of the narrative we're trying to form, so what's presented becomes a crucial factor in the success of the chart—its ability to convey the idea the chart maker wants it to. The manager's boss, seeking meaning, may reasonably conclude from this chart that revenue is steady despite the outage. The narrative he's forming may convince him that he can de-prioritize a proposed customer service overhaul. After all, revenue is unharmed.

But before he can do that, the manager shows him a chart from a previous outage that extends the length of time plotted, shown on the facing page.

In this version he sees a different story: Revenue dropped, but not until nine or ten days after the outage.

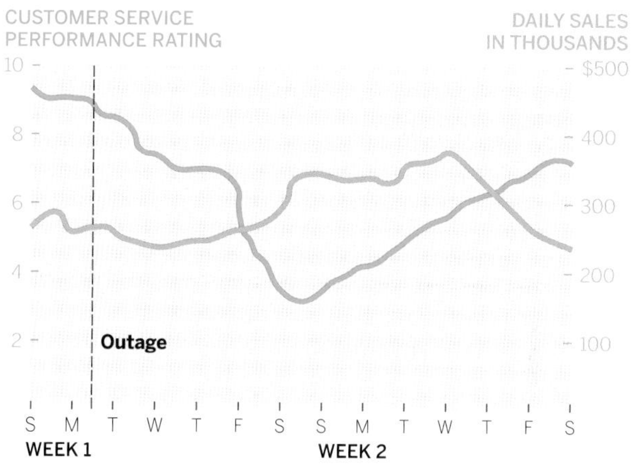

Of course, correlation does not equal causation. Did the outage and customer service's performance eventually affect revenue? Or was the drop related to something not included in the chart? The manager and her boss don't know, but she, knowing that he will seek meaning and make connections, has produced a better chart with which to start the discussion. Good visual communication should be used not just to produce better answers but also to generate better conversations. In this case, the two can wait a few days to see whether revenue starts dropping.

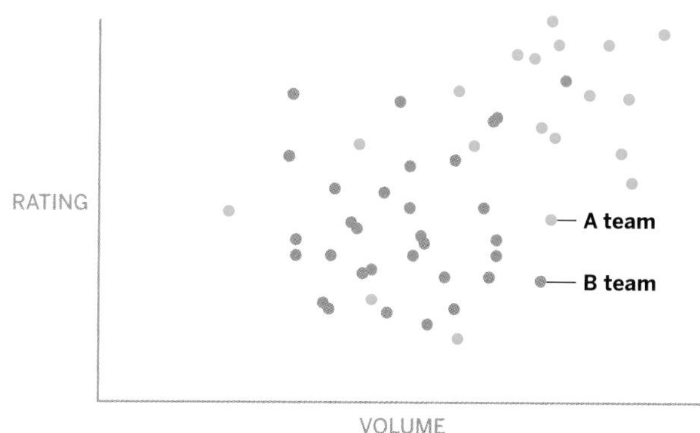

This need to make sense of what we notice is so powerful that it extends to the subconscious. In the Top Performers chart the bold orange headline is one of those instantly noticeable cues. It makes us immediately notice the orange dots and the orange axis labels. Are the orange team members top performers? Orange means *something*.

We're trying to find meaning, but that's not all. Research has shown that our visual system will subconsciously create cohesion among the orange items while tuning out other colors and information in order to increase its focus on the dominant color.[7] Without realizing it, we've prioritized orange over other information. That's unfortunate, because the color connection here is meaningless—a bad

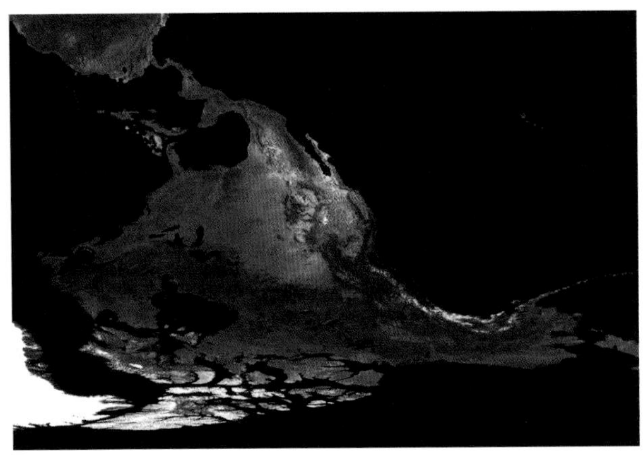

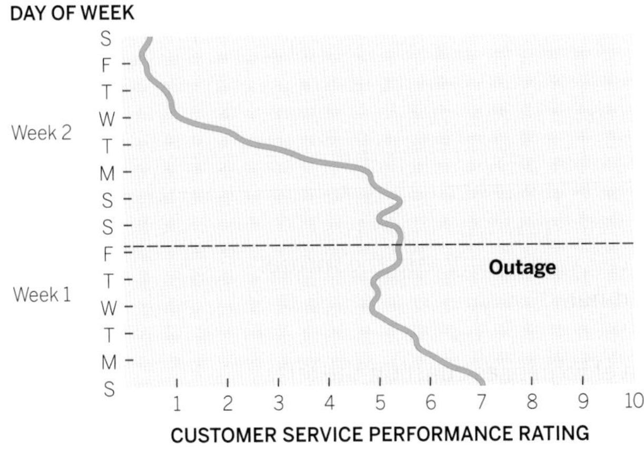

design decision. In fact, the blue team is higher performing.

5. We rely on conventions and metaphors.

It's not just how we're wired to see the world that defines how we see charts. It's also how we're *taught* to see the world. Is this picture of North America wrong?

No. We think it's "upside down" because we've learned that "north is up," even though there is no up or down for a planet in space.

Likewise, the Customer Service Rating chart below it is accurately plotted, but most of us would still say it's "wrong." Once we look at the axes, we find ourselves doing some cognitive gymnastics, expending significant mental energy trying to twist the lines back into a form we're used to seeing. You may have tilted your head to the right in an effort to make the time axis horizontal, only to realize that even then, it still goes right to left. Our minds tell us to rearrange what we see to put time back in its "proper" orientation, because *time doesn't go up.*

In fact, time visualizations can move in any spatial direction and remain factually accurate. But we've learned to *think* of it as moving left to right on a page or a screen, and back to forward in three-dimensional space.

Moving time to the y-axis creates another perception problem. It generates a line that goes down as performance goes up. The highest performance is found at the lowest point. Again, that messes with our learned expectations: "High" performance shouldn't be spatially "low."

Conventions are a form of expectation, and our brains use experience and expectation as cognitive shortcuts so that we don't have to process everything anew every time we see it. In fact, as the neuropsychiatrist Jon Lieff points out, "The over-arching analysis of visual signals depends on what is expected . . . the influence of the brain and expectation are far greater than the raw data."[8]

On the basis of our experiences, we mentally store all kinds of metaphors and conventions about what information means: Up is good, down is bad. North is up, south is down. Researchers have found that we even connect those metaphors to value judgments.[9] For example, because south is "down," we think it's easier to go in that direction than to go north, which requires us to go "up."

There are others: Red is negative, green positive. But *red* sometimes means "hot" or "active" (which can be thought of as positive), and in those cases, *blue* means "cold" or "inactive." Hierarchies move from the top down. Lighter color shades are "emptier" or lower than darker ones.

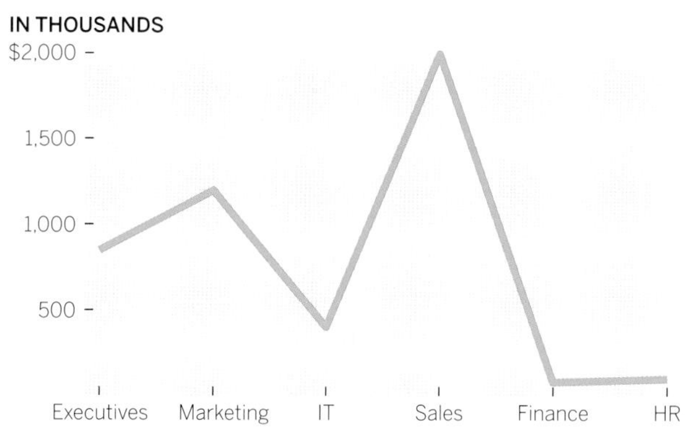

Anytime conventions like these are flouted, confusion, uncertainty, and frustration will weaken a chart's effectiveness. Some of the heuristics are so powerful and obvious that we rarely see them violated. Virtually no one maps the world "upside down." Desert temperatures aren't a deep blue. Imagine a CEO announcing to her employees, "We're going to take this company into the future!" as she points behind her.

Or consider the Travel Expenses chart on the left. Conventionally, we connect data points only when there's a relationship from one value to the next. But here each value is an unchanging category.

NELSON DAVIS

SEEING WHAT NO ONE HAS SEEN BEFORE

"I've never seen myself as a data expert. A lot of people have better data skills than I do. I sit between the data world and the art world."

Nelson Davis's path to becoming a dataviz consultant was, like many others', circuitous. After undergraduate study at Oglethorpe, a small liberal arts college, Davis went to Georgia Tech to study civil engineering. Then he got a master's. Three degrees in six years. He says, "I did some work internationally, came back in the middle of the recession, and there were no jobs."

He took a data internship at a hospital, which was, he says, really the first time he thought about data. "I realized there that I could play with spreadsheets all day long." Eventually he found a civil engineering job. "Turned out I hated it. So when a job offer to become a transportation data analyst came up, I jumped at it, realizing I'd get to play with spreadsheets again."

In an effort to impress his new bosses, Davis mapped some of the geographic data he was working with. The feedback was positive: "One of my bosses said, 'Great, but could you create a dashboard of that with live data?' I said, 'Sure.' Then I had to Google *dashboard* and *live data*."

Today he does visualization for a living. "Four years ago I was just another transportation engineer," he says. "Then I switched into dataviz. Now I feel like I'm on the cutting edge. From a career perspective, it has set me apart, absolutely."

Davis remembers one of the first moments he sensed that he loved visualization and the powerful effect it had on colleagues. The Georgia transportation department manages any number of devices on highways—cameras, sensors, signals—that all have to work together to manage the transportation system. But no one had ever come up with a comprehensive list of the 2,600 devices in the system. So Davis found them all and mapped them by location and type. His map was lightly interactive, with zoom and detail available on rollover. Still, it was a reasonably simple visual. No one had thought or tried to create it before, because of the work required to gather the data. It took Davis five or six weeks to build his spreadsheet of devices. Sometimes the most powerful visuals aren't the prettiest or the most complex or ingenious—they're just the ones no one has yet put the effort into.

"I remember feeling like it was this Christopher Columbus moment," Davis says. "I remember thinking, 'I've just created something no one has ever seen.' We sort of knew it was there, but no one had really *seen* it." His team was impressed and grateful. "It was instant engagement. They immediately started to think about ways to use it."

Since then, Davis has had several similar moments. He says, "You have to hold the client back from jumping up and taking over. It's that instant engagement, and everyone feels it."

Davis says it's useful to approach any visualization effort by putting yourself in the audience's shoes and understanding what they want or need. The transportation map, he recalls, was partly inspired by conversations he'd had that indicated that such a visualization would be valuable to the organization.

"Sales" doesn't change as a value; there's no inherent connection between executives' and marketing's expenses. One value doesn't *go to* the next as this line, literally, does. Each value here should get its own plot, most likely a bar.

The real challenge with conventions comes from subtler violations of our expectations. Here's a re-creation of a published chart I encountered:[10]

HOW INTERESTED ARE YOU IN THIS PRODUCT?

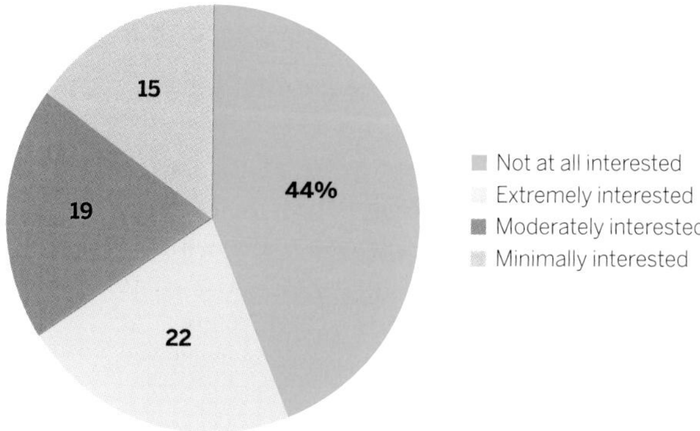

SOURCE: COMPANY RESEARCH

More is happening here than may first appear. Without thinking about it, we access three conventions in our minds to help explain the meaning of the chart:

- Like colors mean like items—the blue things go together.

His process involves plenty of sketching and talking to others, asking them to look at his sketches—all techniques we delve into in detail in chapter 4. He also believes in asking clients *why* questions instead of *what* questions: "Sometimes the boss will say, 'I want you to build this thing,' and then the person goes and creates the charts and brings them back, and the boss says, 'This doesn't tell me what I need to know.' The person who made the chart is thinking, *I built what you asked.* But I'll bet you he never asked the boss, 'Why do you need that?'"

There's a decided creative streak in the way Davis, an amateur photographer, approaches visualization. He says, "In one presentation, I showed the famous photograph of the sailor kissing the nurse in New York on VE Day. I talked about the picture. It shows a man kissing a woman. It's black-and-white. It appears to be New York City. It's old. That's some of the data. Then I talked about the *story*: This is what victory looks like. This is joy. This massive, terrible conflict, World War II, is ending. That's the art. The story is what makes you feel something about the picture.

"I think that's part of what makes me unique. The number of people who can do both the science and the art is small. Some people are good at data. Some are good at design. I feel like I'm in between.

"But I like it there. I like connecting dots."

- Color saturation indicates higher and lower values—lighter colors have lower values than darker ones.
- Categories are arranged and plotted from one extreme to another—we can read this in order from most to least interested.

We're making meaning before we know it: there are two groups of people here with varying levels of interest, and the blue group is bigger than the orange group. But a closer look shows just how far off we are.

Like colors mean like items. You probably assumed that the blues are a pair and so are the oranges. But the key shows that the blue pieces represent diametrically opposed viewpoints (no interest, high interest), and the orange represent middle viewpoints (some interest, little interest). Our expectation is that "not at all" and "minimally" will be in one color because they represent the pessimists, while "moderately" and "extremely" describe another group, the optimists.

Color saturation indicates a progression of values. We expect light-color values to be lower than dark-color values, but here light blue has a higher value (22%) than dark orange (19%). If we match hues to actual numerical values, descending order *should* be: rich blue, pale blue, rich orange, pale orange. Here the color groupings aren't in order either. Optimists are pale blue and rich orange, while pessimists are rich blue and pale orange. The color differences provide no guidance here.

Categories are arranged and plotted from one extreme to another. Our minds want information to be arranged in order, either ascending or descending. But the key here lists categories "out of order," starting with not at all interested and jumping to extremely interested. If we think of "extremely interested" as category 1 and "not at all interested" as category 4, then this key is arranged 4, 1, 2, 3.

What at first glance appeared to be a simple, well-constructed pie chart turns out to repeatedly disrupt our expectations, forcing us to reset them and think hard about what we're looking at. We can't take advantage of the mental shortcuts that help us get to meaning more quickly. Instead, we have to parse.

To show just how much disrupting expectations can affect viewers' ability to find meaning in a chart, look again at the pie chart for a few seconds and see if you can answer these two questions:

- Which group makes up the majority, optimists or pessimists?
- Which single category represents the smallest proportion of people?

Now look at this version and see if it's easier to answer those questions.

CREDIBILITY AT STAKE

That's enough theory to make you an amateur composer. Understanding what people see, and what their minds do when they set eyes on a chart, is the best way to guide you in deciding what to show and how to show it.

The stakes here may be higher than you suspect. Perceptual fluency research suggests that we make qualitative judgments about information on the basis of its presentation.[11] If something is hard to perceive, people not only struggle to find the right meaning, but judge it less favorably.

There's a fine point here that mustn't be lost: It's not the *chart* that they'll judge harshly if the meaning is hard to find; it's the *information itself.* They'll consider it less credible.

If you don't understand these basic tenets of how we see information—if your charts don't make what's important stand out; if complex data doesn't coalesce into a few clear ideas; if the information visualized fosters a false narrative; if unconventional visual techniques confuse your viewers—then you've promised music but delivered noise.

RECAP

WHEN A CHART HITS OUR EYES

Unlike text, visual communication is governed less by an agreed-upon convention between "writer" and "reader" than by how our visual systems react to stimuli. And just as composers use music theory to create music that produces certain predictable effects on an audience, chart makers can use visual perception theory to make more-effective visualizations.

Five high-level, mostly agreed-upon principles are enough to guide you:

1. We don't go in order.
Visuals aren't read in a predictable, linear way, as text is. Instead, we look first at the visual and then scan the chart for contextual clues about what is important.

What this means:
Whereas we write sequentially (in the West, left to right and top to bottom), we should "write" charts spatially, from the visual outward, other elements provide clues to the visual's meaning.

2. We see first what stands out.
Our eyes go directly to change and difference, such as unique colors, steep curves, clusters, or outliers.

What this means:
Whatever stands out should match or support the idea being conveyed. If it doesn't, it will distract from and fight for attention with the main idea.

3. We see only a few things at once.
The more data that's plotted in a chart, the more singular the idea it conveys. A visual that contains tens, hundreds, or thousands of plotted data points shows us a forest instead of individual trees.

What this means:
If we need to focus on individual data points, we should plot as few as possible so that the visuals don't disappear into an aggregate view.

4. We seek meaning and make connections.
Our minds incessantly try to assign meaning to a visual and make causal connections between the

elements presented, regardless of whether any real connections exist.

What this means:
If visual elements are presented together, they should be related in a meaningful way; otherwise, viewers will construct false narratives about the relationship between them.

5. We rely on conventions and metaphors.
We use learned shortcuts to assign meaning to visual cues on the basis of common expectations. For example, green is good and red is bad; north is up and south is down; time moves left to right.

What this means:
In general you should embrace, not fight, deeply ingrained conventions and metaphors when creating visuals. Flouting them creates confusion, uncertainty, and frustration, which will weaken or eliminate a chart's effectiveness.

PART TWO

CREATE

CHAPTER 3

TWO QUESTIONS → FOUR TYPES

A SIMPLE TYPOLOGY FOR CHART MAKING

IF A FRIEND SAID TO YOU, "Pack your bags, we're going on a trip," what would you do next? Here's what you wouldn't do: You wouldn't say "Okay, great," grab a suitcase, and start filling it with clothes. How could you? You have so many questions: *Where are we going? For how long? How are we getting there? Why are we taking this trip? Where will we stay when we get there?* You can't pack until you know what you're packing for.

But when it comes to information visualization, the impulse is to immediately choose a chart type and click a button to create it. You should resist this impulse and instead start by thinking about the questions that will make packing easier later on.

THE TWO QUESTIONS

A good way to start thinking visually is to consider two questions about the nature and purpose of your visualization:

1. Is the information *conceptual* or *data-driven*?
2. Am I *declaring something* or *exploring something*?

If you know, generally, the answers to these two questions, you can plan what resources and tools you'll need and begin to define the type of visualization you may finally settle on using.

CONCEPTUAL OR DATA-DRIVEN?

	CONCEPTUAL	DATA-DRIVEN
Focus	Ideas	Statistics
Goals	Simplify, teach "Here's how our organization is structured."	Inform, enlighten "Here are our revenues for the past two years."

The first is the simpler of the two questions, and usually the answer is obvious. Either you're visualizing concepts and qualitative information or you're plotting data and information. But notice that the question is about the information itself, not the forms that might ultimately be used to show it.

CONCEPTUAL

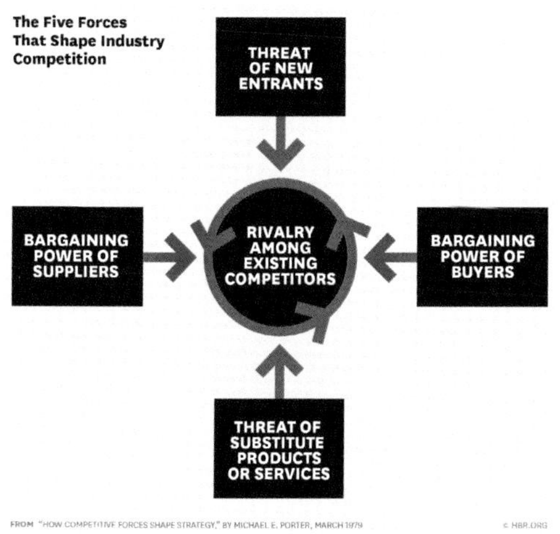
The Five Forces That Shape Industry Competition
THREAT OF NEW ENTRANTS
BARGAINING POWER OF SUPPLIERS
RIVALRY AMONG EXISTING COMPETITORS
BARGAINING POWER OF BUYERS
THREAT OF SUBSTITUTE PRODUCTS OR SERVICES

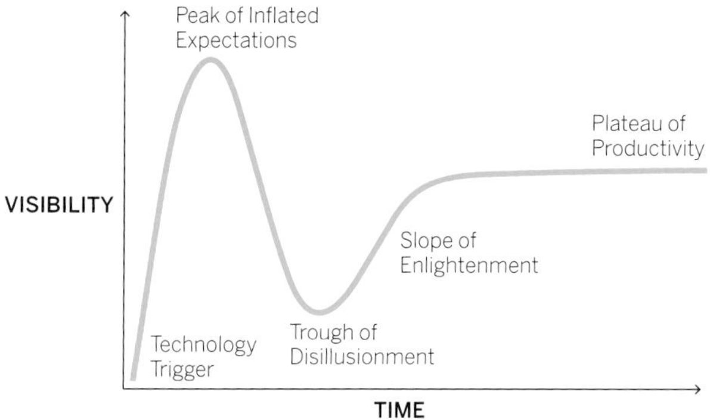
GARTNER'S "HYPE CYCLE"
Peak of Inflated Expectations
Plateau of Productivity
VISIBILITY
Slope of Enlightenment
Technology Trigger
Trough of Disillusionment
TIME

DATA-DRIVEN

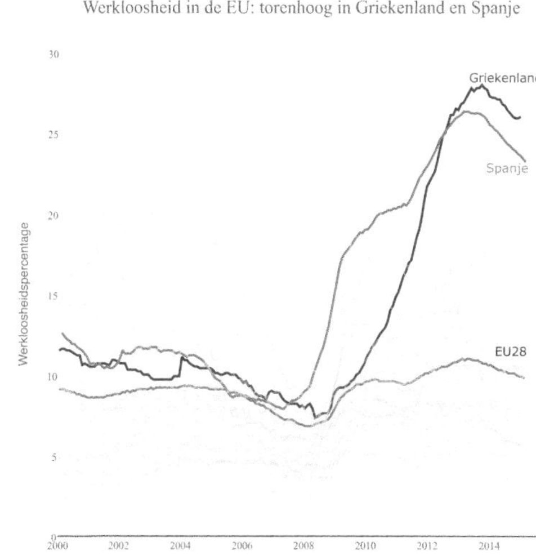
Werkloosheid in de EU: torenhoog in Griekenland en Spanje
Werkloosheidspercentage
Griekenland
Spanje
EU28

TOP BRANDS PER STATE
DIRECTCAPITAL

Sometimes a data-driven chart will take on a conceptual form, and vice versa. The map on the previous page doesn't obviously plot statistics, but the brands shown represent quantitative values. Conversely, the Hype Cycle chart uses a common data-driven form, a line chart, but no real data values exist here. It's a concept.

DECLARATIVE OR EXPLORATORY?

	DECLARATIVE	EXPLORATORY
Focus	Documenting, designing	Prototyping, iterating, interacting, automating
Goals	Affirm: "Here are our revenues over the past five years."	Corroborate: "Let's see if marketing investments contributed to rising profits."
		Discover: "What would we see if we visualized customer purchases by gender, location, and purchase amount in real time?"

If the first question identifies what you *have*, the second one elicits what you're *doing*. The second one is more complicated to answer, because it's not a binary proposition. There are three broad categories of purpose—declarative, confirmatory, and exploratory—the second two of which are related.

Managers most often work with declarative visualizations. These make a statement to an audience—usually in a formal setting. They tend to be well-designed, finished products. That doesn't mean they're unassailable. Declarative viz shouldn't preclude conversation about the idea presented; a good one will generate discussion. If you have a spreadsheet workbook full of sales data and you're using that data to show quarterly sales or sales by region in a presentation—your purpose is *declarative*.

But let's say your boss wants to understand why the sales team's performance has been lagging lately. You think that seasonal cycles have caused the dip, but you're not sure. Now your purpose is *confirmatory*, and you'll dip into the same data to create visuals that will show whether or not your hypothesis holds. Charts like this are less formal, and designed well enough to be interpreted, but they don't always have to be presentation-worthy. The audience is yourself or a small team, not others. If your hypothesis is confirmed, it may well lead to a declarative visualization you present to the boss, saying, "Here's what's happening to sales." If it turns out that seasonality isn't the culprit, you may form another hypothesis and again do confirmatory work.

Or maybe you don't know what you're looking for. Instead, you want to mine this workbook to see what patterns, trends, and anomalies emerge. What will you see, for example, when you measure sales performance in relation to the size of the region a salesperson must manage? What happens if you compare seasonal trends in the Northern and Southern hemispheres? How does weather affect sales? This is *exploratory* work—rougher still in design, usually iterative, sometimes interactive.

Managers don't do as much exploratory work as they do declarative and confirmatory; they should do more. It's a kind of data brainstorming that can deliver insights. Big strategic questions—*Why are revenues falling? Where can we find efficiencies? How do customers interact with us?*—can benefit from exploratory viz.

Other ways to ask the purpose question: "Do I need to give the answers, to check my answers, or to look for answers?" Or "Am I presenting ideas, researching ideas, or seeking ideas?"

As you move from the declarative toward exploratory, certainty about what you know tends to decrease, and the complexity of your information tends to increase. Also, when your purpose is declarative, you're more likely to be able to work alone and quickly. As you move along the spectrum, you're increasingly likely to work in a team, lean on experts, and invest much more time in the process.

THE FOUR TYPES

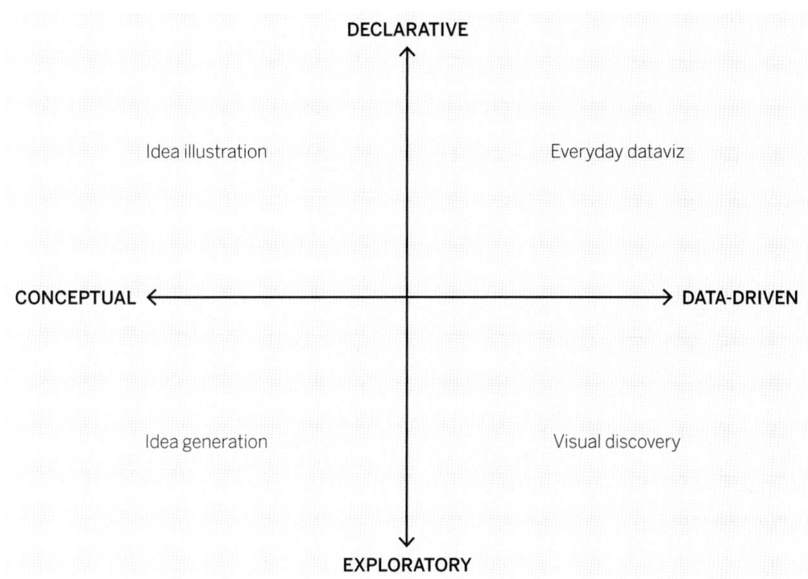

THE FOUR TYPES

The nature and purpose questions combine in a classic 2×2 to create four potential types of visualizations that managers will use.

Knowing which quadrant you're working in will help you make good decisions about the forms you'll use, the time you'll need, and the skills you'll call on. Let's start at the top left of this 2×2 and proceed counterclockwise.

IDEA ILLUSTRATION: CONCEPTUAL, DECLARATIVE VISUALIZATIONS

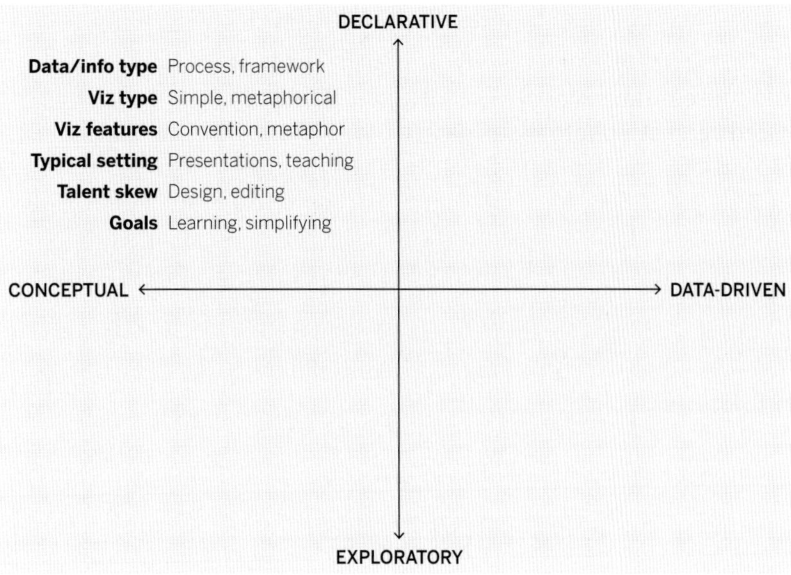

Idea illustration. We might call this the "consultants' corner," given that consultants can't resist process diagrams, cycle diagrams, and other idea illustrations—sometimes to deleterious effect. (Gardiner Morse, an editor at *HBR*, has coined a term for these sorts of overwrought diagrams: "crap circles."[1]) But at their best, declarative, conceptual visualizations simplify complex ideas by drawing on people's ability to understand metaphors (trees, bridges) and simple conventions (circles, hierarchies). Org charts, decision trees, and cycle diagrams are classic examples of idea illustration. So is the 2×2 that frames this chapter.

Idea illustrations demand clear and simple design, but they often lack it. They don't face the constraints imposed by axes and accurately plotted data. Their reliance on metaphors invites unnecessary adornment aimed at reinforcing the metaphor. If your idea is "funneling customers," for example, the impulse may be to show a literal funnel, but literalness can lead to unfortunate design decisions. Because the discipline and boundaries of data sets aren't built in to idea illustration, they must be self-imposed. Focus on clear communication, structure, and the logic of the ideas. The skills required here are similar to what a text editor brings to a manuscript, channeling the creative impulse into the clearest, simplest thing.

Say a company hires two consultants to help its R&D group find inspiration in other industries. They will use a technique called the *pyramid search*.[2] But how does a pyramid search work? The consultants have to sell it to the company's R&D leaders. They present something like this:

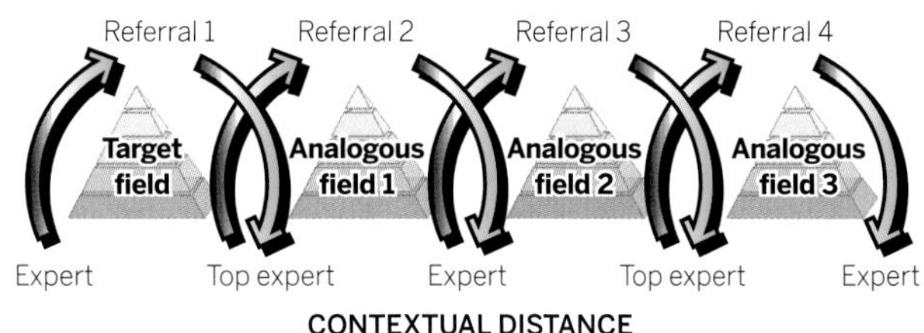

This idea illustration suffers from overdesign. The color gradient, arrows with drop shadows, and the sectioned, 3-D pyramids dominate, drawing our eyes away from the idea and toward the decoration. Stylization like this is a red flag. Additionally, the consultants haven't effectively channeled the metaphor. They're selling a pyramid search, but they present interlocking cycles; the pyramids are simply imagery doing little work. This is confusing. They have also put experts and top experts on the same plane (at the bottom of the diagram—another missed metaphor) instead of using height to convey relative status.

They'd be better off presenting something like this:

CLIMBING PYRAMIDS IN SEARCH OF IDEAS

LEVEL OF EXPERTISE

Top expert
Top expert
Top-level expertise
Referral 1 Referral 2 Referral 3 Referral 4
Below top-level expertise
Expert
Expert
Expert
Target field
Analogous field 1
Analogous field 2
CONTEXTUAL DISTANCE

SOURCE: MARION POETZ AND REINHARD PRÜGL, *JOURNAL OF PRODUCT INNOVATION MANAGEMENT*

Here the pyramid metaphor fits the visual representation. What's more, the axes use conventions that viewers can grasp immediately—near-to-far industries on the x-axis and low-to-high expertise on the y-axis. The pyramid shape itself serves a useful purpose, showing the relative rarity of top experts compared with lower-level ones. The title words help, too—*climbing* and *pyramids* both help us grasp the idea quickly. Finally, they don't succumb to the temptation to decorate. The pyramids, for example, aren't three-dimensional or sandstone-colored or placed against a photo of the desert.

IDEA GENERATION: CONCEPTUAL, EXPLORATORY VISUALIZATIONS

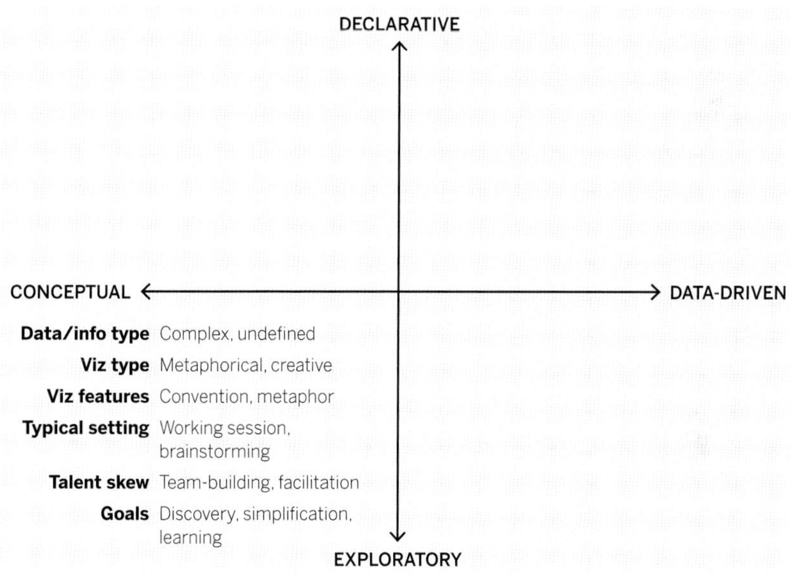

Idea generation. For many people, this quadrant is the least intuitive. When would you ever produce nondata visuals to explore ideas? The very notion of clarifying complex concepts seems to run counter to exploration, in which ideas aren't yet well defined. It differs in setting and media from the other three visualization types, and managers may not think of it as visualization, but they use it often. It happens at a whiteboard, or on butcher paper, or, classically, on the back of a napkin.

Like idea illustration, it relies on conceptual metaphors and conventions, but it takes place in more-informal settings, such as off-sites, strategy sessions, and early-phase innovation projects. It's used to find answers to nondata challenges: restructuring an organization, coming up with a new business process, codifying a system for making decisions.

Idea exploration can be done alone, but it benefits from collaboration and borrows on design thinking processes: gathering as many diverse points of view and visual approaches as possible before homing in on one and refining it. Jon Kolko, the founder and director of Austin Center for Design and the author of *Well-Designed: How to Use Empathy to Create Products People Love*, fills his office with conceptual, exploratory visualizations strewn across whiteboard walls. "It's our go-to method for thinking through complexity," he says. "Sketching is this effort to work through ambiguity and muddiness and come to crispness." Managers who are good at leading teams, facilitating brainstorming sessions, and capturing creative thinking will do well in this quadrant.

Suppose a marketing team is holding an off-site. The team members need to come up with a way to show executives their proposed strategy for going upmarket. An hour-long

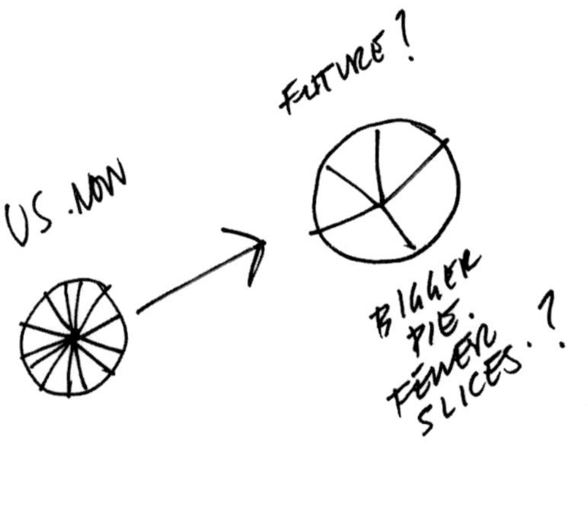

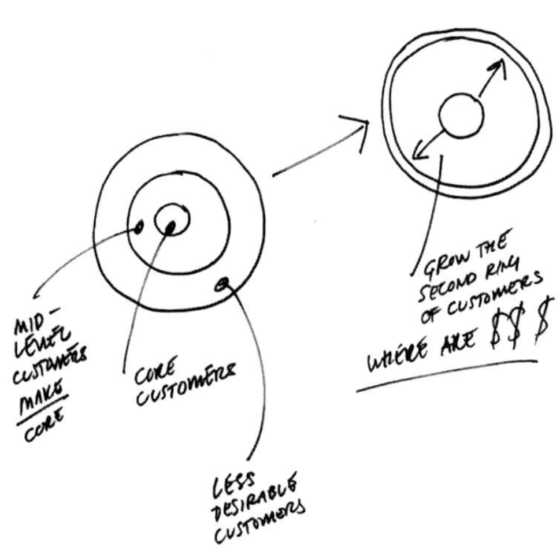

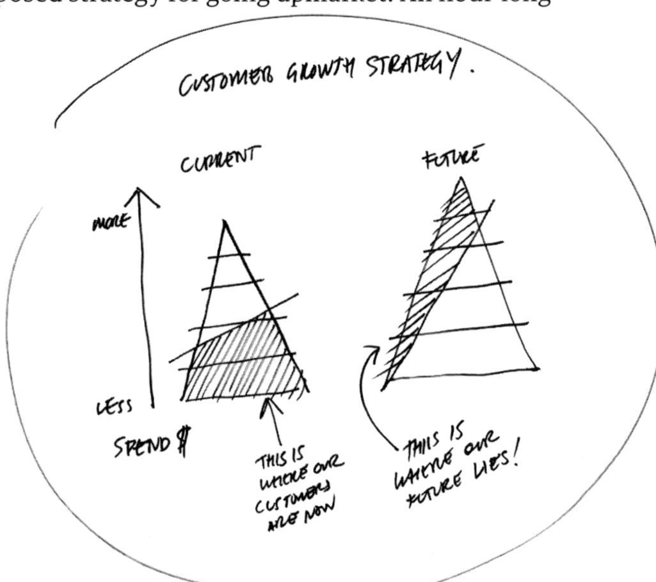

whiteboard session yields several approaches and ideas (none of which are erased) for showing their transition strategy. Ultimately, one approach gains purchase with the team, which thinks it best captures the key points of its strategy: get fewer customers to spend much more.

The facing page shows rough sketches of a whiteboard at the end of the idea generation session. Of course, visuals that emerge from idea exploration often lead to more formally designed and presented idea illustrations.

VISUAL DISCOVERY: DATA-DRIVEN, EXPLORATORY VISUALIZATIONS

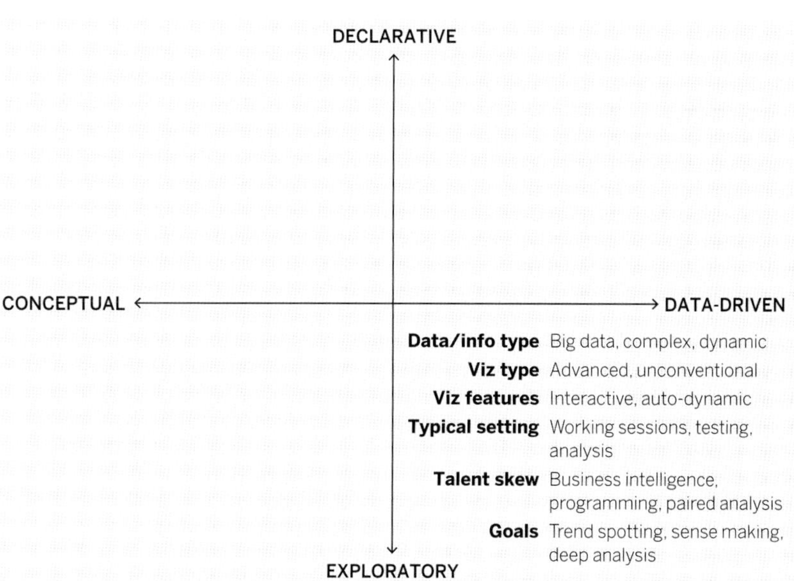

Visual discovery. This is the most complicated category, because in truth it's actually two categories. Remember that the purpose question led to three possible types of tasks: declarative, confirmatory, and exploratory. But I left confirmatory out of the 2×2 to keep the basic framework simple and clear. Now, while we focus on this quadrant, I will add that information in, as seen on the adapted 2×2 on the next page.

Note that confirmatory applies only to data-driven charts. A hypothesis can't be confirmed or disproved without data. Also, the division is shown as a dotted line because it's a soft distinction. Confirmation is a kind of focused exploration, whereas true exploration is more open-ended. The bigger and more complex the data, and the less you know going in, the more exploratory the work. If confirmation is hiking a new trail, exploration is blazing one.

Visual confirmation. You're answering one of two questions with this kind of project:

1. Is what I suspect is true actually true?
2. What are some other ways of looking at this idea?

The scope of the data here is manageable, and the chart types you're likely to use are common—although when you're trying to see things in new ways, you may venture into some less common types. Confirmation usually doesn't happen in a formal setting; it's the work you do to find the charts you want to create for presentations. That means your time will shift away from design and toward prototyping that allows you to iterate on the data and rapidly visualize and revisualize.

Suppose a manager in charge of travel services wants to research whether the plane tickets the company buys are worth the investment. She goes into her visual confirmation project hypothesizing that comfort increases with ticket cost. She pulls data on cost versus comfort for both economy and business class flights and quickly generates a

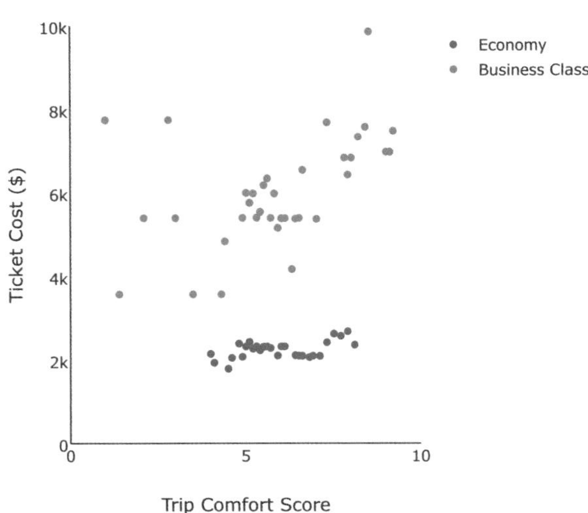

scatter plot. She's expecting to see correlation—dots splayed up and to the right.

Notice that the chart she creates, above, is a prototype. The manager hasn't spent much time refining the design or refining the axes and titles. It's more important for her to see if her idea is right than to make it look great. Immediately she sees that the relationship between cost and her other variables is relatively weak. There is an upward trend in comfort on business class, but it's not strong. She's startled to find her hypothesis doesn't hold. Higher cost of flights may not be worth it. She thinks about what other ideas to test before making any decisions.

VISUAL CONFIRMATION AND VISUAL EXPLORATION

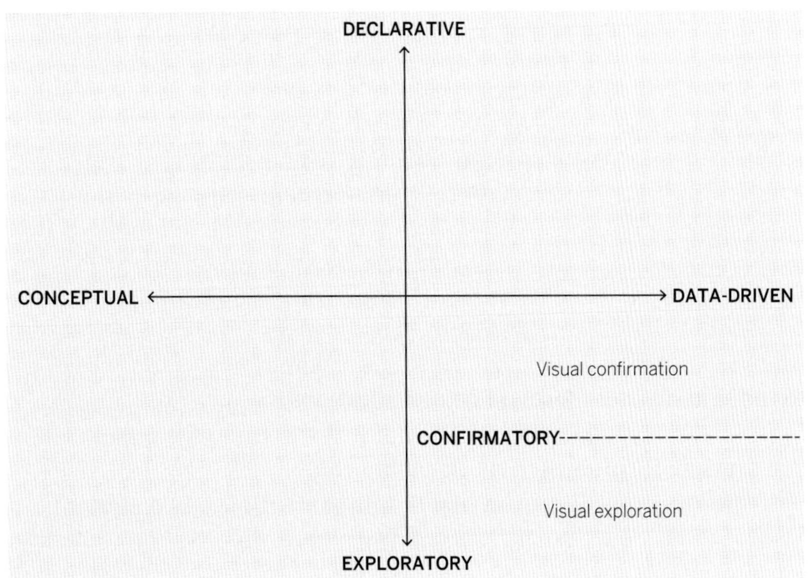

Visual exploration. Exploratory, data-driven visualizations tend to be the province of data scientists and business intelligence analysts, although new tools have begun to engage general managers in visual exploration. It's an exciting kind of visualization to try, because it often produces insights that can't be gleaned any other way.

Since we don't know what we're looking for, these visuals tend to be more inclusive in the data they plot. In extreme cases, this kind of project may combine multiple data sets or even dynamic, real-time data that updates automatically. It may even venture beyond the data. David Sparks, a political scientist and statistical analyst who now works for the NBA's Boston Celtics does visual exploration. But he refers to his work as "model visualization." In Sparks's world, data visualization focuses on real, existing data. Model visualization passes data through statistical models to see what *would* happen under certain circumstances.

Exploration lends itself to interactivity—allowing a manager to adjust parameters, inject data sources, and continually revisualize. Complex data sometimes also lends itself to specialized and unusual visualization types, such as force-directed network diagrams that show how networks cluster, or topographical plots.

Function trumps form here: software, programming, data management, and business intelligence skills are more crucial than the ability to create presentable charts. This quadrant is where a manager is most likely to call in experts to help create the visualizations. In chapter 4 we'll explore one such method of partnering with pros, called paired analysis.

A manager at a social media company has been asked to look for new markets for its technology. He wants to find opportunities that others won't see. He connects with a data scientist who tells him how semantic analysis can be used to map thousands of companies in multiple industries according to the similarity of their text communications.

The manager loves the idea but can't do it himself. He hires the data scientist, who develops and adjusts the data set with the manager until they can generate a rough visual that maps thousands of companies. Semantic analysis links similar companies; the more similar the companies, the "stronger" the link and the more closely they're mapped. This

MODELING MULTIPLE FUTURES

"I remember when I learned about regression, in my undergraduate statistics class. It seemed like magic."

David Sparks was a poli-sci major, not a stats major, at Vanderbilt. But the way regression models could show multiple potential futures excited him. After learning how they worked, he grabbed some baseball statistics and tried one on his own. "It worked," he says. "It was really cool."

Graduate-level political science, which he took on at Duke, proved to be more statistically intense than he had expected. He knew that he'd have to learn how to use data analysis software such as Stata and R. "So during the day, I was a research assistant doing typical research assistant things," he says. "When office hours were over, I'd open up Stata, grab some baseball or basketball statistics, and teach myself how to use it."

Why sports data and not political data sets? "Political data can be messy. I was trying to learn, and in sports the data is clean and I'm interested in it."

To offset the deeply technical learning he was doing with the stats software, he sought out less taxing, more-popular writing: *Freakonomics*, *The Undercover Economist*. Eventually, he found Edward Tufte. "I hadn't been excited about visualization before that," he says. "The stats packages didn't do visualization very well, so I never thought about it much."

He found visualization challenging, but also deeply rewarding. "It's such a powerful way to show regression and uncertainty. These are important ideas when you're modeling the future, and it's hard to keep many numbers from a table in your head at once. Finding ways to represent these abstract concepts visually intrigued me."

The practice on sports data sets led to an internship and later a consulting gig with the Boston Celtics. "I still wanted to be a political scientist," he says, "but this was perfect. I could work on basketball data sets and tell myself it would make me a better political scientist, because I was learning the tools and methodologies and how to think about problems."

He was right. His dabbling in visualization for sports led Sparks to map the history of the US Congress's ideological polarization (using a data set called Nominate) for his "real" job. Despite the deep analysis that went into it, and its sophisticated form, it was a simple chart: When blue and red lines converged, Congress was less polarized. As they diverged, it became more polarized.

But Sparks added another layer of information, distinguishing between northern and southern Democrats: "A major narrative in twentieth-century American history is how northern Democrats were isolated as southern Democrats, who were already more conservative, became even more conservative, until they eventually became Republicans."

The chart is detailed and possibly not accessible to a lay audience, but he knew his audience of professors and students would understand what he had captured. He knew his context.

"I remember the day I showed it to my advisers at Duke," he says. "These guys are top congressional scholars. This is what they teach. I was so nervous." No need: They were impressed that Sparks had summed up in one graph what they used full lectures to explain. They requested copies to use in their classes and to display as a poster. "That's when I thought, 'Okay, I can do this.'"

As for his process, Sparks doesn't sketch. His investment in those statistical packages has enabled him to go straight there. The software allows for rapid prototyping and lets him try multiple chart types quickly.

Because he works with complicated data, he rarely makes charts that plot only two variables. "There's almost always some z-axis—color, size of bubbles. Something." This has forced him to become good at the design part of visualization, because the more information he encodes in his charts, the more complicated they become. Sometimes he sacrifices instantaneous recognition, demanding that his audience spend time analyzing. It's necessary, he says, because modeling the future isn't simple. But it's also worth it, because the ideas it can surface are so powerful. "Is it that important that they get it in under a second? Sometimes. But for some ideas, if they invest a few seconds, they can get a richer, more rewarding experience."

When presenting visuals, "the chart needs to be making an argument," Sparks says. "Supplying all the data you have isn't really useful. You wouldn't write a paragraph that includes everything you know about a topic."

Sparks finished his doctorate at Duke, but he found the market for poli-sci profs underwhelming. So all that practice visualizing with sports paid off. He signed on with the Celtics, where his role, he says, is to "quantify and visualize what we believe about basketball and basketball players." Consistently, Sparks describes what he does as "model visualization" rather than "exploratory visualization." The difference: he's using statistics to represent potential futures and their uncertainty. "Visualizing uncertainty is not a trivial challenge. We're already showing complicated ideas about the future to people who don't do data, and then we have to have this layer of uncertainty over it. It's one of the most important challenges for the viz community to work on."

He didn't model his own future, but he's happy to be in it.

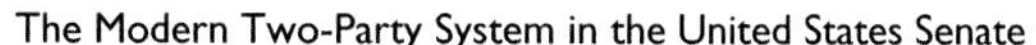

The Modern Two-Party System in the United States Senate

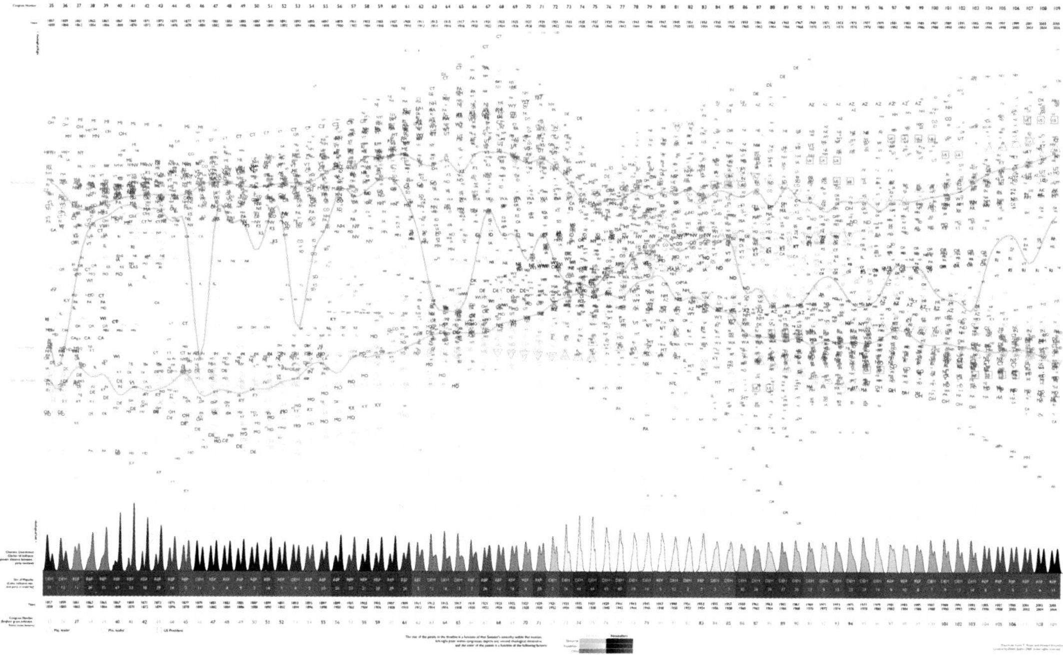

INDUSTRY CLUSTER SEMANTIC ANALYSIS

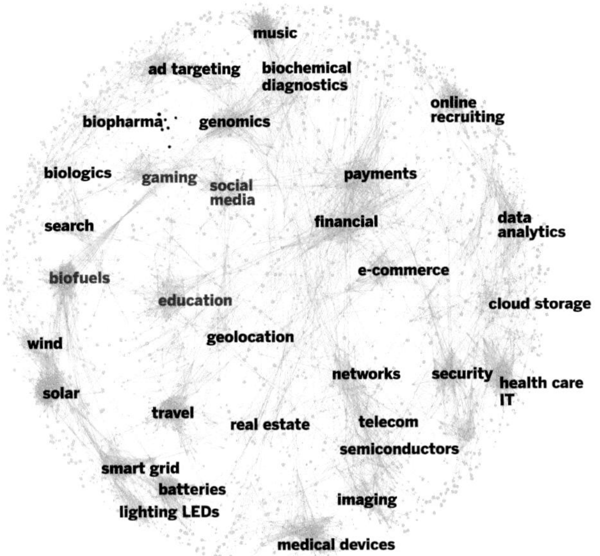

results in this network diagram, which exposes easy-to-see industry clusters. The white space between proximate clusters represents opportunities to connect one industry to another, because although the data shows that those clusters are similar, no companies have yet emerged to fill the gap.[3]

The manager is not surprised when he immediately notices that social media and gaming don't have much white space between them; he's played Candy Crush Saga. But he does see white space between social media and other industries, such as education and biofuels—potential new markets for his technology.

Everyday dataviz. Unlike data scientists, who do more exploratory work, managers focus here. These are the basic charts and graphs you normally spit out of an Excel spreadsheet and paste into a PowerPoint. They are most often simple forms, such as line charts, bar charts, pies, and scatter plots.

The key word here is *simple*. The data sets tend to be small and simple. The visualization communicates a simple idea or message, charting no more than a few variables. And the goal is simple: give people factual information based on data that is, for the most part, not up for debate.

EVERYDAY DATAVIZ: DATA-DRIVEN, DECLARATIVE VISUALIZATIONS

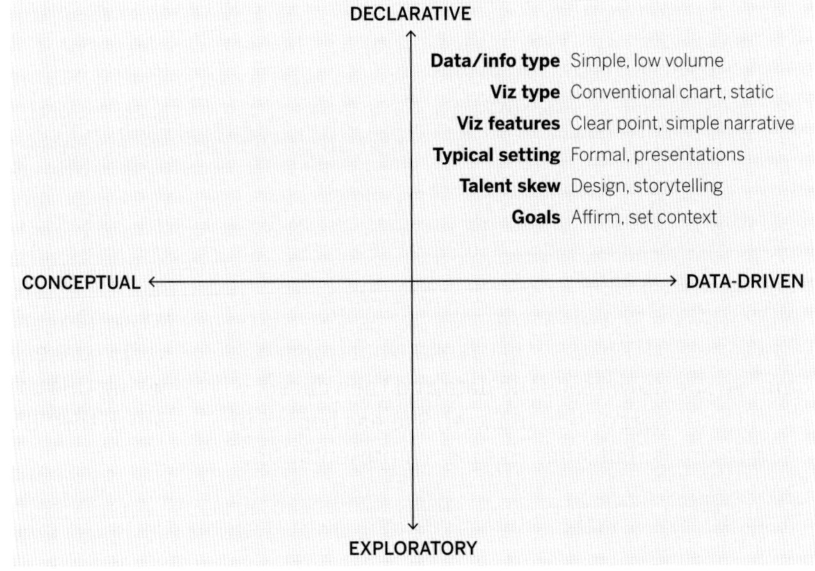

Simplicity is primarily a design challenge. Clarity and consistency make these charts most effective in the setting where they're typically used—a formal presentation. In a presentation, time is constrained. A poorly designed chart will waste that limited time by creating questions that require the presenter to explain the structure of the visual or the information that's meant to come to the fore. A manager should be able to present an everyday dataviz without speaking at all. If it can't speak for itself, it has failed like a joke whose punch line needs explanation.

That's not to say that declarative charts shouldn't generate discussion. They should. But the discussion should be about the ideas in the chart, not the chart itself.

An HR vice president will be presenting to the rest of the executive committee about the company's health care costs. A key message she wants to convey is that the growth of these costs has slowed significantly, giving the company an opportunity to think about what additional services it might offer.

She's read an online report about the slowing growth that includes a link to some government data. So she downloads the data and then clicks on the line chart option in Excel. She has her viz in a few seconds. But since this is for a presentation, she asks a designer colleague to add even more detail from the dataset about GDP and recessions, to give a more comprehensive view of the data.

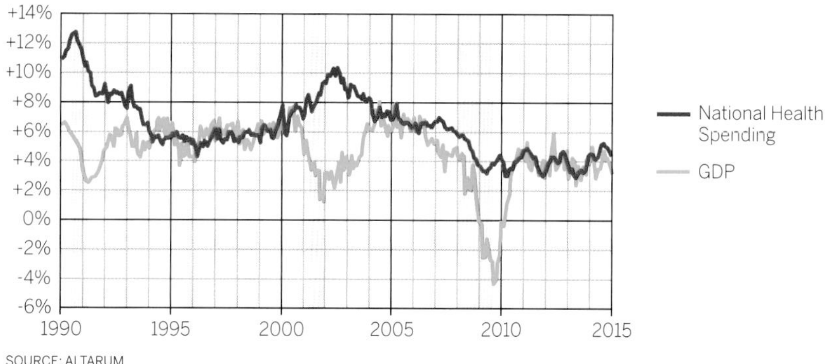

This is a well-designed, accurate chart, but it's probably not the right one. The HR exec's audience doesn't need two decades' worth of historical context to discuss the company's strategy for employee benefits investments. The point she wants to make is that cost increases have slowed over the past few years. Does that jump out here?

In general, charts that contain enough data to take minutes, not seconds, to digest will work better on paper or a personal screen, for an individual who's not being asked to listen to a presentation while trying to take in so much information. Health care policy makers, for example, might benefit from seeing this chart in advance of a policy hearing in which they'll discuss these long trends.

But our exec needs something simpler for her context. From the same data set, she creates the Annual Growth chart on the next page.

ANNUAL GROWTH IS DECLINING

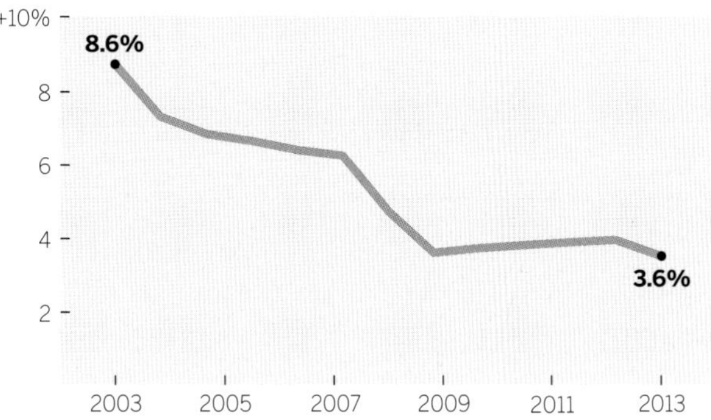

SOURCE: CENTERS FOR MEDICARE & MEDICAID SERVICES

She won't have to utter a word for the executive team to understand the trend. Clearly and without distractions, she has set the foundation for presenting her recommendations.

USE THE "FOUR TYPES" 2×2

The "four types" 2×2 is a useful structure. Just as you can layer many types of information over a basic road map—where the gas stations are, what traffic and the weather are like—you can layer any number of ideas, resources, rules of thumb, over the map of visualization types, to help plan the time, resources, and skills you'll need. Here are five examples:

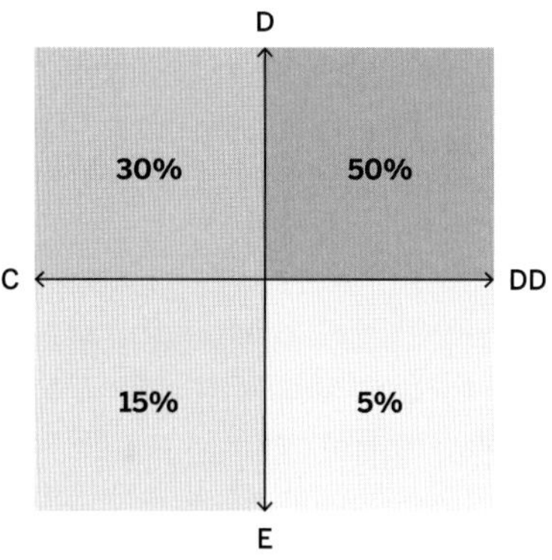

Usage frequency. Your numbers may vary. I've put in my own starting point. Most managers will spend the majority of their charting time with everyday dataviz. However, new software and online tools are making discovery and exploration much easier. I expect that number in the bottom right quadrant to grow.

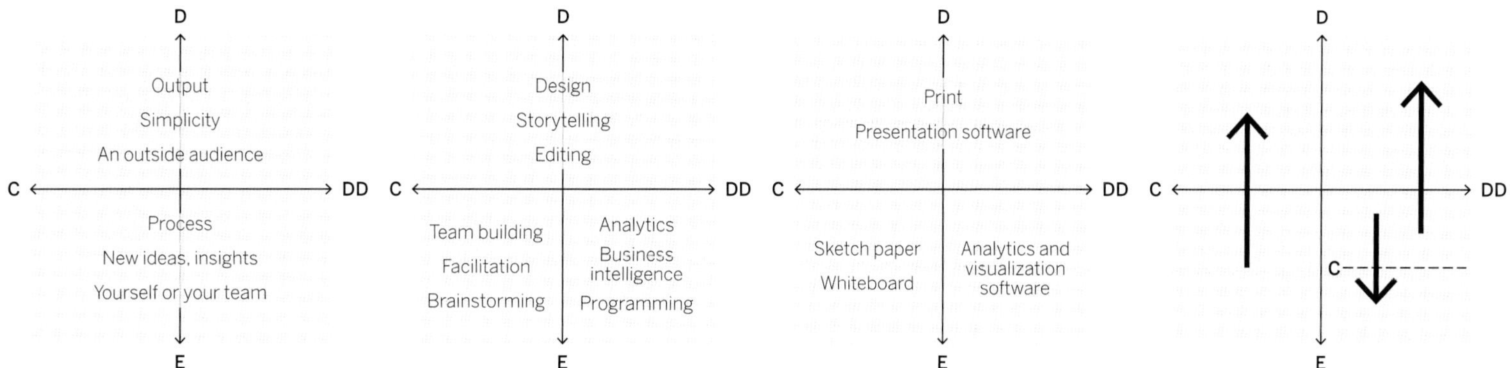

Focus. For declaratives, focus on output—creating great visuals that will move others. For exploratories, worry less about how your visualizations look and more about generating ideas and allowing you and your team to learn.

Skills. A project's importance, complexity, and deadline will dictate whether skills should be developed or hired. You're most likely to need to contract with others in the discovery quadrant and for crucial presentations, such as to the board. And managers should develop idea exploration skills whether or not they're applied to infoviz.

Media. In general, tools in the exploratory half enhance your ability to interact and iterate, whereas tools for declaratives support great design. But expect more good design to be built into exploratory software tools as they're developed.

Workflows. Exploratory work often results in insights that you want to share in well-designed declarative charts for a broader audience. All the 2×2 idea illustrations in this chapter, for example, started as idea explorations before being designed for publication. Sometimes testing a hypothesis in confirmatory work will produce unexpected results that you can't explain, and thus will send you into deeper exploration.

You can keep layering over the frame. You might, for example, add the names of colleagues you'll call on when doing a certain type of visualization. You might add links to the software tools you use in the various quadrants, or links to courses you want to take to improve your skills with visualization.

Looking at information visualization this way makes it seem less like one thing and more like a group of related but different things. The skills you'll call on, the tools you'll use, and the media you'll visualize with can vary significantly from quadrant to quadrant. What makes an idea illustration a good chart may be different from what makes an everyday dataviz a good chart.

Spending just a few minutes asking the two questions at the beginning of this chapter—Is the information *conceptual* or *data-driven*? and Am I *declaring something* or *exploring something*?—will prepare you to visualize well. You'll have packed for the right trip.

RECAP

TWO QUESTIONS → FOUR TYPES

Visualization is a diverse craft. Different types require different skills and resources. Before making visuals, plan for them. Determine what skills and resources you'll need by defining your visual communication as one of four kinds. You'll put yourself in the right mind-set for the project and save time by having planned ahead.

Answer two questions to learn which kind of visual communication you're about to undertake:

1. **Is my information *conceptual* or *data-driven*?**
   - Conceptual information is qualitative. Think of processes, hierarchies, cycles, and organization.
   - Data-driven information is quantitative. Think of revenues, ratings, and percentages.

2. **Are my visuals meant to be *declarative* or *exploratory*?**
   - A declarative purpose is to make a statement to an audience—to inform and affirm.
   - An exploratory purpose is to look for new ideas—to seek and discover.

Match your answers to the type of visual communication shown the Four Types 2×2 matrix:

THE FOUR TYPES

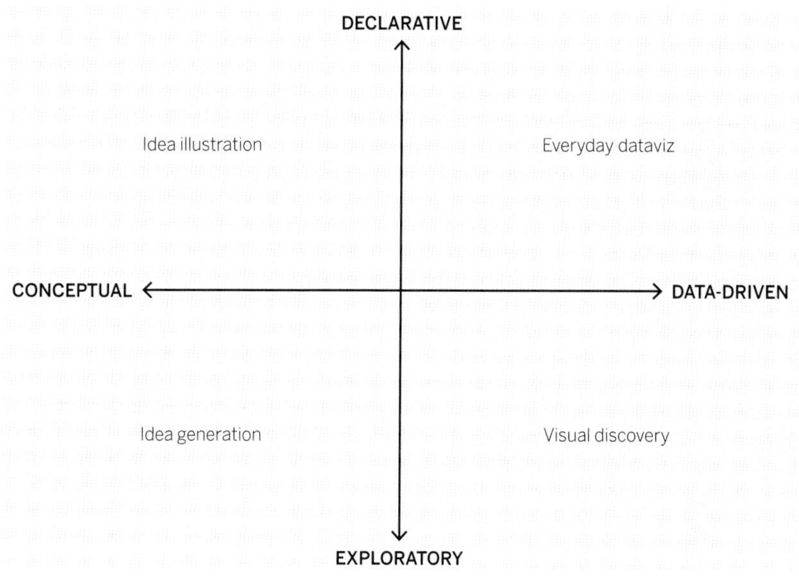

Idea illustration
A visualization of an idea that's not connected to statistical data. Often uses metaphors, such as trees, or processes, like cycles. Examples include organizational charts, process diagrams, and this 2×2 matrix itself.

Idea generation

Rapidly sketched concepts for visualizing ideas not connected to statistical data. Often done in groups as brainstorming sessions, on whiteboards, or, famously, on the back of a napkin.

Visual discovery

Visualization in which data is used to confirm hypotheses or find patterns and trends. *Visual confirmation:* the more-declarative subset of visual discovery that is generated to test a hypothesis or look at data in a new way. It's often done by an individual, usually with statistical software, such as Excel or any number of online tools. *Visual exploration:* the more-exploratory portion of visual discovery, which uses data in its rawest form to see what patterns or trends emerge. Relies on large data sets and dynamic data sets that change often. Usually requires advanced software tools and data science or business analysis skills.

Everyday dataviz

Standard charts and graphs used to express an idea to an audience. Usually well designed and based on a manageable amount of data, and often used in a presentation setting.

You can use this 2×2 as a template to make notes about each type of visualization, the skills you want to build for developing them, the tools you'll call on, and any other hints you'll find useful whenever you start a visualization project. For example, here's a version that provides reminders of what to think about for each type:

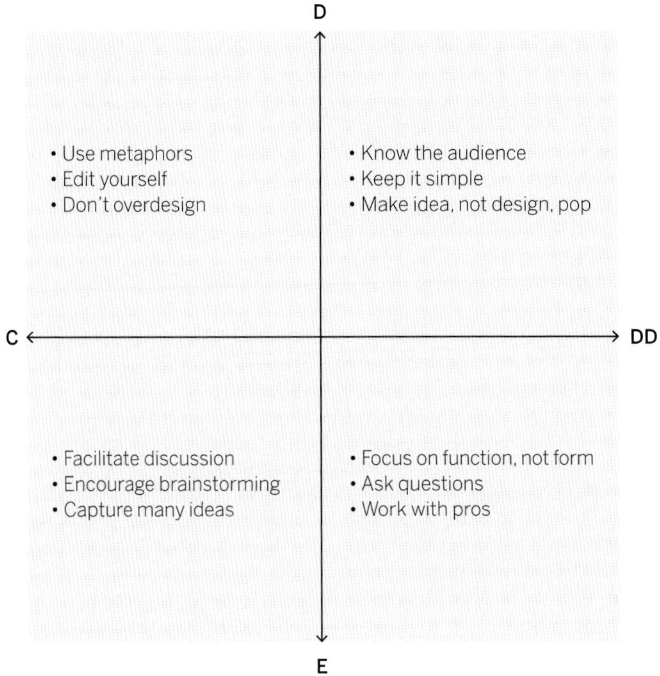

CHAPTER 4

BETTER CHARTS IN A COUPLE OF HOURS

A SIMPLE FRAMEWORK

MOST OF THE STRESS MANAGERS feel about creating charts relates to picking the right kind, which often amounts to scanning preset options in Excel or Google Sheets and trying out a few until one looks right or just seems pleasing. They might adorn it with a few more clicks—3-D, color. The tools make it so easy to produce a visualization that the biggest challenge in crafting good charts is overcoming the inclination—temptation, really—to just click and build. It seems hardly worth putting more time and effort into the process.

Of course, that's flat wrong. That approach might be fast, and it might spruce up the look of a chart, but it doesn't refine the ideas that the chart conveys. Recall the Good Charts matrix in the introduction that crosses design execution with context setting: Good charts

It takes less time than you'd expect to transform your thinking so that instead of producing the two bar charts on the right—which were created by a consultant for a pitch to clients—you produce the four line charts below.

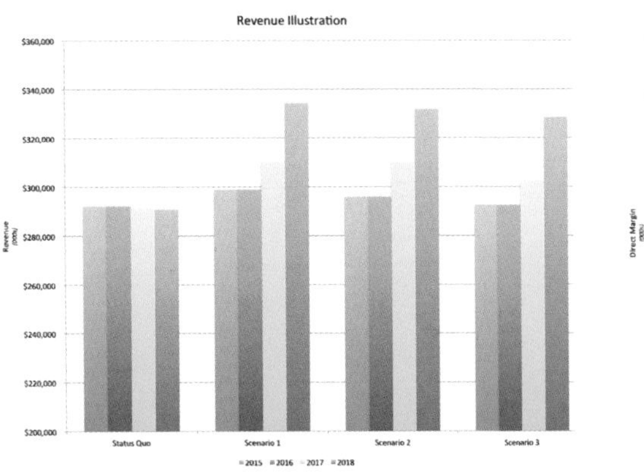

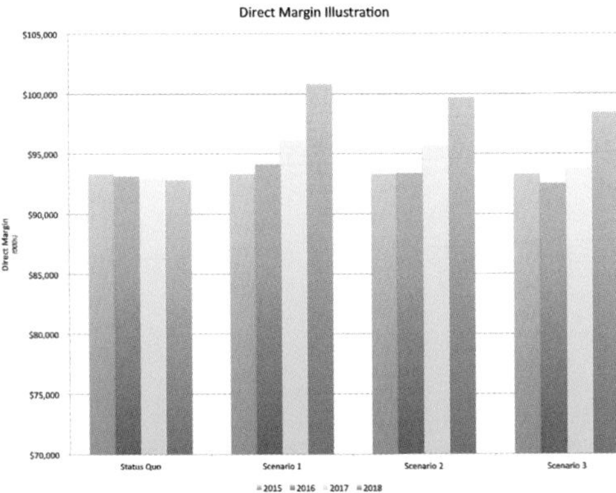

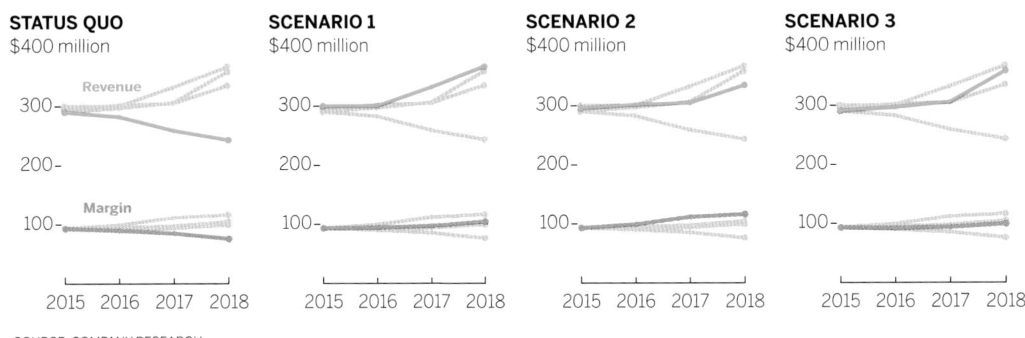

are a positive combination of those two elements. Even if software programs automatically generated well-designed charts (most of them don't), none sets context to any meaningful degree; a spreadsheet doesn't know the chart's audience or purpose. Programs visualize data. People visualize ideas.

So instead of jumping right to chart types and design, you need more inputs to help define your context and identify the visual approach that will be most effective. This isn't a waste of time and effort; it's the antidote to unthinking, automatically generated charts. With just a little effort we can turn the bar charts on the facing page—which are charts from a real presentation by a consultant to clients—into the line charts below them.

An upgrade like that doesn't take as much time or effort as you might suspect. This one took 45 minutes. In some cases you can make major gains in the quality of your visual communication in less time than that. In others you may spend an afternoon on a chart. On average, you can radically improve your charts in an hour or so.

Here's how. Let's start with these steps and time frames:

BUILDING BETTER CHARTS

MINUTES SPENT AT EACH TASK

Prep time usually doesn't take more than a few minutes. But as you might expect, ensuing steps' time will vary according to the type of visualization and the complexity of the project. For one or two good charts, start with this time distribution.

PREP

Cooks would call this *mise en place*—all their ingredients and their kitchen organized to prepare for cooking. Do these three things:

Create three kinds of space.

- **Mental space:** Block out time on your calendar. Turn off e-mail and social channels. Focus.
- **Physical space:** If you're in an open-concept office, get a room. Even if you have an office, find a quiet, closed-off area away from your desk to minimize interruptions. You'll be seeking others' ideas and opinions, but you don't want random, unsolicited comments from passers-by.
- **White space:** Bring plenty of paper and whiteboards. A rolling whiteboard will allow you to take notes back to your desk. If you can't get one, bring a phone to snap pictures of your sketches. It's helpful to have markers and pens in three or four colors.

Put aside your data. This may seem counterintuitive, but it's key to allowing for more-expansive thinking. Don't ignore the data—make sure you understand it—but don't lead with it. "When you start with the data set in mind, it limits how you think," says Jeff Heer, an associate professor of computer science who teaches data visualization. "First you need to step back and think more broadly."

Focusing on the cells of data can lead to banal results—charts that just convert tables to visual form. If you start with a more open point of view, you may discover ways to make your idea come through more strongly by introducing new data, or crunching the data you have.

Here's a simple example. A general manager for an e-commerce site is looking at customer purchase activity by time of day. Visualizing the data from one of his spreadsheet's columns yields this:

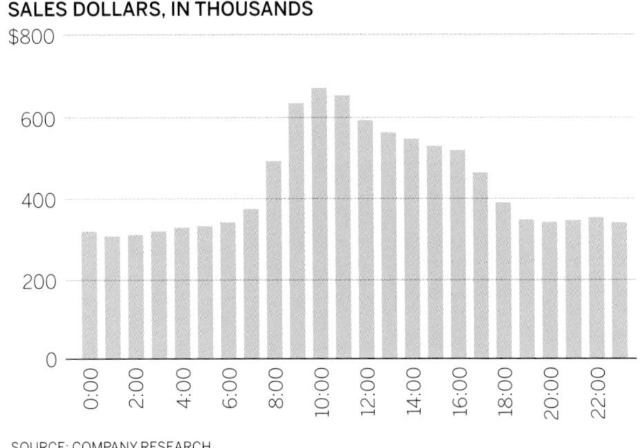

This is not bad, and it was simple to execute. But if the manager had put aside the data and talked through what he was trying to show (a process I'll get to in a minute), he'd have realized that the data was normalized to Eastern Standard Time, in the location where the purchase was registered, not to time in the location where the purchase was made. It would be more useful to show volume of sales by the *purchaser's* time of day:

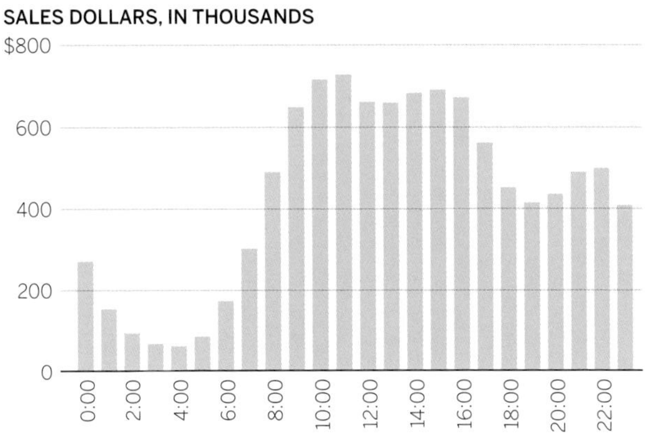

Starting from what he wanted to show rather than from what data he had on hand led to a different, more useful chart.

Write down the basics. You've created space. Now document a few key pieces of information on your paper or whiteboard to help frame your thinking. Include:

- what you'll call it
- who it's for
- what setting it will be used in
- which of the four types of visualization you're creating
- where on the Good Charts Matrix between context and design you should aim

For example, take a look at the Sales Team Performance sketches below.

Add keywords and notes as prompts and reminders. This will serve as a launching point, or as a buoy you can return to if you drift off in the talking and sketching you're about to do (which should be encouraged; think expansively).

TALK AND LISTEN

If you want your charts to get better, talk about what you're trying to show, listen to yourself, and listen to others. Conversations contain a trove of clues about the best way forward. Words and phrases will steer you to the data you need, the parts of it to focus on, and possible chart types to use.

Of all the things you do to make better charts, this will be the most revelatory, but also possibly the least natural. It takes getting used to. Practice doing these three things:

Find a colleague or friend. Although you can talk out loud to yourself or take notes, having someone to chat with works better. Who? That depends. If you feel uncertain about your approach, ask an outsider, someone who doesn't know much about either the data or what you're doing, whose reactions will be free from the assumptions and biases of those who are familiar with the data and its audience. That will force you to explain even basic information, organize your ideas, and provide context. It will feel like brainstorming.

Conversely, if you're confident about your approach but you want to refine it or to make sure that it's sound, connect with someone closer to the project who knows more about the data and may even be part of the audience. This will feel more like a gut check.

Talk about specific questions. Don't wander into the conversation without a plan. Start with these questions:

- What am I working on?
- What am I trying to say or show (or prove or learn)?
- Why?

The first question is straightforward and factual, most useful if your counterpart is an outsider. It gives rise to necessary exposition; his ensuing questions may signal when you're making assumptions that he's not and help you notice when you're veering off topic.

Imagine starting one of these conversations this way:

I'm working on showing the bosses we have an opportunity to invest in new HR programs—

Wait—smaller programs for the upcoming fiscal year, or more like big, long-term investments?

Already the conversation is forcing you to focus more precisely on what you want to show.

The second question will vary according to whether you're in the declarative space (*What am I trying to say or show?*) or the confirmatory or exploratory space (*What am I trying to prove or learn?*). Notice that you're still explicitly avoiding your data. You don't want to ask, *What does the data say?* Even if you're reasonably certain that your viz will be a straight translation of some of your data, this is your chance to think more broadly about your approach, which may in turn lead you to seek out other data or information to incorporate into your visualization.

It will help with subsequent activities if, while you're talking, you find and jot down a short phrase or sentence that becomes the working answer to *What am I trying to say?* Here's a conversation that arrives at such a statement:

I'm trying to show my boss that we're doing better than she thinks in terms of customer retention.

Why does she think you're doing poorly?

Well, our retention rate has fallen for three straight quarters. I know it looks bad right now, and everyone is panicking.

So how is it better than she thinks?

Well, it's not what we're doing, as far as I can tell—it's what's happening in the industry. Although our retention rate is falling, it's not falling nearly as dramatically as our two main competitors'. Something systemic is going on, I'd guess.

Ah!

If I can show her that clearly, I can tell her that we should focus our worry, our energy, on figuring out what's going on in the market, not on changing how we're executing as a company.

The manager has found a visual starting point. He starts by suggesting that what he wants to tell his boss is "We're doing better than you think." His partner recognizes that as a qualitative statement, and does well to press the manager into explaining. This leads the manager to a description of what he can show to prove it to his boss: "Although our retention rate is falling, it's not falling nearly as dramatically as our two main competitors'."

The third question is the most difficult and, frankly, the most annoying. Keep asking "Why?" and encourage the person you're speaking with to challenge you as well. If you become exasperated, find yourself unable to come up with a good answer, or hear yourself saying "Just because!" that's a good sign that you need to think more critically about what you're trying to show. This conversation and its litany of "Why?" forces a manager to admit that she's not prepared to create the declarative she's proposing:

I want to compare financial results to key productivity data like time spent on e-mail and in meetings.

Why? What's the connection there?

It just seems like there's probably a relationship between the two. Revenues are down. I ask myself, *Why?* We're in meetings so much now. We never have time to work!

But don't you get work done in meetings? Why are they the problem?

I mean, I know I'm getting less done because of all this time spent on other stuff.

Why does one lead to the other, though? How can you actually prove that more meetings and e-mails equals lower revenue?

I'm not sure, but of course there's some connection there. There has to be!

Why? What if they're helping you get work done, too?

Just because! I'm sick of sitting in meetings!

If you're trying to create a declarative dataviz and you can't adequately answer the "Why?" you might want to stop, form a few hypotheses, and test them with exploratory visuals to see what emerges.

Listen and take notes. As you talk, listen to your counterpart, but listen to yourself, too. Pick out visual words and phrases that describe how you *see* the ideas and information and write them down. If, for example, you hear yourself using words like *distributed* and *spread out over,* or *different types* and *clusters*, they are clues to your potential approach. Listen for metaphors: *The money's flying out of our department. We saw a huge dip. Revenues fell off a cliff. It's a crazy maze of choices.* They evoke powerful imagery that could inform how you design your information.

Take this statement: "I want to compare the number of job postings to hires to see what the ratio is for different types of jobs." That sentence contains enough information to suggest a strong visual approach. Here it is again, with the visual cues emphasized:

I want to **compare the number** of job postings to hires to **see** what **the ratio** is for **different types** of jobs.

Compare the number suggests a chart that plots data points along a numbered axis. *The ratio* tells you you're comparing one number with another. *Different types* suggests that you can repeat the comparison across several categories, and maybe create subgroups. (You may also notice some of the other nouns describe potential variables: *Postings*, *hires*, and *jobs* are all important categories of data. Note these, too.)

Let's skip ahead for a moment. Pulling those keywords from that one sentence could bring the manager to the following final visualization. Reread the sentence the manager captured: It's all reflected in the chart:

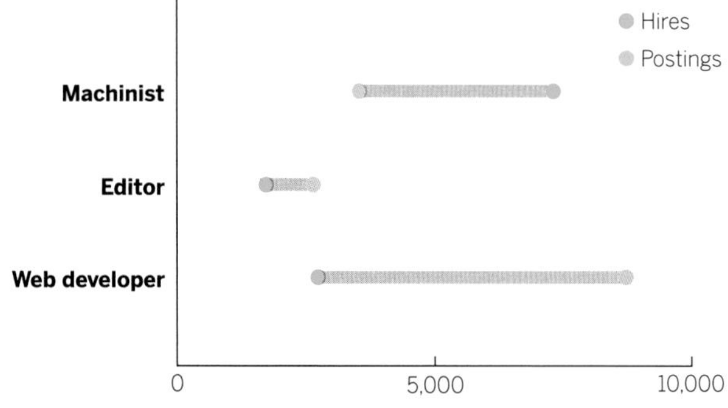

Here's another example, this one of a sales manager who wants to do some exploratory visualization of his teams' sales performance. "It's not clear," he says to his friend, "that there's any regular pattern to our sales. I'm really trying to understand how and when they make sales—how sales are happening over time. Is it mostly smooth, or are there bursts of sales with periods of nothing? Is it the same month to month or not? Are different seasons showing different sales patterns?"

If he's been doing this for a while, he will have jotted down several keywords and phrases from his chat:

It's not clear there's any regular **pattern** to our sales. I'm really trying to understand how and **when** they make sales—how sales are **happening over time**. Is it **mostly smooth** or are there **bursts** of sales with **periods of nothing**? Is it the same **month to month** or not? Are different **seasons** showing different sales **patterns**?

It's a bit strange at first, listening to yourself talk in such an active way, but it's undeniably valuable. Time and again I've watched people's eyes light up as someone utters a phrase that creates a *Eureka!* moment. Suddenly they realize how they'll visualize something. A favorite example comes from when I worked with the venerable business professor Clay Christensen. He wanted to visualize the fact that his *Harvard Business Review* feature article "The Capitalist's Dilemma" was the product of dozens of ideas that people had posted to an online discussion forum created in part by IDEO.[1] The forum allowed participants to note which posts had influenced their own, and tracked how many people read a post and how many commented on it. I'm paraphrasing him here, but in effect he said, "I want to show how a network of contributors helped shape this article into its final form."

Christensen's team created a rough sketch of what they thought might work to show the interconnections in the conversations. It looked like a cross between a constellation and a flow chart and was peppered with quotations from the forum discussion. A version of it is displayed to the right, on top.

It was a start. It conveyed the idea of interconnectedness, but it also felt somewhat haphazard. What did the colors mean? What did the dots represent? We wanted to improve it. We spent 30 minutes in a conference room talking and listening. I jotted down many keywords and metaphors from the session, including *network of ideas*, *interconnectedness*, *back-and-forth exchange*, *over time*, *crowdsourced*, *big influencers*. Eventually, as Christensen continued to explain how the forum helped him write the article, he said (again paraphrasing), "All the ideas from the forum flowed into the article." *Flowed into.* That was it. We had hit on a good visual metaphor, and we started sketching rough versions of two types of charts that represent flows: alluvial and Sankey diagrams. We continued to talk, until someone in the small group (there were five of us) uttered another keyword when he mentioned how the conversation in the forum *cascaded*.

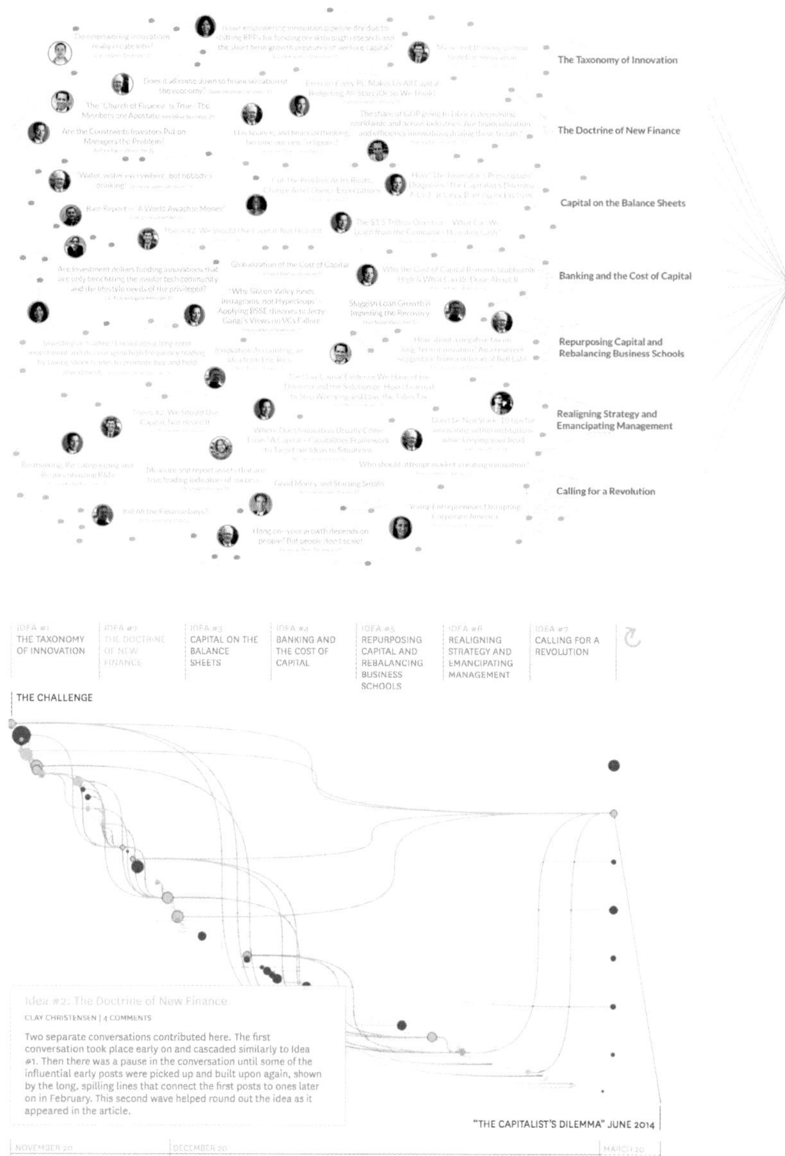

That was enough to begin building the chart. Ultimately, it became the interactive visualization (previous page, bottom) in which *flow* and *cascade over time* are plainly evident.[2]

When you're talking and listening, force yourself to answer that fundamental question out loud: *What am I trying to show or say (or learn, or prove)?* More than you may suspect of the answer to that question lurks in a brief conversation. Once you extract those words, it's time to draw.

SKETCH

Finally, you're drawing. You should come out of this step with an approach and a rough draft that can be refined. Here's how to start:

Match keywords to approaches. The words you wrote down can now be put to use. Start drawing examples of the visual words you captured. Match those words to types of visual forms. You can match them to the types of visualizations that typically best show what they describe.

You may have seen or used a chart cheat sheet like Andrew Abela's. The university provost and former dean of the business school at Catholic University of America, he has written books about effective presentations.[3] Abela's guide, on the facing page, organizes typical charts well, but it comes with caveats. For instance, not everyone will agree on which chart types should be included and which excluded. Some people will take exception, for example, with Abela's inclusion of pie charts and spider charts (Abela calls spiders "circular area charts" here), which they consider difficult or suboptimal. Others will ask why unit charts and slope graphs *aren't* included. And what about tables?

Also, a guide like this could narrow our thinking at a stage when we should be broadening it. It's something like pouring out a bucket of Legos in front of a child and then telling her she can make only the ten things in the instruction booklet. At the beginning of the sketching phase, we're better off just messing around with the Legos.

Still, Abela's guide is here for two reasons. First, it's as good as any typology out there (an online search will yield many more) at helping us understand categories of forms—comparison versus distribution, for example. Remember that no cheat sheet will encompass all options. Under every common chart type shown here is a remarkable diversity of variations. New chart species are being spawned all the time. Trying to identify and document every variation of every chart type would be a quixotic effort at best.

It's better to just learn basic categories and types and then become a collector. Look around; collect examples of infoviz that appeal to you or that you

ABELA'S CHART TYPE HIERARCHY

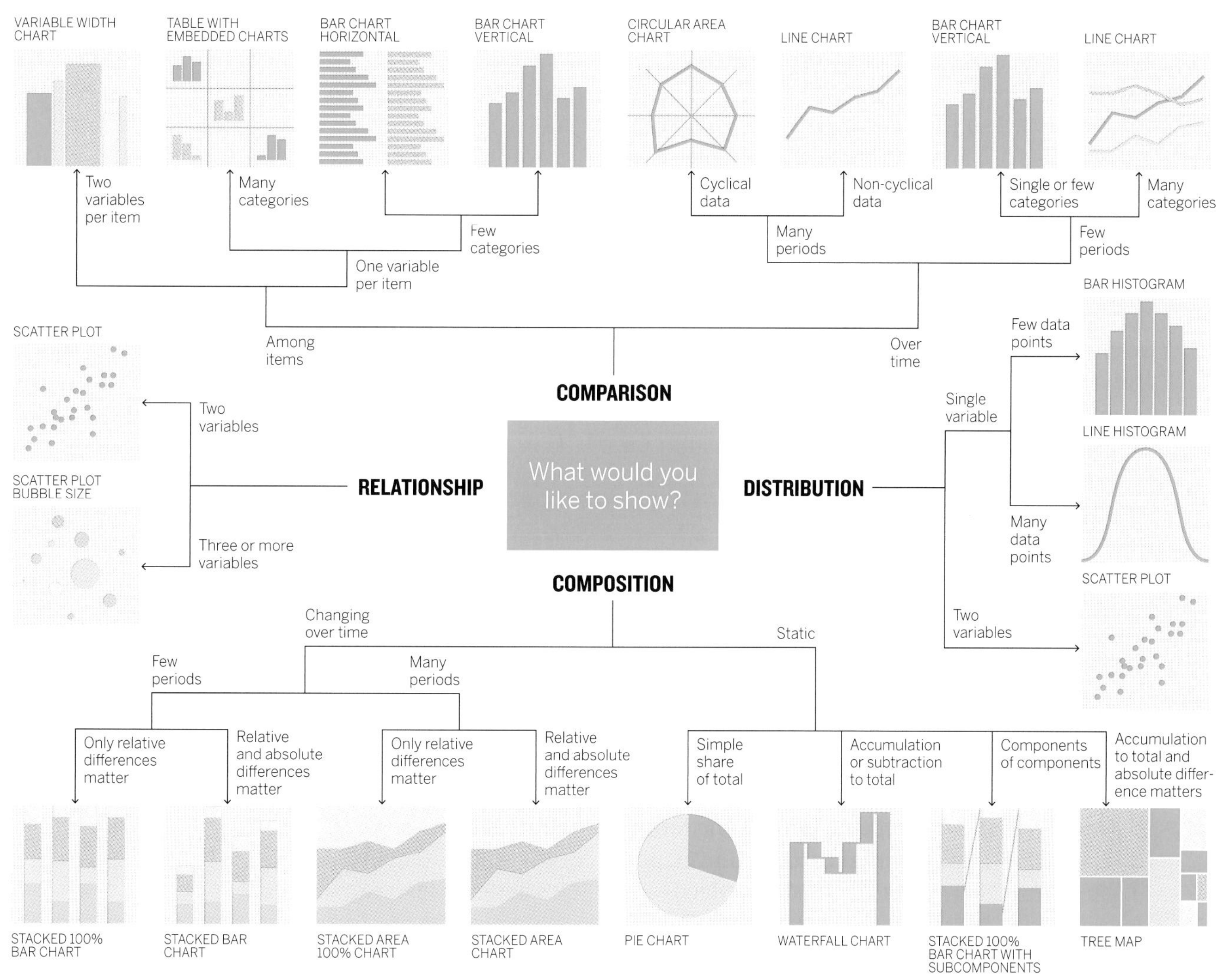

SOURCE: ANDREW V. ABELA

find exceptionally effective. Make notes about what you think works well or caught your eye. Visit websites devoted to infoviz and follow people on Twitter who post new charts daily. (Shortcut: make a list for #dataviz, #visualization, #viz.)

The second reason I'm showing Abela's chart is that I've adapted it. The variation on the facing page matches typical keywords you may find yourself jotting down during the talk and listen stage to the types of charts you might try to sketch.

This transforms Abela's decision machine into more of an inspirational guide. I've simplified the categories and types but added conceptual forms, such as networks and hierarchies, that don't appear in Abela's chart. (Ironically, the type of visualization Abela used to create his typology—a hierarchical decision tree—isn't listed *on* the typology, because he shows only data-driven forms.) To use this guide, take a look at the keywords you recorded during your talk and listen stage and start in that quadrant. For instance, if you wrote down *proportion* and *a percentage of*, you might consider starting with stacked bars or a pie.

Keep in mind that this chart is neither complete nor definitive. It's not meant to tell you what chart type to use, only what types to play with as you start sketching. You may find that some projects, for example, can benefit from multiple chart types or hybrids (say, a bar chart overlaying a map). It's just meant to help you get started.

Start sketching. Sketching is the bridge between idea and visualization. Good sketches are quick, simple, and messy.[4] Don't think too much about real values or scale or any refining details. In fact, don't think too much. Just keep in mind those keywords, the possible forms they suggest, and that overarching idea you keep coming back to, the one you wrote down in answer to *What am I trying to say (or learn)?* And draw. Create shapes, develop a sense of what you want your audience to see. Try anything.

Sometimes the form will seem so obvious that you won't feel the need to sketch a lot of alternatives. A basic comparison between categories can often result in a bar chart. Trends over time are usually plotted as line charts. Still, don't forgo the exercise altogether. Hannah Fairfield, a graphics editor behind some of the most celebrated data visualizations in the *New York Times*, always tries out at least two completely different forms to check her assumptions about the best approach and to stay creatively open.

For an article comparing the price of various Apple products to median monthly household income, my coauthor on that piece, Walter Frick, and I thought we'd show a simple bar chart, with one bar for the cost of a product and the other for income.

It would have been a natural choice, because we were comparing values within categories. The bar chart is valid. But, in keeping with Fairfield's advice to always sketch a couple of options, we decided

MATCHING KEY WORDS TO CHART TYPES

COMPARISONS

NOTES

before/after
categorics
compare
contrast
over time
peaks
rank
trend
types
valleys

BARS · BUMP · LINES · SLOPE · SMALL MULTIPLES

DISTRIBUTIONS

NOTES

alluvial
cluster
distributed
from/to
plotted
points
spread
spread over
relative to
transfer

ALLUVIALS · BUBBLE · HISTOGRAM · SANKEY · SCATTER

COMPOSITIONS

NOTES

components
divvied up
group
makes up
of the whole
parts
percentage
pieces
portion
proportion
slices
subsections
total

PIE · STACKED AREA · STACKED BAR · TREEMAP · UNIT

MAPS NETWORKS LOGIC

NOTES

cluster
complex
connections
group
hierarchy
if/then
network
organize
paths
places
relationships
routes
structure
space
yes/no

FLOW CHART · GEOGRAPHY · HIERARCHIES · 2 X 2 · NETWORKS

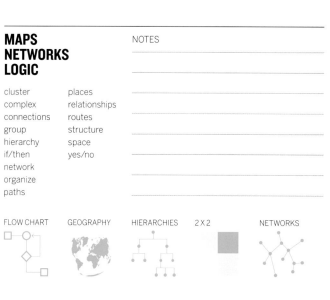

to look for other ways to show the comparison. One phrase kept recurring while we sketched: how much monthly income the cost of an Apple product would *take up*. This led us to think about the product's cost as a piece of monthly income, rather than just a comparative value. Eventually, we settled on the less likely but arguably more effective approach of mini treemaps. Sketches of both the simple approach and the alternative are below.

Even if you're confident that you should be using a simple line chart or a scatter plot, sketching these basic forms is still important. Just as rough drafts improve even staff memos and other prosaic writing, sketches will make even simple charts better.

Remember the manager in chapter 2 who wanted to show her boss that customer service performance was declining in spite of, not because of, a website outage? She could have thrown together a basic line chart showing the data she'd collected: customer service calls and customer service performance. As a reminder, that chart is shown on the facing page.

Even if you think a standard chart type will work for your visual, sketch an alternative to check your assumptions and stay creatively open. Sometimes it will lead to a better form.

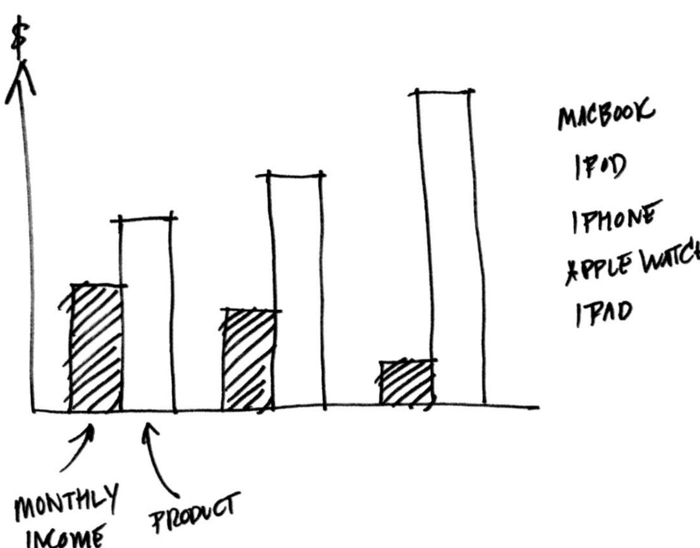

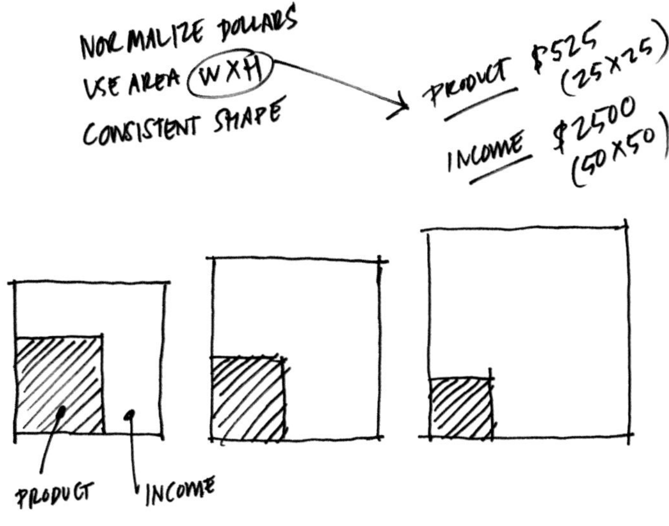

CUSTOMER SERVICE CALLS VS. PERFORMANCE

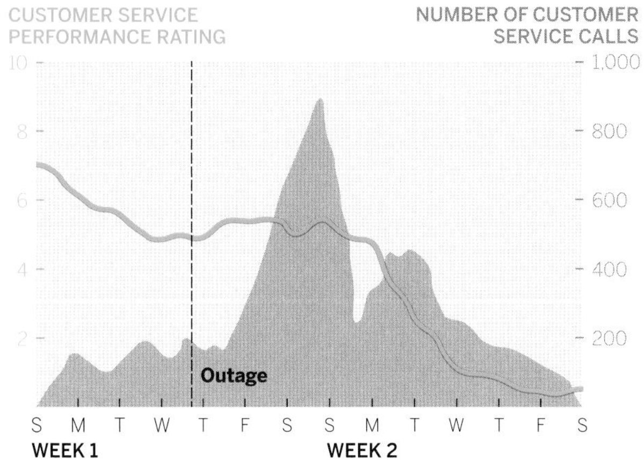

SOURCE: COMPANY RESEARCH

But when she sketched the basic chart, she saw that the dramatic shape of the call volume would probably fight for attention with the performance trend. So she spent a few minutes drawing alternatives (shown to the right), looking for ways to increase the focus on customer service performance. She kept referring back to the statement she had jotted down to describe what she wanted to communicate to her boss: *Even when service was restored after a website outage, customer service ratings continued to decline. And they started declining before the outage.*

The breakthrough came when she realized that her statement didn't mention customer service calls at all. The data was there, and she had plotted it unthinkingly. So she sketched a version *without* the outage data and immediately felt it was better. Then she added two key points that were reflected in her statement: *after service was restored* and *before the outage.*

As she sketched, she didn't try to portray the data accurately; she knew the trend was downward—that was good enough for the time being. She added notes about possible treatments, such as magnifying and shading. But few decisions were actually made. The most important decisions at the sketching phase are what *not* to pursue and what form to use. This is illustrative brainstorming. In 15 minutes the manager went from visualizing some cells of data to visualizing what she wanted to say.

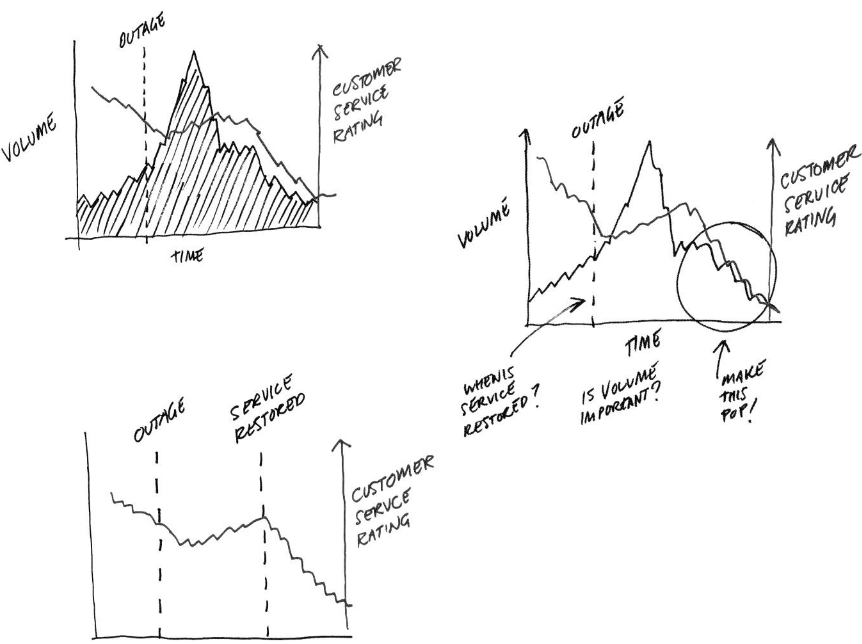

Sometimes sketching lasts longer. The sales manager from earlier in the chapter who was looking for seasonal and month-to-month patterns in his team's sales performance noted some keywords from his conversation with a friend about his project:

It's not clear there's any regular **pattern** to our sales. I'm really trying to understand how and **when** they make sales—how sales are **happening over time**. Is it **mostly smooth**, or are there **bursts** of sales with **periods of nothing**? Is it the same **month to month** or not? Are different **seasons** showing different sales **patterns**?

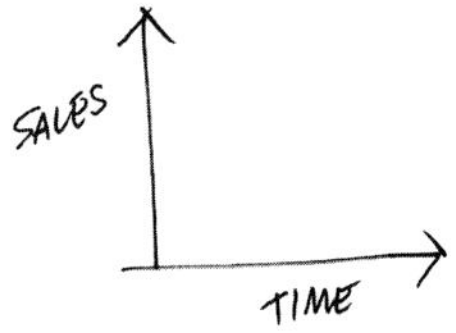

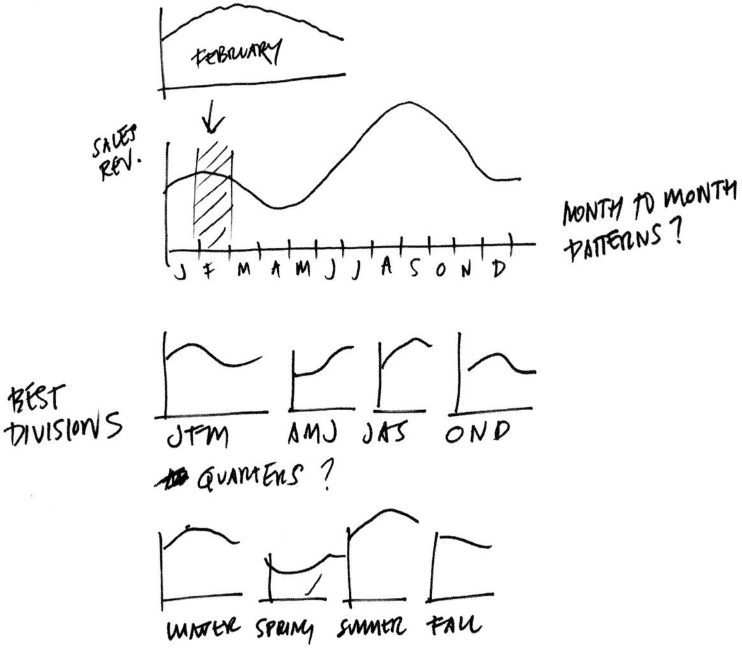

Looking at his notes, he saw that he was really talking about two things here: patterns and time. He actually used a phrase that was *the* potential visual approach: *sales over time*. He sketched those two variables as axes and then started to think about how to use them.

Line graphs are usually a good starting point for trends. So he drafted one of those over a year. From there his sketches reflect an effort to find the right set of line graphs based on some of his words—*seasons, periods,* and *month to month*—which suggested ways to organize his visuals. As he proceeded, his approach came into focus; but again, his charts weren't accurate or to scale. He was just homing in on the approach.

Sketching is also useful to help us try different approaches to complex stories. Here's part of a conversation from the talk and listen stage for an economics student. The student extracted lots of keywords from his conversation:

I'm trying to show **a lot of things**, actually. I want to see where the **greatest growth** is in jobs in the **coming decade, compare** sectors that are **strong or weak**. But also how is pay in those jobs **relative to** the **total number** of jobs that will be created? That's the tricky part, because it's easy to show a **super high growth** of jobs, but if it's growing from 10 jobs being available to 20, what does that **percent growth** really mean? If **high-growth** jobs are **low-paying** ones, what does that mean? What about manufacturing versus knowledge work? Could I **divide** the data that way? There's just a lot going on in the data.

Why is it important to show so many things? That's just it. Many times you see **one piece** of this data highlighted and it ignores these other factors, so it's like, "Look at all that **job growth**," but it doesn't take into account **pay** or **raw numbers** of jobs. I'm looking for a **holistic picture**, a smarter look at this.

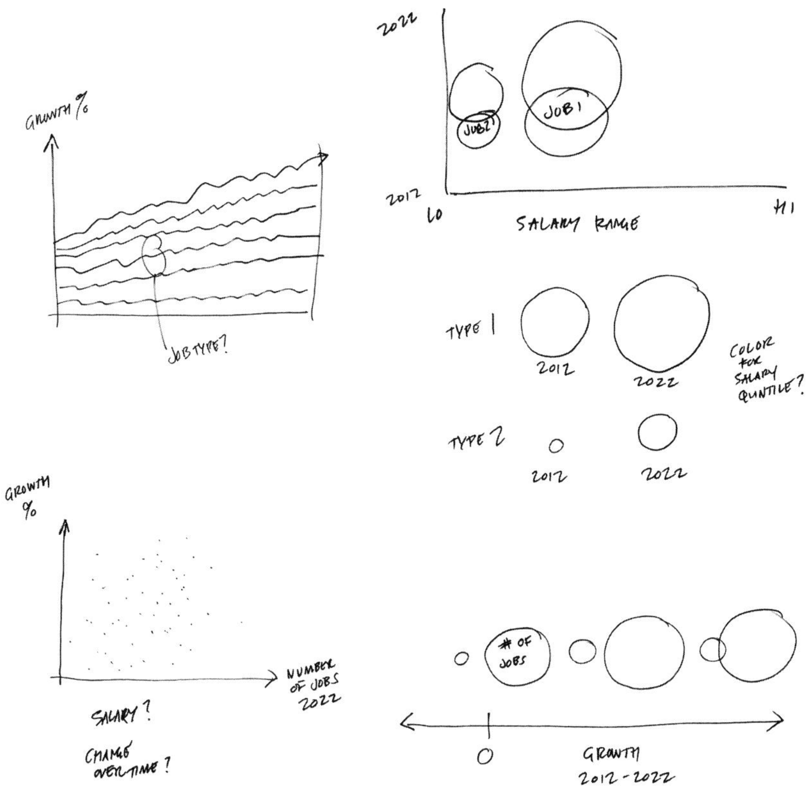

It's silly to think the student could extract one chart style or approach from this conversation. On this page, sketching is meant to explore options for organizing this student's *holistic picture*.

Whether it takes five minutes to confirm the approach you sensed you should use, or an hour of slogging to find a good way to organize your information, sketching is a crucial habit to form. For many professional designers and dataviz pros, it ranks at or near the top of their list of activities that improve visual communication.

PROTOTYPE

At some point, you'll have done enough sketching and will be ready to start making more-realistic pictures. But when? Watch out for these signs that you can begin to prototype:

- Your sketches reasonably match your *What am I trying to say or show?* statement.
- Your sketches are becoming refinements of one idea, rather than broad stabs at different ideas.
- You find yourself plugging actual data or axes and labels into your sketches.
- You find yourself designing the charts, focusing on color, titles, and labels.
- You feel that you don't have any more ideas.

Sketching is generative; it's meant to bring up ideas. Prototyping is iterative; it's meant to hone good ones.

Prototypes should incorporate real data, or *realer* data. Don't try to be perfect with your plotting, but use realistic axis ranges and approximate values that give a sense of what the actual shape of the thing will be. Often, it's useful to prototype on the basis of a small subset of the data to create accurate pictures without feeling the burden of having to prototype everything. The manager plotting seasonal sales data might focus on one season for his prototypes.

Prototypes should also begin to incorporate broad design decisions such as use of color, and the media you'll be building it for. Compare the sketch and the prototype below to see the difference between the two stages.

The prototype, which plots only three categories even though the final chart will catalog many more, is cleaner and more realistic than the quick sketches. It uses real labels and

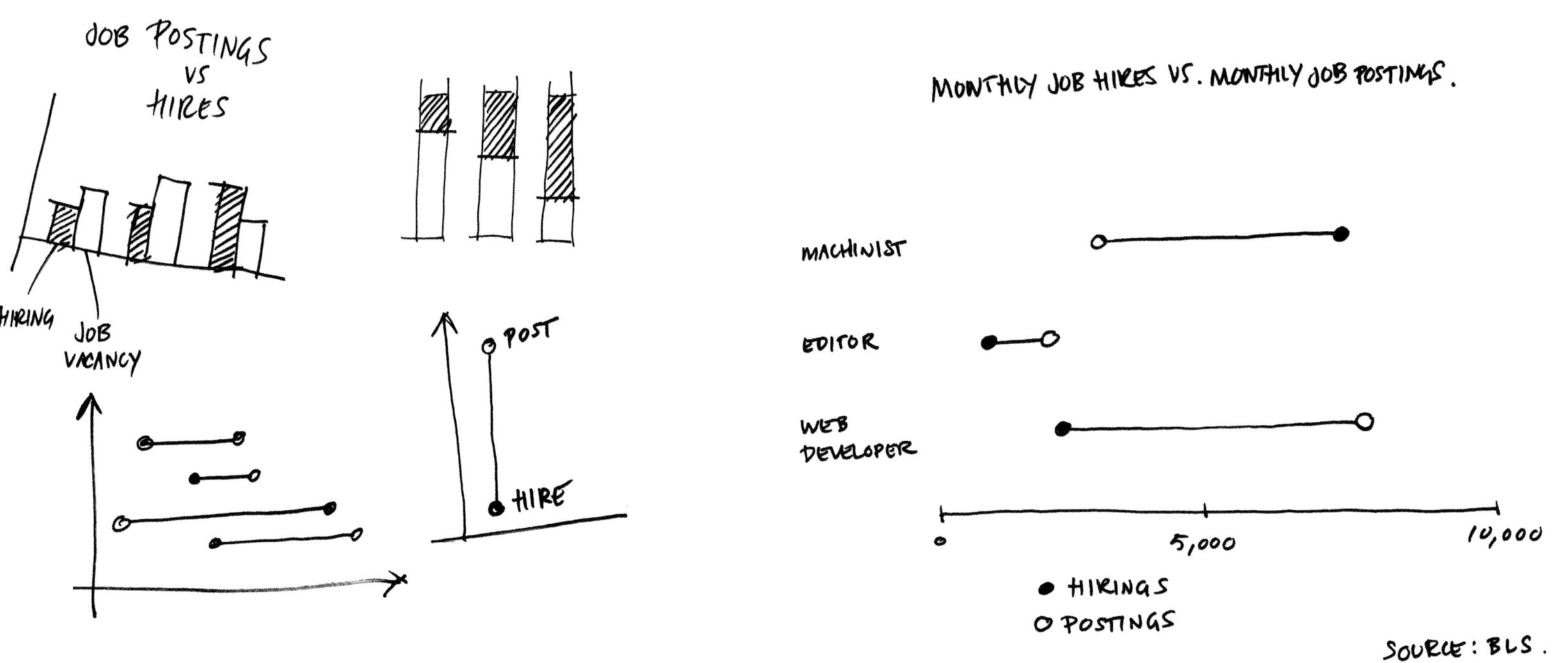

includes a key. It also raises questions—*Will this x-axis range work, given the data? Should color be used for categories*—that can be addressed in ensuing iterations.

Most prototyping you'll do falls into one of three categories:

- **Paper**, done on paper or a whiteboard
- **Digital**, done in software or on the web
- **Paired**, done with a partner who has skills you lack, such as programming or design

Paper prototyping requires virtually no setup beyond what you've already done. Even if you plan on doing digital prototypes, a paper prototype is a good transition from sketching; a first paper prototype is like a final-draft sketch. Paper prototyping is good for simpler data sets (or subsets of larger data sets) and simpler visualizations, because it's slow. A chart with ten categories could become difficult and tedious to draw by hand. It's also harder to maintain clean plotting on paper as the amount of information piles up.

Digital prototyping is much faster than drawing and manages more information more cleanly. Here you can use tools built into the software where your data exists (such as Excel or Google Sheets) to quickly build visuals, or you can upload some data to a website that offers the ability to try multiple approaches. Digital prototyping is rapid prototyping. It's especially powerful for confirmatory and exploratory dataviz.

The good news for managers is that the number of tools suited to digital prototyping is exploding—they are part of the democratizing moment that's making these tools affordable and easy to use. Their functionality and requirements vary considerably. A primer on some of the popular tools is provided on the following page.

Some of these programs have been designed such that the default color and labeling on their output makes it potentially good enough to use as a final draft; certainly it's suitable for exploratory work that's not meant to be presented to others. Those that generate vector graphics (SVG) output can be imported into Adobe Illustrator and other designer's programs for refinement. Many of them generate HTML output that is by default interactive, such that when you hover over data points, their values appear. But right now they all still work best as a way to rapidly tweak and hone a visualization.

WHICH TOOL IS RIGHT FOR YOUR DATAVIZ PROJECT? A sample of available options.

CATEGORY	QUALITIES: Pros	QUALITIES: Cons	TOOLS	TIERS: Free	TIERS: Register	TIERS: Pay	CHART TYPES: Basic	CHART TYPES: Advanced	EXPORT FORMATS
Data manipulation	• Easy to use • Quick output good for testing, prototyping • Good for everyday dataviz, visual confirmation	• Tools focused more on data than visualization • Templated designs not necessarily optimal • Not many advanced chart types	Microsoft Excel		●	●	●	some	bmp, gif, jpg, pdf, png
			Google Sheets		●		●	some	html, png
			Numbers (Apple)			●	●		pdf, png
Prototyping	• Easy to use and free online • Relatively good-looking output for prototyping, export • Good for everyday dataviz, visual confirmation	• A little harder to adjust data and revisualize than with data manipulation tools • Feature sets/chart types inconsistent between tools • Some features require pay	Datawrapper	●	●	●	●		html, pdf, png
			Raw	●	●			●	html, png, svg
			Chartbuilder	●			●		png, svg
			Infogr.am	●	●	●	●		html, png
			Vizable	●	●		●		png
Online and desktop workspaces	• Deeper feature sets than prototyping tools • Good, somewhat customizable design output • Good for visual confirmation, exploration, everyday dataviz	• Steep learning curve • Feature sets still somewhat inconsistent between tools • Pay tier required to keep charts private	Plot.ly	●	●	●	●	some	eps, html, pdf, png, svg
			Quadrigram	●	●		●	some	html, png, svg
			Silk		●	●	●		html
			Tableau Public	●	●		●	●	bmp, html, jpg, png
			Qlik Sense	●	●	●	●	●	html, jpg, pdf, png
Analytics and visualization platforms	• Powerful data and visual analytics systems • Good for building visual analysis teams • Good for visual confirmation, exploration, everyday dataviz	• Steep learning curve, requires formal training • Probably too much power for one-off chart making • Requires significant investment	Tableau Desktop		●	●	●	●	bmp, html, jpg, png
			Qlik View	●	●	●	●	●	html, jpg, pdf, png
Design	• Powerful and flexible design tool • Presentation- and publication-worthy design output • Good for everyday dataviz, idea illustration	• Steep learning curve, requires formal training • Not well suited to visual analysis, prototyping • Requires significant investment	Illustrator			●	●	●	ai, bmp, eps, jpg, pdf, png, svg
Development	• Flexible tools for creating charts, dashboards • Customizable, interactive output, many chart types • Good for everyday dataviz, visual exploration	• Steep learning curve, requires professional development skills • Chart types available and quality of design output varies	D3	●			●	●	html, svg
			Google Charts	●			●	some	html, svg
			Highcharts	●			●	some	html, svg

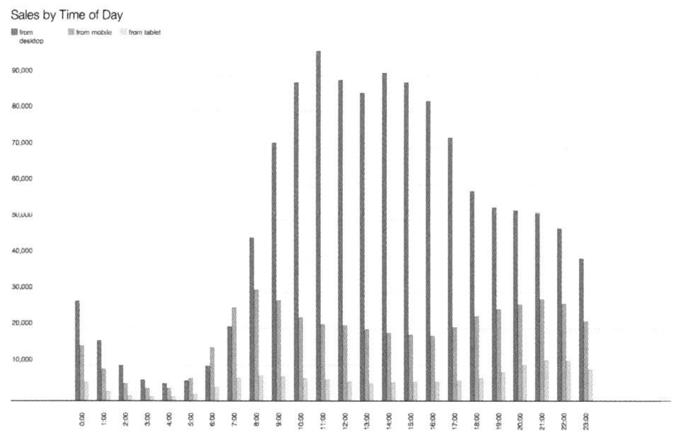

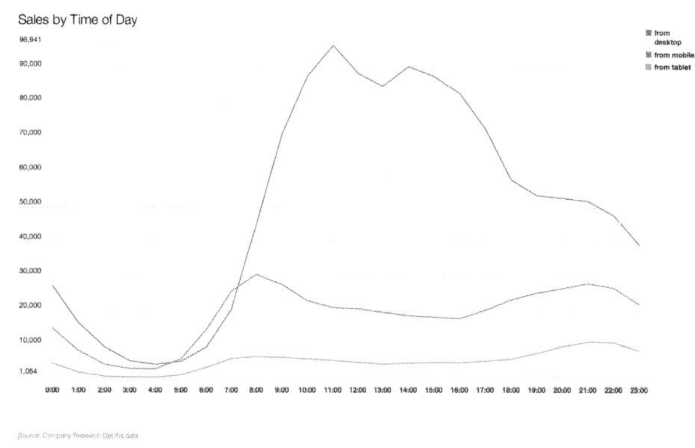

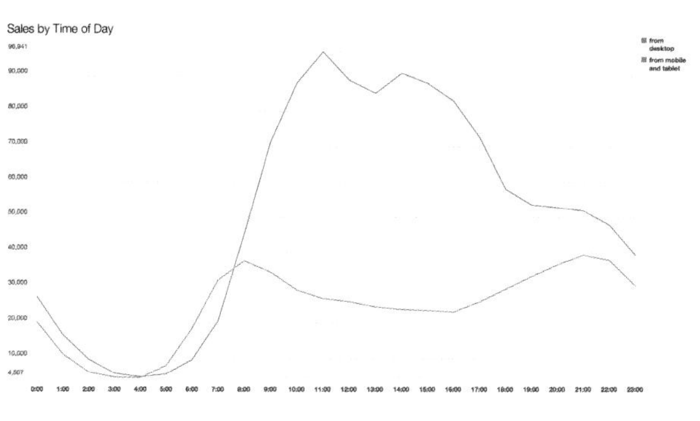

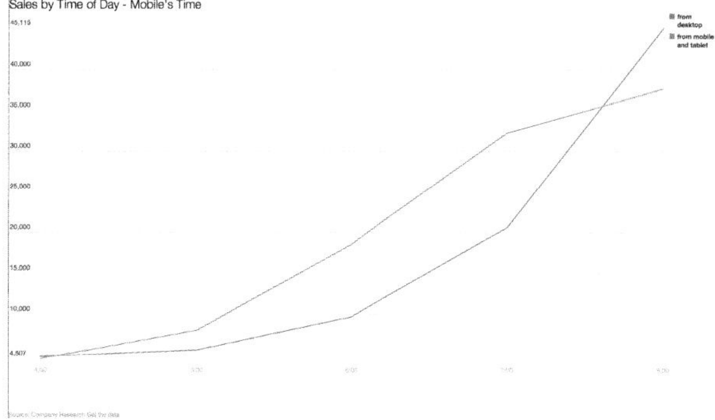

The four Sales by Time of Day prototypes above were created with Datawrapper in less than ten minutes of exploring online sales traffic data.

That you can move a visualization so far in ten minutes demonstrates the power of digital prototyping. You can almost read the manager's thoughts in the iterations: *This is way too much information crammed into a single chart. The trend is what matters anyway, so let's try a line chart. Mobile and tablet can go together, and it's simpler to have just the two trends to compare. Now let's zoom in on this interesting slice of the data that I want to focus on.*

It has its drawbacks, though. For one, the tools that do most of what you want to do in digital prototyping well are the ones you need training to use. The free online ones have a lower learning curve but more-sporadic feature sets. Each has its strengths and weaknesses, so you may find yourself jumping from tool to tool depending on your project or even within a project. Digital prototyping may also be overkill for simple visualizations in which paper prototypes get you to where you need to be. And few of these tools are designed to help prototype conceptual forms, which often require more sketching and prototyping than data-driven ones. When working on conceptual graphics, paper and whiteboard are probably your best options. Still, you'll find yourself using these tools often.

Paired prototyping is something else altogether. The previous techniques are defined by the tools you use. Paired prototyping is defined by the way in which you work: with an expert partner. The concept is based on a system of data analysis called paired analysis, which itself borrows from a method called extreme programming and other sources.[5] In each of these the idea is to pair a subject matter expert—that's you, the manager—with a tools expert who can manipulate data and visuals to suit your needs.

Brian Fisher and David Kasik cocreated the method at Boeing.[6] "This turns out to be highly effective," Kasik says. "The key is to have them actually sit and work together, not throw things over the wall."

Paired analysis has proved powerful at Boeing. In one case, the company used it for some deep exploratory sessions in which a team of two wanted to visualize information about bird strikes on

JOSHUA BLACKBURN

SAVING LIVES WITH REAL-TIME EXPLORATORY VISUALIZATION

"I'm a programmer, so I work with code all day, but it's just easier for me to actually see things."

Joshua Blackburn is a software engineer at IEX Group in New York, the protagonist firm in *Flash Boys*, Michael Lewis's best seller about high-frequency stock trading. Blackburn plays a small but crucial part in the book. Because it's easier for him to see things, he took the massive and complex data set that was IEX's trading activity and visualized it. In a dramatic moment in the book, Blackburn tells IEX CEO Brad Katsuyama to refresh his browser to *see* the trading activity.[7] "The screen was now organized in different shapes and colors," Lewis writes, with anomalous trades "bunched together and highlighted in useful ways." For the first time, the CEO "could see patterns. And in the patterns he could see predatory activity neither he nor the investors had yet imagined."

Blackburn, a mostly self-taught programmer, excels in what he calls "operational environments"—a term he no doubt picked up from his years in the Air

Force. What he means is that he builds exploratory visualizations on the fly to solve an immediate problem with a large data set. Then he adapts that visualization as the situation demands. "The way I build stuff is flexibly," he says. "It's high feedback. I do it. They use it. They give me feedback and I update it. I'm trying to help people answer questions in real time. Definitely here I'm the go-to visual guy."

From a dataviz perspective, that means Blackburn's visuals are utilitarian rather than polished. In many ways, prototypes are his final product, because operational environments change quickly and constantly. "The visual aspect is important," he says, "but it's always a question of not taking too much time with it, because you won't get the answers you need when you need them."

Whatever points he may lose on presentation, though, he gains back many times over with the types of fast insight he generates. The predatory activity his IEX dataviz confirmed is a good example. The word Blackburn uses most often to describe his visualizations is *patterns*. When mining big data sets, the goal is to find any pattern at all, and then try to make sense of it. That is true visual exploration.

Blackburn starts the visualization process by observing his users and listening to them. He says in *Flash Boys* that he zeroes in on people's complaints, such as "I wish I could see" this or "I wish I knew" that.

What he's doing reflects the talk and listen phase of visual thinking described in this chapter—only Blackburn does a lot less talking and a lot more listening. "I have no background in finance, so I might ask them, 'How do you do this?' or 'What are you looking for?'" he says. "But mostly I want to hear them describe things. Then they'll tell me about some stream of information and the tables that contain all that information. That's how they're used to seeing the data."

Blackburn then becomes the user and asks himself how he'd want to *see* the information. "It's always easier for me to develop something I can see. It's natural for me to look at data and immediately think about how to make it visual."

The deeply exploratory nature of the work Blackburn does, coupled with the fact that he iterates so rapidly, has led him to be much more experimental with forms. "I feel like I break with tradition a little," he says. "You see a lot about how everything has to fit into these certain forms. Most of the time we don't know what we're looking for. If I'm confined to bar charts and line charts and scatter plots, I might not see the patterns I need to." Those forms, he notes, wouldn't have exposed the predatory trading patterns very well. "Allowing someone to look at data in different, unique ways can be beneficial. I made one visualization that's really just things flying around the screen, exploding. At first it seems like eye candy, but pretty quickly you realize it's not. The movement of things tells a story. The patterns and the motion aren't just to look cool. They *are* the story."

Being a key player for the good guys in Lewis's book may be a point of pride, but it's not what Blackburn thinks of when asked to remember a time he realized that his visualization was making a difference: "The highest point for me I can't talk about much, but it was working with the military. It was at the height of the surge."

The military, like a lot of companies, had gotten very good at collecting data but less adept at using it effectively. Blackburn realized he could build a map that aggregated battlefield information. He could use heat maps to show trends over time—for example, when and where IEDs were discovered and detonated. "I was looking for patterns. Could we take all this data and actually see how IED activity moved over the course of the war? Could we predict where they'd be and avoid them?"

He recalls how generals reacted watching his maps on massive screens—how they immediately began to pick out patterns and adjust strategy.

"The chief of operations is using the map. Patrols on routes are using the maps to see IED trends, to see the movements, the patterns of the enemy. And I just remember being there, thinking, *I'm helping answer these big questions. I'm supporting decision makers. Giving them answers they didn't have before.*"

airplanes. Bird strikes are a serious safety issue (a strike by Canada geese on an Airbus A320 passenger jet caused the notable "Miracle on the Hudson" water landing in New York in 2009)—at the time of the analysis, the cost of bird strikes was estimated at anywhere from $123 million to $615 million a year, but very little was known about the patterns of bird strikes and how they might be mitigated.

Little was known in part because the data analysis required to understand bird strikes was a tedious process of finding and reading through thousands of records from dozens of sources, correlating them, and then updating the results as new events occurred. To speed things up, Boeing paired a subject matter expert (an aviation safety specialist) with a tools expert (in this case, an expert in both Tableau and IN-SPIRE visualization software). They worked together over several days. The following example shows the workflow. Think of the images as responses from the tools expert to requests from the subject matter expert. Obviously, in a real-life setting they'd be discussing each of these steps in depth before the person visualizing went ahead and created charts.

We need a way to identify and extract data on bird strikes from XYZ data sources. And once you have that system set up, we really want to see *when* bird strikes happen, by both month and time of day.

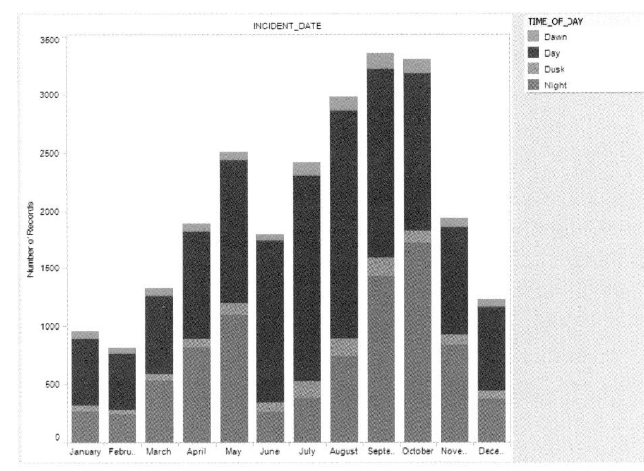

That's good, but is there a way to map this by geography? I'd like to know where the most bird strikes happen. And can each spot break down the type of bird that was involved?

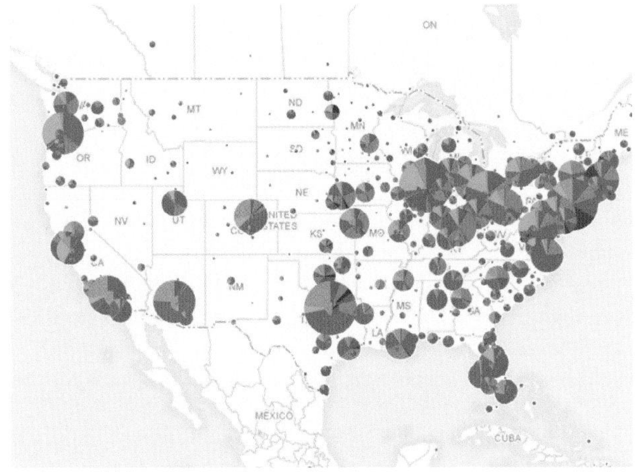

Wow. Great. Can we combine those two? Time of day and location? But less detail. I want to be able to show this to management and discuss the findings.

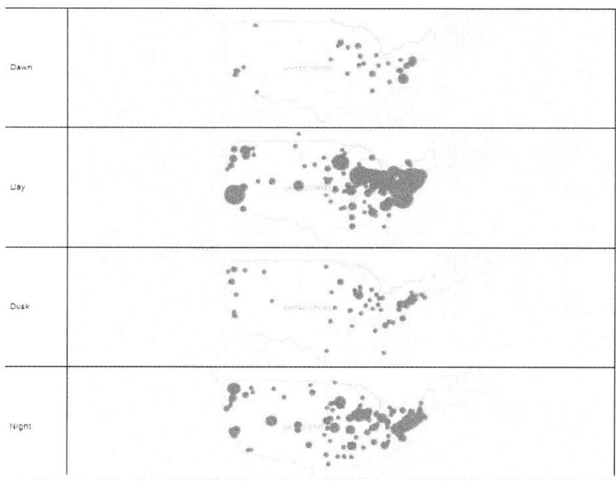

Great. Finally, for the presentation, we should show frequency of where on planes birds strike. Something simple.

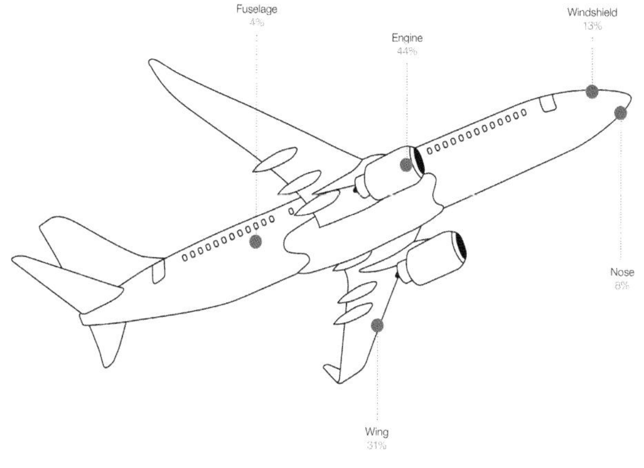

Can we also see altitude versus speed? Maybe see if there's any pattern there.

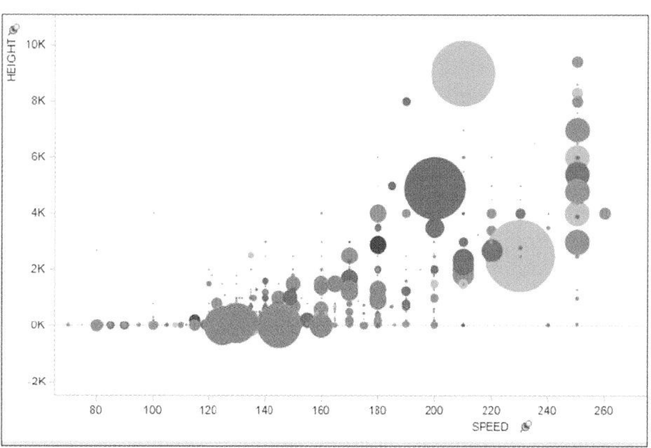

Obviously, this is a radically simplified and abbreviated version of the work the two put in on the project. But it shows how the subject matter expert focused on articulating the problems and explaining the context he was trying to create. The tools expert, meanwhile, drew on his knowledge of good visualization techniques to give his partner what he needed.

Kasik says this process brought new insights faster than other methods and has led to design improvements to shield airplanes and better pilot training to recognize and react to bird strikes.[8]

You can borrow this framework to achieve similarly powerful results with your prototyping: You are the subject matter expert. Recruit a tools expert, someone with expertise in some aspect of visualization that you don't have. That could be:

- **A developer** who can create interactivity with complex programs like D3—the most popular JavaScript visualization library for programmers
- **A designer** who can help you visualize a complex or unusual form using professional design tools like Adobe Illustrator
- **A data analyst** who knows how to find, scrape, clean, and manipulate data in business intelligence and visualization software systems like Tableau or QlikView so that you can find patterns and relationships that you'd otherwise miss.

Sit together. Describe to the expert what you're trying to achieve. Talk. (More talking!) Show the expert your sketches, the keywords you jotted down; clarify your ideas. Then begin the back-and-forth exchange. Even better, you can go through the whole development process with the expert.

As far back as Willard Brinton's foundational *Graphic Methods for Presenting Facts* (1914), some form of paired analysis was implicitly understood to be a prerequisite for creating good charts. In 1914, no one expected a manager to learn a draftsman's trade. In 1969, Mary Eleanor Spear likewise assumed that charting was a team effort. She even laid out how a "communicator," a "graphic analyst," and a "draftsman" would work together on charts. It wasn't until the 1980s, with the arrival of software that could automatically spit out charts, that companies de-emphasized the value of professional visualization output in favor of efficiency. Excel charts became "good enough," and visualization became the job of the manager.

Paired prototyping techniques, and recent increased investments in information design, show that the pendulum is swinging back. Today, Spear's graphic analyst may be a business analyst, and the draftsman may be a programmer, but the collaborative approach is similar. Encourage your company to invest in specialized talent. Many companies now contract with "data designers" and programmers who specialize in visualization. Even if your company doesn't use specialists, set aside some budget to have your own small team on call. Routine projects may not call for paired prototyping or design, but complex data sets, large projects, and visualizations for which you want to go beyond the standard chart forms will benefit from a team and free you up to focus on the ideas. You'll use paired analysis less often than paper and digital prototyping, but when you're set on finding profound new insights, or you want people to see something in a powerful new way, it's a worthwhile investment.

IN PRACTICE, START TO FINISH

Here's an example of thinking through a visualization from beginning to end. Lisbeth is a marketing manager at a company that provides streaming music services. The company is trying to understand what other activities customers engage in while they're streaming music. Data collected by the company will help shape its multimillion-dollar marketing strategy.

Lisbeth has seen the data. She's even quickly generated a pie chart from her spreadsheet program, just to see at a high level what was there:

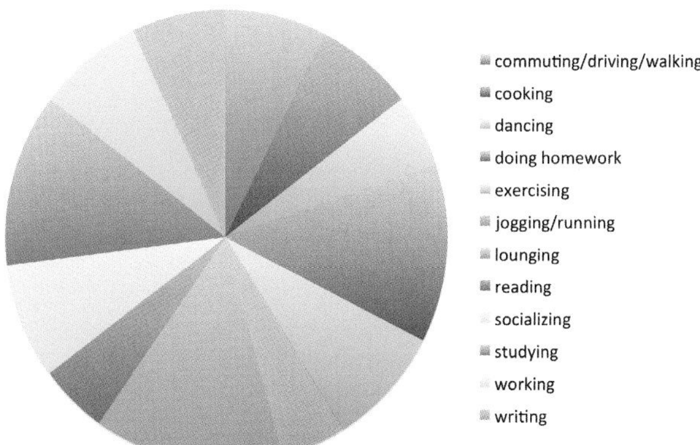

She knows that even a cleaned-up, well-labeled version of this pie won't be effective. She's having trouble herself extracting any meaning from it other than *users do a lot of different things while streaming music*. She blanches at the idea of presenting this to the marketing department as a visual aide to a multimillion-dollar investment decision. She decides to make it better.

Prep: 5 minutes. Lisbeth finds a small workroom with a whiteboard and a few color markers. She brings coffee for herself and a friend she has invited to help. First she spends just a few minutes framing her effort at the top of the whiteboard. In addition to plotting her work in the declarative, data-driven quadrant (everyday dataviz) of the Four Types chart on page 57, she plots what will make this chart "good" on the Good Charts Matrix that crosses context and design, on page 9. Her sketches are shown on the following page.

Her chart should look good, but she's willing to forgo time refining the design to focus on getting the context as close to perfect as possible. After all, she's presenting to her unit, where people will have deep knowledge and opinions on the topic and data. She makes a brief note that if this chart gets it right, she may have to make a better-designed one for other, more formal presentations.

Talk and listen: 20 minutes. Her friend—who's not part of this project—arrives. Lisbeth wants not only to talk through her idea but also to check her

MARKETING STRATEGY

— MARKETING TEAM — CMO

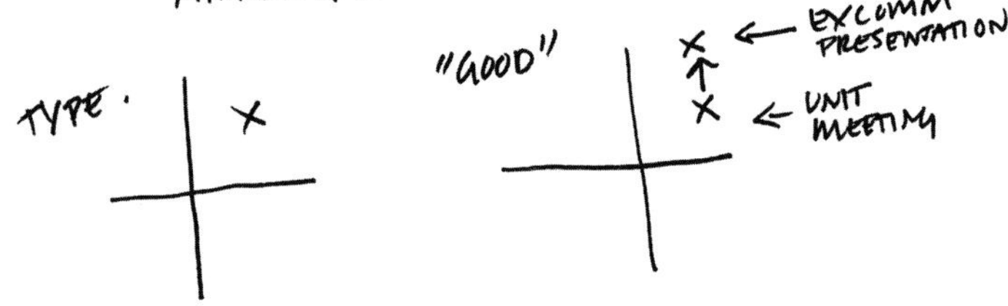

WHAT'S MY SENTENCE?

SIMPLIFY?

FIND THE MAIN IDEA

ACTIVITIES THAT DOMINATE

NOT PERCENTAGES — INDIVIDUALS/PEOPLE

ORGANIZE INFORMATION — TOO RANDOM

CATEGORIES

THINKING	ACTIVITY/EXERCISE	RELAXING
HOMEWORK	EXERCISE	SOCIALIZING
STUDYING	DANCE	COOKING
WRITING	COMMUTE	PARTIES
ETC.	ETC.	ETC.

INDIVIDUALS.

THINKING

EXERCISE

RELAX

?

"IF TWITTER WERE 100 PEOPLE"

ACTIVITY OF 1000 / 10,000?

WHAT WOULD THAT LOOK LIKE?

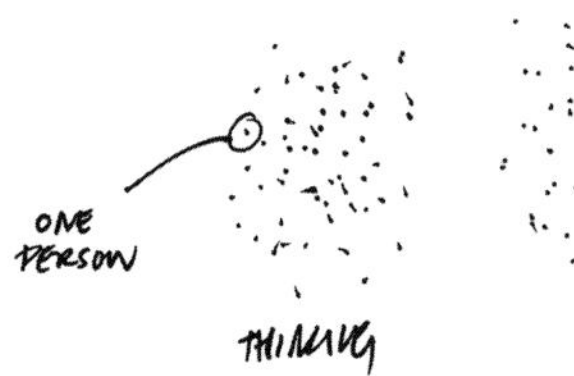

assumptions with someone who doesn't have much knowledge or bias about the project.

So, I need to show my department what people do while they're using our service. I want to be able to show any trends or dominant activities, for sure, but there are a dozen different things they do, and it all seems pretty random.

Why can't you tell your team there's no dominant activity?

We can't market to everyone; we have to figure out who we want to target and know why. Plus I'm not convinced that it's trendless. I just think I haven't figured out the way to group the data that will expose the trends.

Is there a category of activity, or a couple of categories you can focus on, like exercising?

Maybe. Actually, the data wasn't grouped, but that's something to look at.

Their conversation goes on for about ten minutes. Later Lisbeth spends ten more minutes chatting up a colleague who'll be at the meeting. Here's part of what she says to this friend:

So the big meeting is coming up, and I know Tom is going to give me the "So what?" because it's not entirely clear we've found one or two dominant activities that we can focus on. Plus I get frustrated when we just put up these percentages and don't think about the individuals. You can't just market to some 60% because they're all doing the same thing. You have to think about people. Anyway, I'm looking for ways to organize the information so it's not just random. But I also think it'll be more effective if we get people in a mind-set to think about talking to people, not just these aggregate groups.

Sketching: 20 minutes. Even as Lisbeth captures the conversations, she starts sketching as shown on the facing page. She knows right away that grouping the activities in general categories will help make a pie chart more accessible, so she looks over the activities again and assigns each to one of three categories. Although she's pretty sure a pie won't work, she sketches one anyway. She sketches bars and tries out a Venn diagram, with circles for each category overlapping with some of the activities. She scribbles. The word *individuals* keeps staring back at her from the whiteboard. She really wants to make the information feel more personal and less like a generic stat. She draws a few icons of people, remembering a dataviz she found online that went viral called "If Twitter were 100 people," which used a similar technique to show a percentage breakdown of that service's audience.[9]

She writes, "Activity of 1,000/10,000? What would that look like?" And she jabs the whiteboard with dots. Could she put thousands of dots on the screen in her presentation? A unit chart might work.

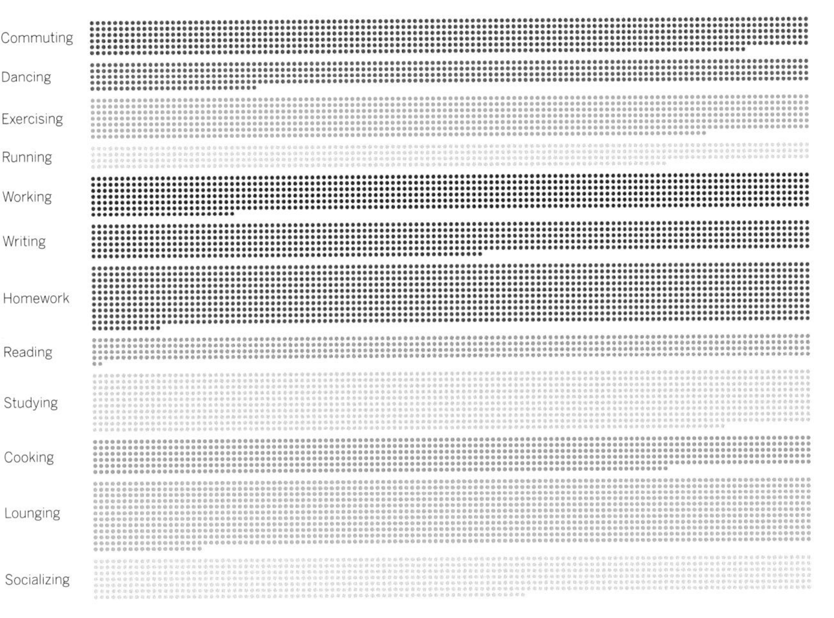

Prototyping: 65 minutes. Lisbeth likes the idea of a unit chart and recruits another friend who can do some light programming to create some, paired-prototyping style. In 30 minutes they have multiple unit charts to evaluate—each showing proportional numbers of participants in activities—including the version to the left.

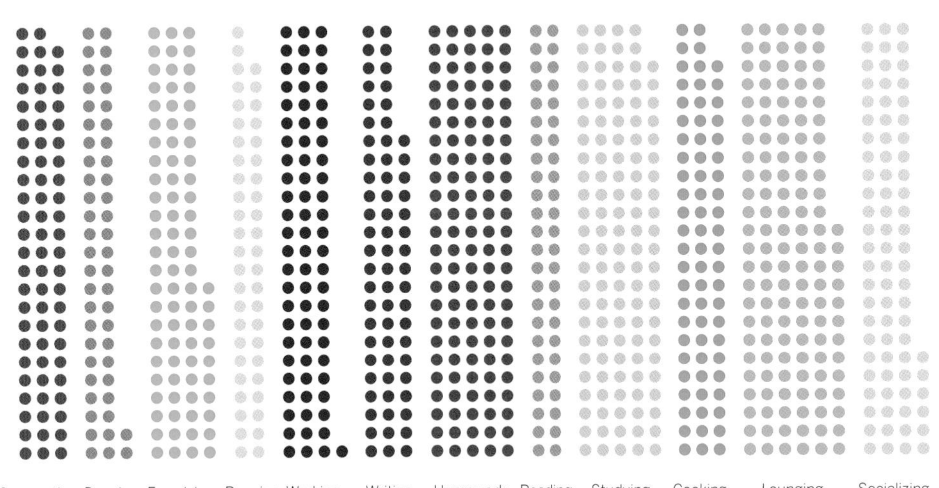

Commuting
Dancing
Exercising
Running
Working
Writing
Homework
Reading
Studying
Cooking
Lounging
Socializing

Lisbeth recognizes that 10,000 dots, although decidedly stunning, is somewhat impractical for a presentation. It's hard to see any values or differences in values in the picture. She asks her programmer to try versions with 1,000 dots. She asks him if he can "make it so the differences in value are easily seen." He iterates. They need just 15 more minutes to produce versions with 1,000 dots, including the two on the bottom of the facing page.

Lisbeth likes the leftmost of these because the differences feel meaningful and the form feels familiar, like a proportional bar chart, but also because each group of dots evokes a group of people. In just 20 more minutes—less than two hours after she started—Lisbeth has a presentation version of her chart, the pair on this page, which organizes activities both by cateogry in one chart and by most-to-least-common in the other. She thinks, *These are visualizations we can have a conversation about.*

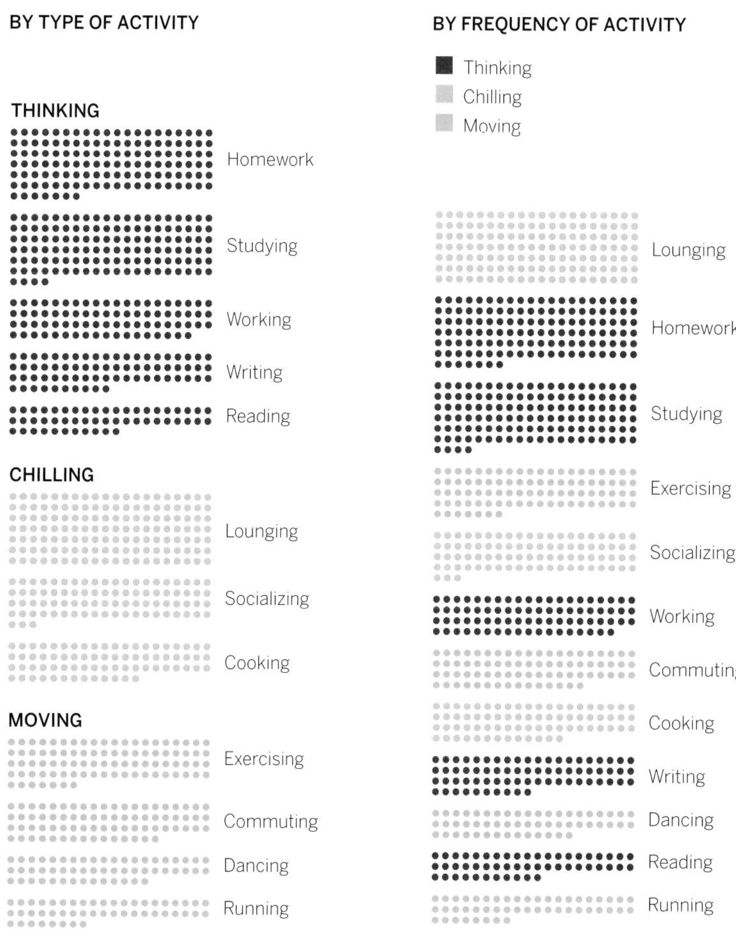

OVERLAPPING, NOT SEQUENTIAL

I've outlined a process that goes from one step to the next with fixed time intervals, largely because that's the easiest, most accessible way to describe the progression of activities.

BUILDING BETTER CHARTS

MINUTES SPENT AT EACH TASK

5 | 15 | 20 | 20

Prep | Talk and Listen | Sketch | Prototype

In practice, the process won't be so linear. The steps will bleed into one another. You may find yourself sketching as you talk, for example. You should: it's hard not to start drawing as you capture keywords and talk through your challenge. Sometimes a prototype will expose a weakness in your visualization (or an opportunity you hadn't seen) that will literally send you back to the drawing board to sketch alternatives.

In short, the process may proceed something more like this, which shows how, in that typical hour, the steps might overlap:

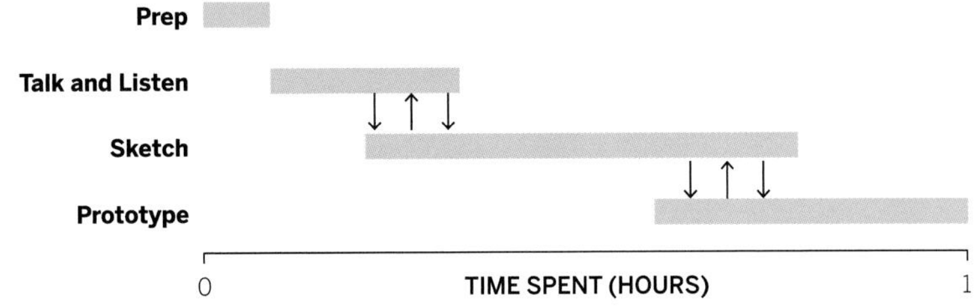

Not every project is typical, though. When the best visual approach isn't clear, talking and sketching may dominate your efforts. Or, if you have a good idea of what you're trying to show, or if prototypes lead you to further manipulate the data to refine the idea, you may quickly settle on the visual approach and spend much more time refining prototypes. You can imagine the length of these bars stretching and shrinking, and the arrows between them shifting.

We've spent time trying and choosing forms, but this process isn't really about finding the right type of chart. It's about refining your ideas and your message, creating the best context possible. It's about pushing yourself as far to the right as possible on the Good Charts Matrix.

Designing charts so that they're beautiful is not the most difficult part of creating good charts. It's this effort to make ideas visual that constitutes the greatest challenge. And now you have a method for accomplishing that. In fact, if you're working in the exploratory space, or in an informal setting, this may be as far as you need to go with a particular visualization. The one-on-one with your boss may not demand a refined and finished product.

More often than not, though, even exploratory projects lead to declarative visuals—some kind of finished product for a presentation or for publication. That's where we'll go next. You can make your well-conceived sketches and prototypes even more effective by making them visually captivating.

RECAP

BETTER CHARTS IN A COUPLE OF HOURS

To improve visual communication, fight the impulse to go right from getting data to choosing a chart type from the preset options in a software program. First spend time creating context and thinking through the idea you want to convey. Usually, an hour or so of prepping, talking and listening, sketching, and prototyping will help produce a superior visualization.

Follow these steps to make it happen:

1. **Prep: 5 minutes**
   - Create a workspace with plenty of paper or whiteboards.
   - Put aside your data so that you can think more broadly about ideas.
   - Write down the basics as constant reminders, including who the visualization is for and what setting it will be used in.
2. **Talk and listen: 15 minutes**
   - Enlist a colleague or a friend to talk about what you're trying to say or show, or prove or learn.
   - Capture words, phrases, and statements that possibly sum up the idea you want to convey.
3. **Sketch: 20 minutes**
   - Match keywords you've captured to chart types that you may try out, using the chart on page 85 as inspiration.
   - Start sketching, work quickly, and try out multiple visual approaches.
4. **Prototype: 20 minutes**
   - Once you have an approach you think will work, prototype it by making a more accurate and detailed sketch.
   - Use digital prototyping tools or paired prototyping techniques if you want to iterate further.

PART THREE

REFINE

CHAPTER 5

REFINE TO IMPRESS

GETTING TO THE "FEELING BEHIND OUR EYES"

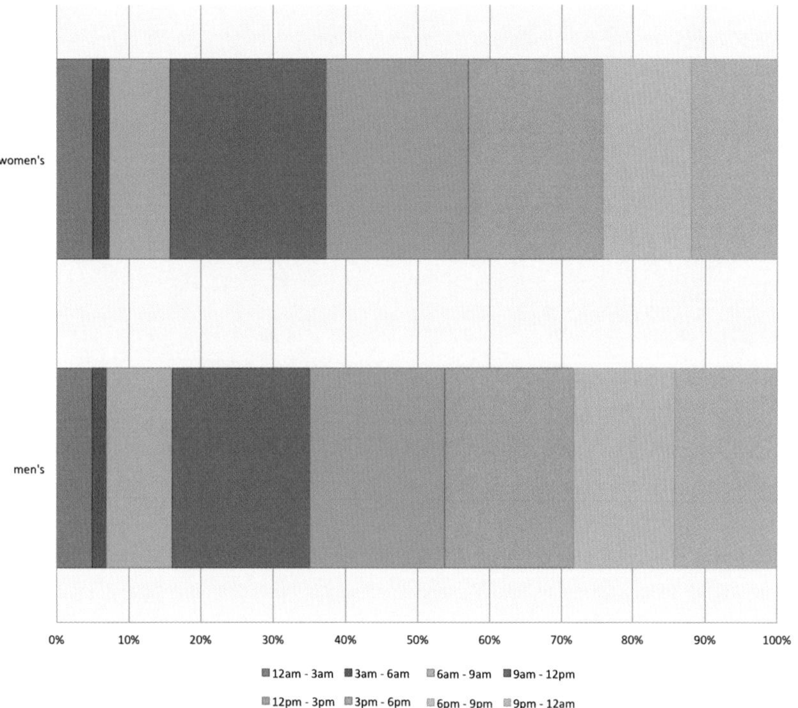

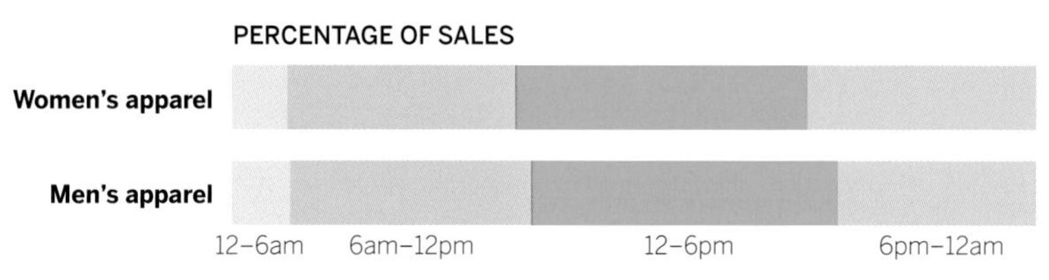

WHICH OF THESE is a prototype and which is a final, declarative dataviz created for a presentation to the CEO?

The top chart is obviously the prototype, generated in Excel with just a few clicks. Most of us would say the bottom chart (designed with Adobe Illustrator) looks better, is "airy" or "streamlined" or "clean," whereas the top one is "busy" or "blocky" or "messy."

In *Style: Toward Clarity and Grace*, Joseph Williams describes impressions of good and bad writing as "a feeling behind our eyes."[1] Charts get behind our eyes in the same way, and it's important to understand why, and what design principles and tactics lead to bad feelings or good ones. Creating something prettier than the average dataviz isn't an end in itself. It's a means to a more important end: *effectiveness*. For example, look at the charts on this page again and try to answer these questions: Do more people buy women's apparel before or after noon? Does the site get more buyers before breakfast or after dinner?

Despite the fact that these charts are of the same type and contain the same data, the design of the second one makes it easier to use. Good design serves a more important function than simply pleasing us: It helps us access ideas. It makes lesser charts good and good charts transcendent.

“THE FEELING BEHIND OUR EYES”

Instead of proffering rules and procedures to help you get from the one-click Excel chart to a well-designed, more effective one, I’ll work backward. Let’s start with some of those feelings we get behind our eyes when we see charts, and explore the design principles used to help create those feelings. The overarching goal here is not perfection, it’s *balance*. To that end, I won’t be telling you how many tick marks or colors to use to keep a chart from getting confusing. The answer is, of course, “That depends.” Instead I’ll simply show the implications of changing your design in one direction or another.

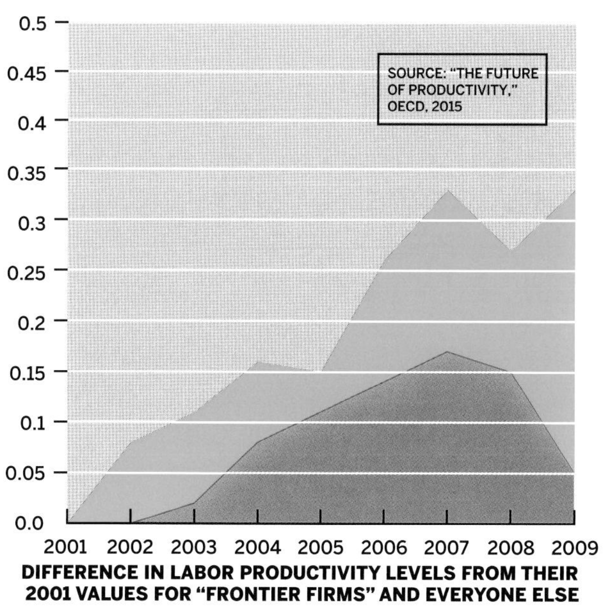

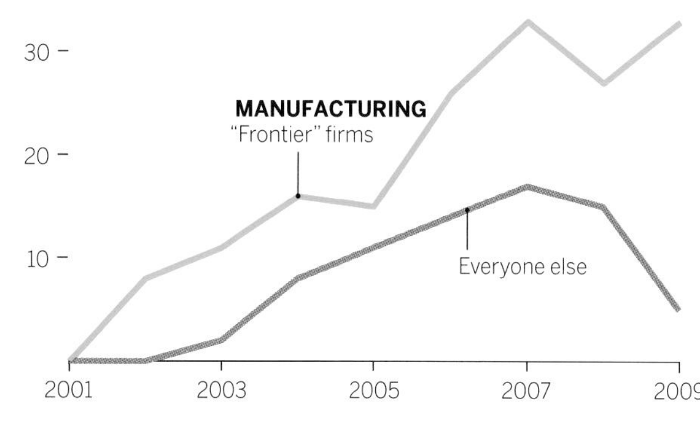

Structure and hierarchy. Does it look neat and clean, or messy and muddled? Impressions of the relative orderliness of a chart come from its *structure* and *hierarchy*. Which of the two charts on this page looks cleaner?

Obviously, the one on the right looks cleaner and much more professional, even if we're not sure why. Here are the techniques that give us that impression:

The chart relies on a consistent structure. Every chart you build for a presentation or for publication should include all or most of these elements:

Title
Subtitle
Visual field (visuals, axes, labels, captions, legend)
Source line

You should be able to map those elements onto any well-designed declarative chart, whether it's a map, conceptual, or statistical.

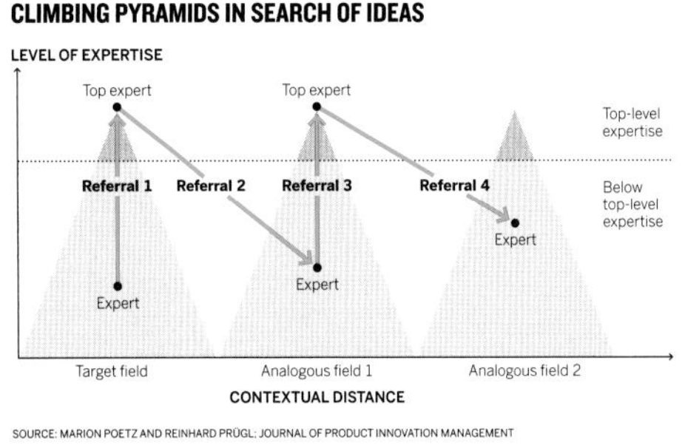

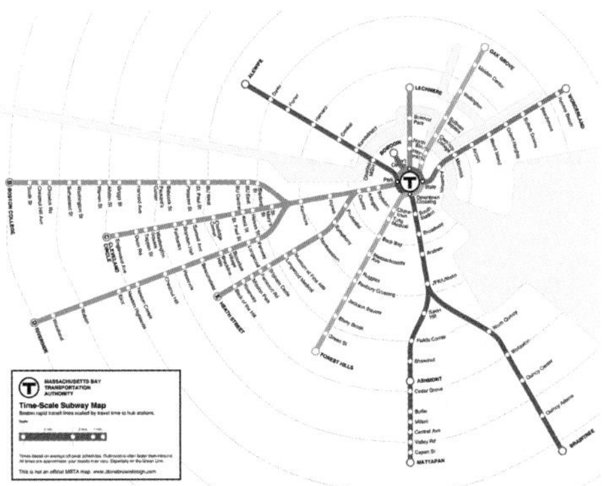

CREDIT: PETER DUNN

How to design each of these elements comes later. For now, just take an inventory. Create a checklist. Sticking to this consistent structure will be useful in two ways. First, it will prevent a presentation from getting derailed by questions about the chart itself because some element is missing. Everything that makes a visual self-explanatory makes it more effective. The less you have to talk about the visualization, and the more you can talk about its ideas, the better.

Second, consistently including all those elements makes charts portable, reusable, and sharable. Your boss may want to put it in a presentation he's making for the executive committee, and he can do so with confidence that it won't raise questions he can't answer about what an unlabeled axis represents. The social team can put it on the company feed. If you want to reference this chart months or years later, its provenance won't be in doubt because you've included a source line.

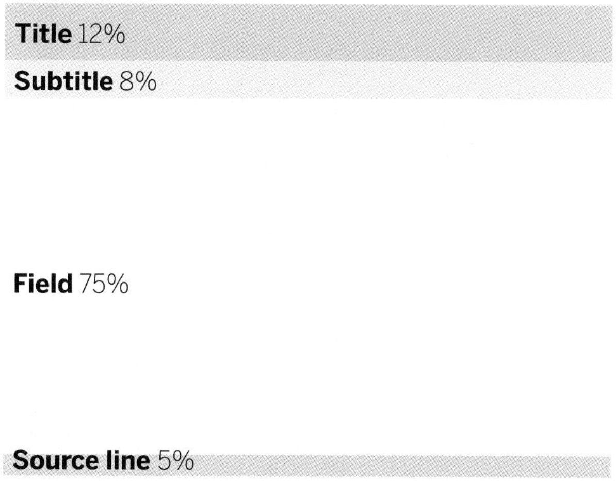

Title 12%
Subtitle 8%
Field 75%
Source line 5%

The chart uses consistent placement and weighting. The structure outlined above is so consistent in chart making that you hardly notice it. It disappears into a convention we're all used to seeing: The title, for the most part, sits atop all, directly over the subtitle, which precedes the visual field. Sourcing is a small footnote at the bottom, and the legend, if there is one, often rests on the right side or in another vacant part of the field where it can't disrupt the visual. Regardless of the shape, most charts' proportions are divided up in about the same way as shown in the diagram on this page. The visual field should dominate the structure. The other elements serve the field. Give the title too much weight, for example, and it will fight for attention with the field. Give it too little, and you may have missed an opportunity to use text to help viewers understand the chart. Compare the first pair of charts in this chapter to see the difference between a title that disappears and one that supports the visual.

Well-designed charts we see every day are built this way, regardless of if they're presented horizontally, as in a presentation, vertically on a phone screen, or as a square in a social media feed. (See the following page for examples of all three orientations using these proportions).

Don't go measuring charts to get your space allocation just so; use these proportions as a guideline, and know when to break them. The Boston "T" commute time map on the facing page devotes even more space to the visual field because it would be difficult to contain all of its useful information in a smaller space and maintain legibility; it moves and

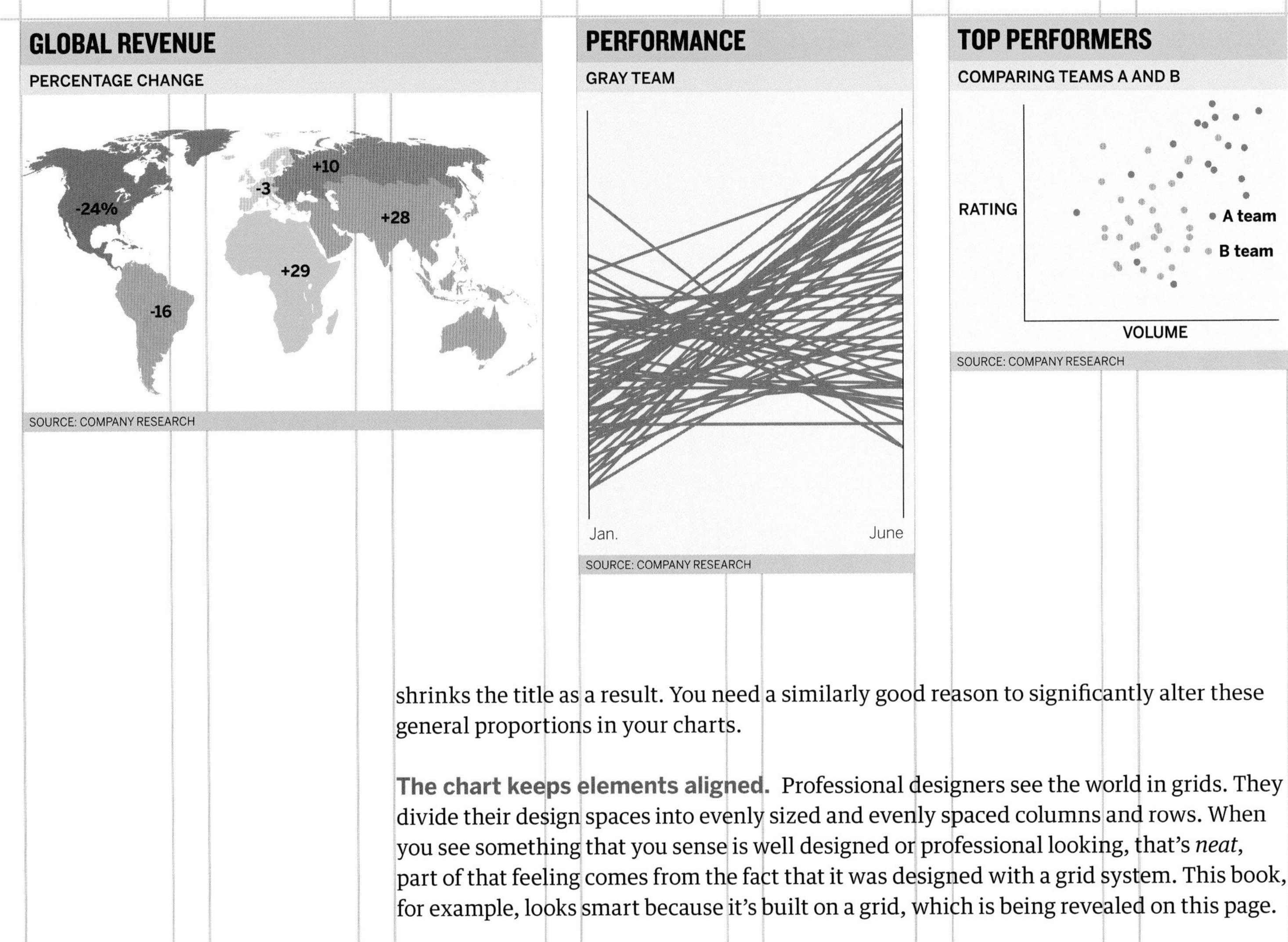

shrinks the title as a result. You need a similarly good reason to significantly alter these general proportions in your charts.

The chart keeps elements aligned. Professional designers see the world in grids. They divide their design spaces into evenly sized and evenly spaced columns and rows. When you see something that you sense is well designed or professional looking, that's *neat*, part of that feeling comes from the fact that it was designed with a grid system. This book, for example, looks smart because it's built on a grid, which is being revealed on this page.

This book's grid is quite complex. Well-aligned charts don't need such sophisticated grids. They will use as few points of alignment as possible, because more makes charts

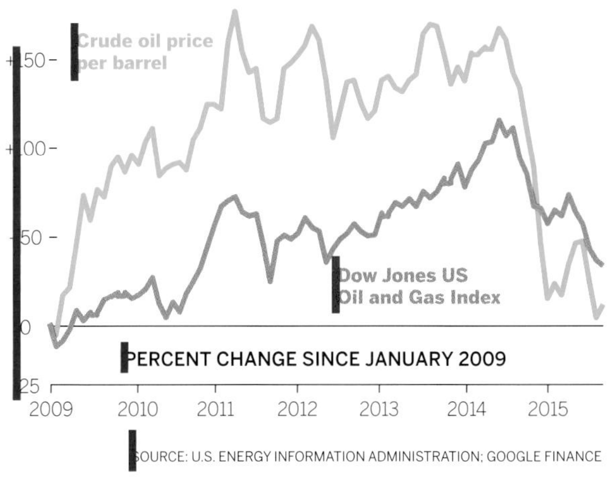
OIL AND GAS POISED FOR A FALL?
Because reserves account for a major portion of valuations in the oil sector, its market cap tends to track crude prices. But when crude prices recently plunged, the sector's market cap did not—a sign that valuations in the industry may be artificially high.
Crude oil price per barrel
Dow Jones US Oil and Gas Index
PERCENT CHANGE SINCE JANUARY 2009
2009
2010
2011
2012
2013
2014
2015
SOURCE: U.S. ENERGY INFORMATION ADMINISTRATION; GOOGLE FINANCE

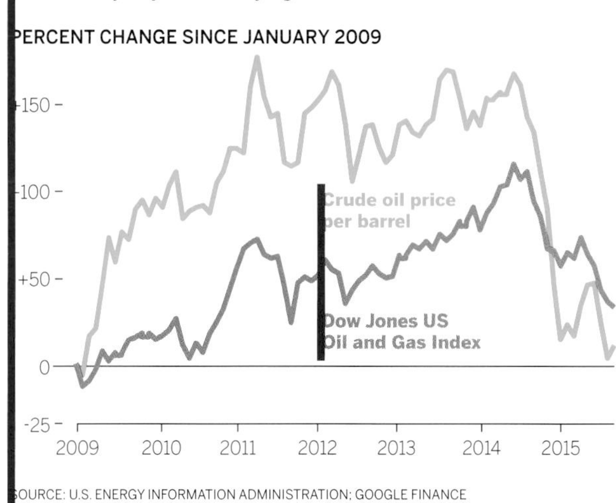
OIL AND GAS POISED FOR A FALL?
Because reserves account for a major portion of valuations in the oil sector, its market cap tends to track crude prices. But when crude prices recently plunged, the sector's market cap did not—a sign that valuations in the industry may be artificially high.
PERCENT CHANGE SINCE JANUARY 2009
+150
+100
+50
0
-25
Crude oil price per barrel
Dow Jones US Oil and Gas Index
2009
2010
2011
2012
2013
2014
2015
SOURCE: U.S. ENERGY INFORMATION ADMINISTRATION; GOOGLE FINANCE

feel busier. Center justification creates multiple alignment points for elements that could share one. And unaligned labels in the visual field create a sense of haphazardness. The title, subtitle, and legend, for example, could all align to a single, left reference point. The difference in the sense of orderliness in the two Oil and Gas charts is plain.

Do you need a grid system for your visuals? Many charts already have one: the axes. They are valuable guides that you can use as baselines for your labels and other elements.

The chart limits eye travel. Keeping elements that work together proximate also supports a clean structure. Keys and legends, for example, can force a lot of back-and-forth eye travel to match values with visual elements. Still, keys and legends are useful

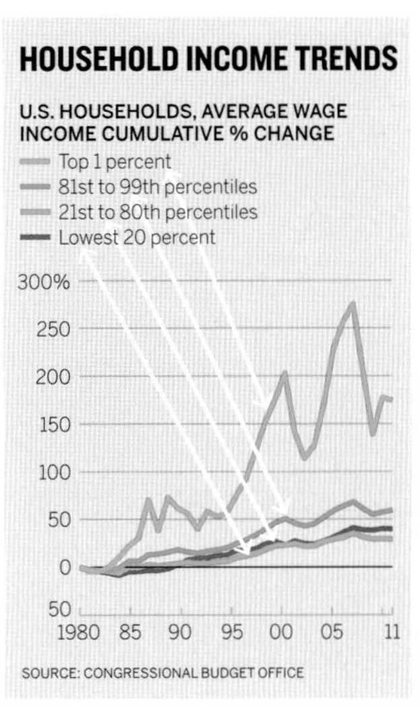

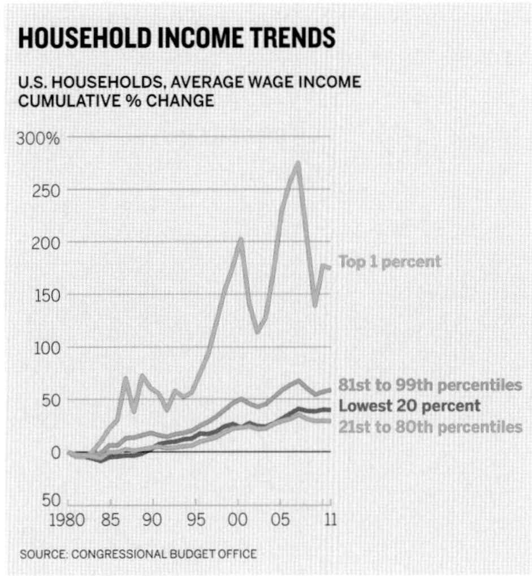

and sometimes necessary, but it's often best to connect values directly to their visual counterparts.

The second Household Income Trends chart *feels* simpler. Your eye travels across the visual and arrives at the label, connecting the elements more naturally than a key can.

Another way to limit eye travel and keep the structure of charts neat is to make pointers and other marks as short and straight as possible, or even eliminate them altogether. Curves and elbows in lines pull your focus away from more important elements. And the further away the label, the harder it is to connect it to its visual counterpart. Compare these two pie charts:

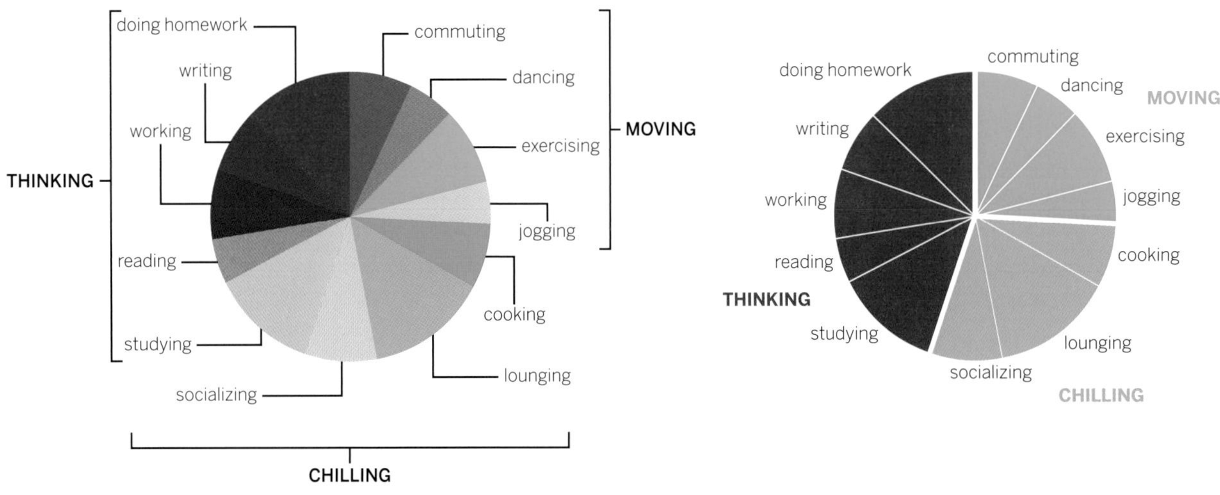

Clarity. Does the chart make sense to you, or are you stuck wondering what you're supposed to see? You may have experienced what the data visualization pioneer Kirk Goldsberry calls a "bliss point"—that *Aha!* moment when a dataviz instantly and irresistibly delivers its meaning to you in a way that feels almost magical, as if it required no effort on your part. Such moments come from a design that achieves *clarity.* Which of these charts sparks that bliss point?

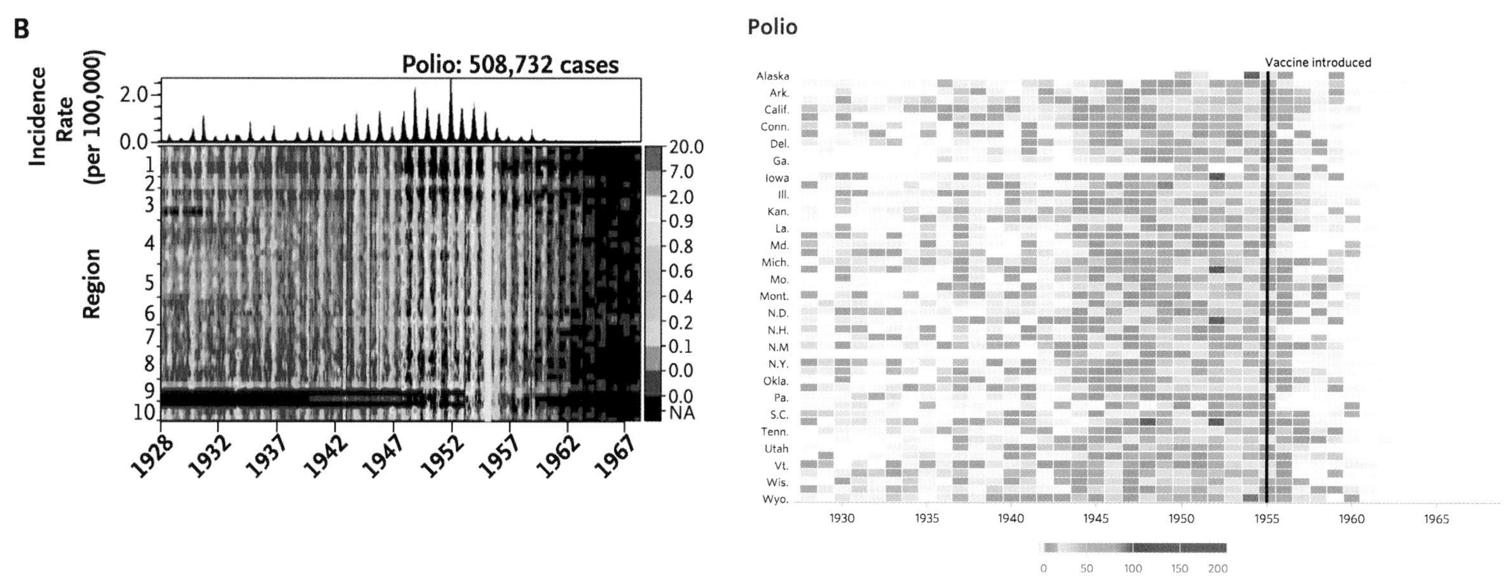

The chart on the right is an astonishing achievement in clarity, part of a set designed by Tynan DeBold, of the *Wall Street Journal.* The chart on the left, which delivers the same information, was presented in the *New England Journal of Medicine* for a specialized audience. It's a good chart for its context, but it's nowhere near as clear as its populist offspring. How does DeBold's chart achieve such clarity?

Nothing is extraneous. Other than labels, only three words accompany this visual, yet it's instantly understandable. DeBold's restraint is remarkable. He doesn't add "States" to the y-axis, or "Year" to the x-axis, because we don't need those words to understand the labels. He even goes so far as to omit "Cases" from the title. (The chart ran as part of an article that briefly notes before a series of graphics like this that they represent "cases per 100,000 people," but even without that the meaning is clear.) Admittedly, this is an extreme example. But it serves to illustrate how clarity can be achieved by removing nonessential information.

Each element is unique and supports the visual. DeBold's chart contains seven elements: title, x-axis labels, y-axis labels, legend, visual, line of demarcation, and caption. Each one does a job that none of the others does. There's zero redundancy.

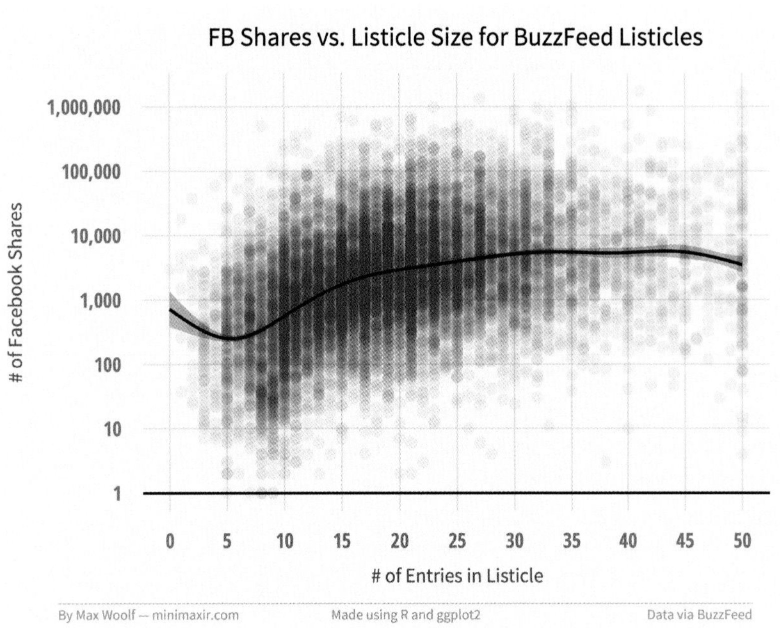

Most charts aren't so purposefully clear. They lack clarity because elements are used to describe the chart's structure rather than support the idea being conveyed. Titles or subtitles repeat axis labels. Captions describe what the visual shows. These are signs of a chart that plots data but isn't making a point, or a chart maker who lacks confidence that the visual can convey the idea on its own.

Supporting elements that have a finer purpose—that augment rather than just repeat—enhance clarity. Start by using such elements to describe the chart's *idea* rather than its structure. Think of a piece of music: Which title helps you understand the *idea* behind it better: Concerto No. 4 in F Minor or *The Four Seasons: Winter*?[2]

One way to create clarity is to make the title or the subtitle the question that the visualization answers. Go back to our core question: *What am I trying to say or show?* This Facebook/BuzzFeed chart is an excellent visualization. But would you more quickly understand what it's showing if it were headed:

Finding the Sweet Spot
How many items make listicles go viral?

The actual number of shares on the y-axis—what the original title refers to—is the data that helps show the *idea* of virality. This title refocuses viewers on that idea, helping them get to what they're looking for a bit more quickly. The words in the title give deliberate clues: "Sweet spot" prompts us to "find" the active region in the visual field. Convention tells us that a sweet spot will be active, positive, dense, so we make a connection between the deep red blotch we see first and the title.

If, instead, we wanted people to notice what types of articles don't go viral, we could change the supporting text:

Viral Dead Spots
Listicles get shared less when they include too many or too few items.

Same visual, completely different effect on viewers as they check the visual and then reference the title and subtitle for context. One final note: The original title of this chart isn't invalid. Sometimes you want a more objective or passive tone that simply describes the data. (This is especially true for analysts, who are meant not to make judgments on the data but only to show it.) As ever, knowing the context is key.

It's unambiguous. If you were quickly approaching the intersection where this sign is posted, and you had to get to Cambridge, would you be able to get in the correct lane in time?

Its ambiguity is paralyzing. Now, instead of using the sign to guide you, you have to assign meaning to the sign itself. You're forced to slow down, shift your focus from driving to thinking about the sign, while trying to continue moving forward. You might feel that your mind is racing, or you might get panicky trying to figure this out as fast as possible. Maybe people are beeping at you. It's stressful.

Ambiguity in visualizations generates a similarly stressful effect (without the beeping). We approach a visual at speed, prepared to parse it quickly, and then an ambiguous label forces us to stop, refocus, and think about the visual rather than the idea. In DeBold's polio graphic, there's no way to misinterpret any element on the page. Compare that with the medical journal version, in which the legend is vertical, snug against the heat map. Is it an axis? What about the lavender line? It's unlabeled. What does it mean? How does the small line chart above the chart relate? Why are there *three* y-axes? We're reading the sign instead of using it to get where we're going.

It doesn't flout metaphors or conventions. DeBold's polio chart uses colors in a way that our brains can swiftly understand: red is more intense, blue is less so. He has created a low-res heat map that plots 2,250 data points (50 states by 45 years). But he's done something clever to his design: he's tacked on a blue-to-pale-gray gradation at the low end of the scale, desaturating the blue until it's nearly colorless, or "empty," at zero. With that he has tapped into another convention we're used to: less color saturation equals less value.

These two conventions combine to create the stunning effect of polio's literally *disappearing*. Compare this with the journal version, in which midnight blue equals zero. The disappearing effect is there, but dark blue transitioning to a darker blue doesn't feel as powerful or immediate. It could just as easily convey full saturation. The lavender line of demarcation for when the vaccine was introduced is harder to see. It doesn't elicit a before-and-after narrative as effectively.

Simplicity. Does the chart look airy, simple, elegant, and pleasing, or cluttered, busy, and complex? The sense of spaciousness, minimalism, beauty, or lyricism we may feel when we see a dataviz comes from its *simplicity*. Clarity and simplicity are related but subtly different. Clarity concerns effective communication: Does the idea come through? Simplicity focuses on effective presentation: Are you showing only what's necessary for the idea to come through? When both are achieved, they hold together like a binary star system, serving each other. Simplicity contributes to clarity, and clarity enhances the sense of simplicity.

But simple isn't always clear, and clear doesn't have to be simple. Which of the two charts on the facing page takes longer to understand?

COMPANY EXPECTATIONS SHAPE RETENTION

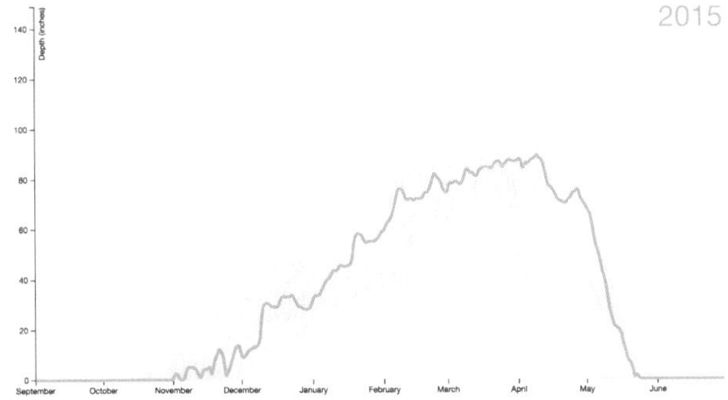

Although the chart on the left is *simpler*, it probably took longer for you to understand. It's less clear. The labels fight with their visual counterparts. How much value does the first bar have? Why are there no values at all on the y-axis? Why are the bars different colors? If the middle bar represents 17% more likely, how can the only slightly larger third bar represent 42% more likely? (In fact, the bars represent some chance of leaving a job that we don't know, because it's not shown; the second and third labels represent the difference in height between compared to the first one.)

The chart on the right is not nearly as simple. It plots 60 trendlines each across 365 x-axis points (one for each day of the year). Still, the point of it is absolutely clear. It uses color effectively. The title and labels are unambiguous.

We tend to think of simplicity as the absence of stuff—that if we just keep taking away more and more information, we'll achieve it. That's true to a point. But excessive simplicity leads to a lack of clarity. What you really need to think about is *relative simplicity*—how little you can show and still convey your idea clearly. Follow the maxim usually attributed to Einstein: "Everything should be made as simple as it can be, but not simpler."[3] Which of the charts about sales rep performance on the following page is simpler?

A REP'S PAST PERFORMANCE DOESN'T PREDICT FUTURE PROFITS

By looking not just at the revenue reps have generated but at their future profitability, you may find that your top performers are even more valuable than you thought—and your low performers even more costly.

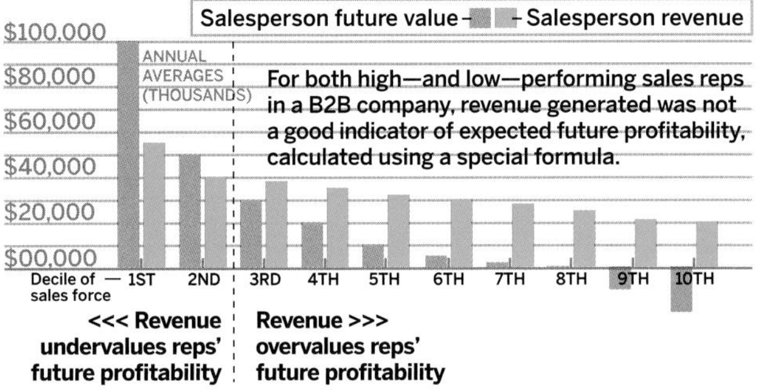

SOURCE: V. KUMAR, SARANG SUNDER, AND ROBERT P. LEONE

A REP'S PAST PERFORMANCE DOESN'T PREDICT FUTURE PROFITS

SALES REPS' AVERAGE ANNUAL REVENUE (IN THOUSANDS)

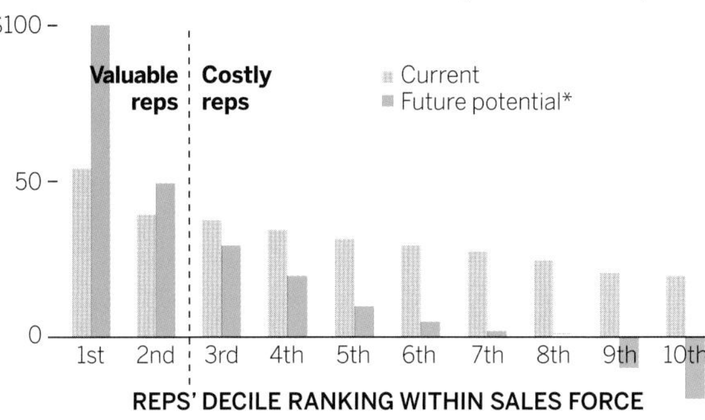

*CALCULATED USING A PROPRIETARY FORMULA.

SOURCE: RESULTS FROM A STUDY OF ONE B2B COMPANY BY V. KUMAR, SARANG SUNDER, AND ROBERT P. LEONE

The chart on the left looks final and reasonably clear. But *simple* and *clean* probably aren't the feelings you get behind your eyes. The simplicity of the version on the right is impressive, given that it manages to convey the same point with so many fewer elements. What makes that version simpler?

It removes stuff. The most obvious path to simplicity is to remove unnecessary things from the chart, leaving only what's valuable to communicating your message. Edward Tufte mathematized this idea as the "data-ink ratio"—the higher the share of ink on the page that's devoted to necessary elements, the better.[4]

Tufte's concept sounds precise, but he's really just saying don't waste ink on decoration or redundancy. In text editing, this is more colorfully referred to as "removing the dead-wood." It's a sound principle. But the trouble with such aphorisms is that "necessary" is a slippery, subjective thing. What is valuable to communicating your message depends, as always, on context. Who is the visual for? Do you already have their attention? How much detail do they need? How and where will they use the visual? Do they have seconds or minutes to look at it?

It's also hard to edit yourself. If you didn't think some element was necessary, you probably wouldn't have included it in a prototype in the first place. It takes discipline to "kill your babies," as text editors sometimes say.

A good way to force yourself to look critically at what you've included is to evaluate the elements one by one, using this simple question flow:

WHICH ELEMENTS SHOULD YOU KEEP?

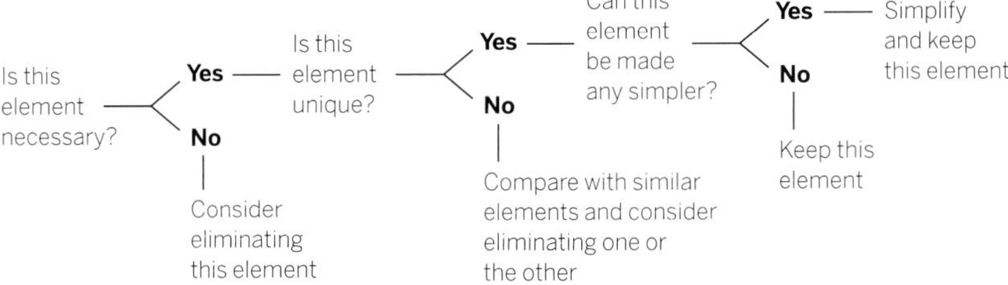

If you've been through a talking and sketching process, and your answer to *What am I trying to say or show?* is written down, you can use that to determine whether an element is necessary. The manager who created the Rep's Past Performance chart on the facing page did write down his statement: *Past sales aren't a good predictor of future performance. Highest performers are more valuable than you think, and lower performers are less valuable than you think.*

With this in mind, we can spend a few minutes applying the question flow to every element in the original version of his chart.

A title is nearly always necessary. But is this one unique? No. In fact, one of the captions repeats it nearly verbatim. Keep the title, kill the caption. Is there a simpler way to present the title? Not really. It can stay as is. The subtitle is a tougher call. It sums up the statement of purpose well. But is it really necessary? It's not unique: it recapitulates the visual. The captions below the x-axis also repeat the idea. That's three ways to say the same thing. Kill the subtitle.

The information in the visual field is necessary, unique, and couldn't be made much simpler. Keep it as is. We've already decided that the caption is redundant, but it does contain bits of unique information, about the formula for future value and the source of the data at a B2B company. This is minor information that doesn't need to distract from the visual. It can be moved to the source line. The other two captions, about over- and underperforming, are necessary to describe the division between the two types of salespeople.

Axes are nearly always necessary on data plots, but how many demarcations they should contain is both endlessly debatable and a major factor in how simple a chart feels. The "airiness" of a simple visualization is often achieved by diminishing or removing a chart's background structure—reference

VISUALIZING IDEAS, SIMPLY

"Visual thinkers aren't born; they're made out of practice."

Jessica Hagy, formerly the creative director at an advertising firm, is now a full-time artist. "If you can visualize ideas," she says, "you have another way to present information. Another way to pop the neurons in people's brains."

Hagy's art focuses mainly on creating apparently simple, sometimes lyrical conceptual visualizations at her site Indexed. Her medium is ink on index cards. Her style is ultra-minimalist. Her subject, often, is work. She uses her simple charts to expose the deep-seated truths and patent absurdities of modern office life. They are a new generation's *Dilbert*, except Hagy accomplishes with a few pen strokes the kind of incisive commentary that required three panels and dozens of words in *Dilbert*.

Hagy continues to publish cards like this weekly. Recently she took on a new challenge: *The Art of War Visualized,* an infoviz version of Sun Tzu's legendary primer on military strategy. She expanded her style somewhat for the project, adding a bit of color and thick, organic brush strokes to reflect the bold, militaristic text. But the conceptual visualizations remain minimalist and restrained.

If you find yourself thinking, as kids sometimes do when they look at a Jackson Pollock painting, *That's so simple, anyone could do that,* you're wrong. Simplicity is an earned skill that takes practice. Hagy works at it every day. "People see simple and think that's the same as simple to create," she says. "I can tell you that to make something *feel* simple but still create insight, or a new way to look at something, or even a punch line, takes work. So much goes into it, including deciding what doesn't go into it." In some cases she reads an entire book to realize one chart.

Hagy says she feels lucky, because although simplicity is hard, "getting there is fun for me." For inspiration, she takes whatever is around her. "I eavesdrop. I wander around. Sometimes I just have news on in the background and jot down an interesting sentence I hear."

She works from a sentence structure—not unlike the process in chapter 4 of capturing ideas from a conversation to describe what a visual should show. "I write

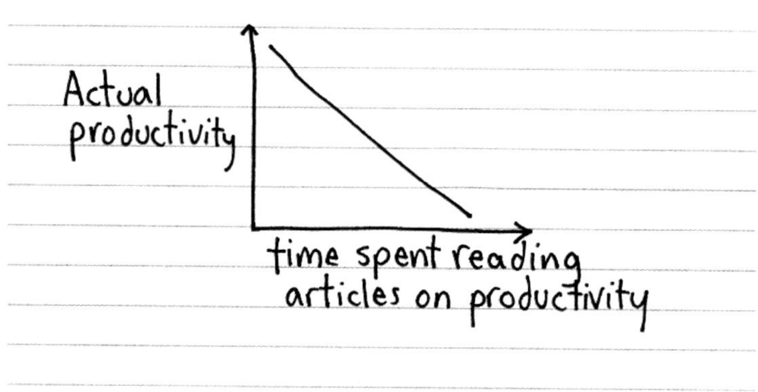

Jessica Hagy's ultra-minimalist index cards are astonishing achievements in simplicity.

down the sentence and then see if I can make it visual," she says. "I might change the subject of the sentence to see where that takes the visual. I'm really tinkering with vocabulary in the sentence, and the form changes with it."

She also ruthlessly edits—a task, she says, that is always difficult—to see how little she can show and still capture the essence of the sentence she's working from. For every index card she creates, Hagy goes through five or more drafts to achieve her hallmark simplicity.

And it's worth it, she says, because she finds that people respond more deeply to simpler visualizations. They reach a "bliss point" when they see an idea that might take them five or six sentences to explain summed up in a chart and processed instantly. For example, you might listen to an HR director explain the relationship between job skills, performance, and wages as one in which how much money you earn depends both on how unique your talent is and on how well you perform, and that the most valuable type of hire combines high performance and unique talent. Or you might look at this:

VISUALIZE YOUR NARRATIVE | 109

> To be near the goal while the enemy is still far from it, to wait at ease while the enemy is toiling and struggling, to be well-fed while the enemy is famished: This is the art of husbanding one's strength.
>
> To refrain from intercepting an enemy whose banners are in perfect order, to refrain from attacking an army drawn up in calm and confident array: This is the art of studying circumstances.

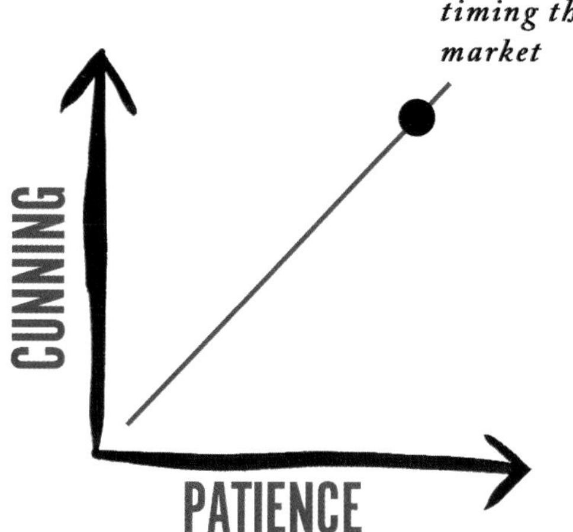

Translating two paragraphs into a single, simple visual requires time, discipline, and multiple tries.

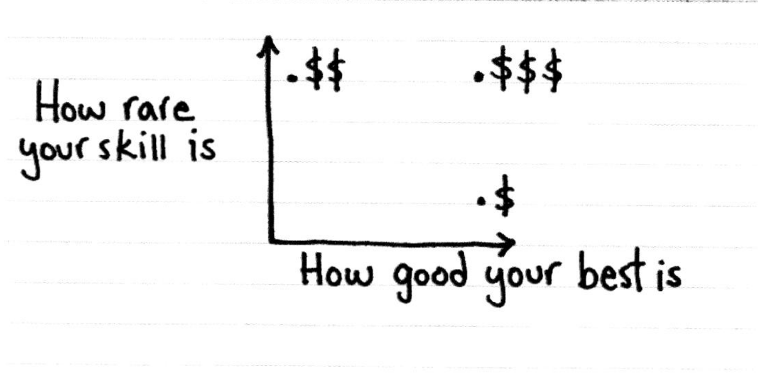

Hagy says that the simpler the chart, the more deeply people connect with it.

lines, ticks, value intervals. Take a look at the three gold price charts below (we'll come back to the sales performance chart).

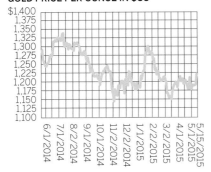

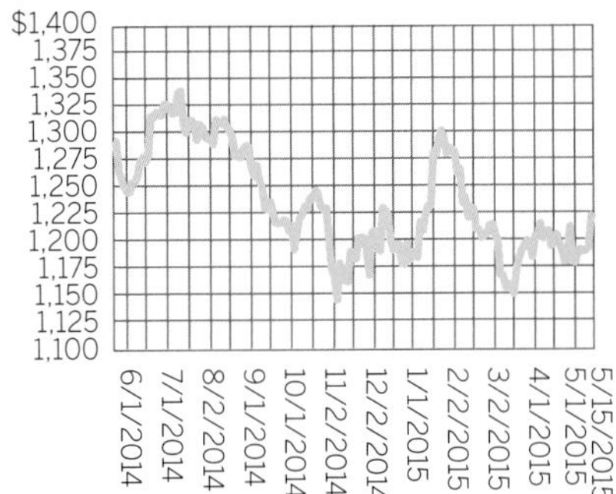

Context: Prototype
Use: Research, individual, informal
Media: Personal screen, paper

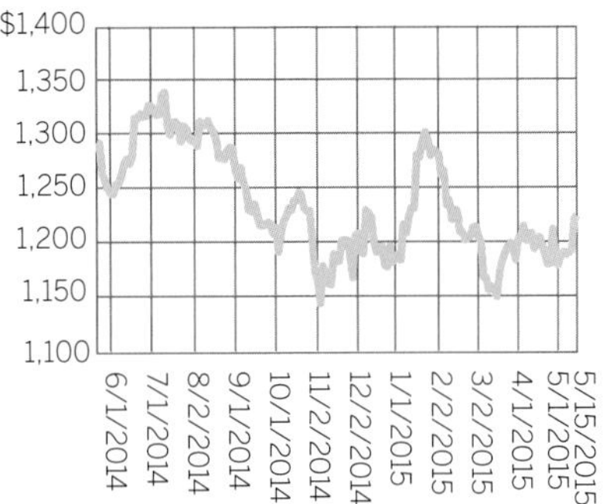

Context: "Let's talk about gold prices"
Use: Analysis, informal or formal, one-on-one, small group
Media: Paper, personal screen, public screen

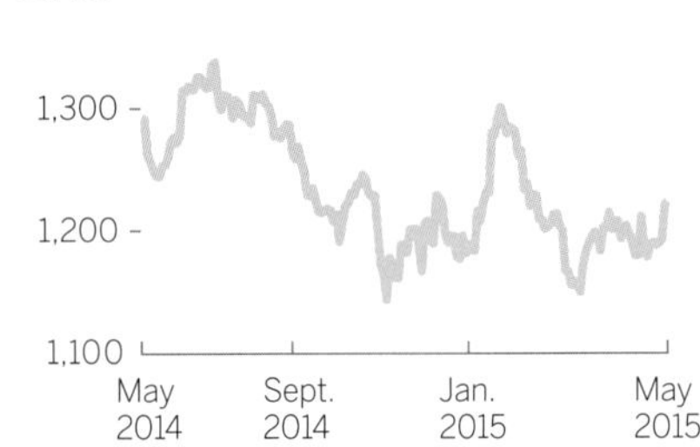

Context: "Gold prices are dropping this year"
Use: Presentation, formal, small or large group
Media: Paper, small screen or large screen

SOURCE: BULLIONVAULT.COM

Clearly the chart without gridlines and fewer labels feels simplest, but is that kind of minimalism always a good thing? Think about display media: A chart presented on paper or on a personal screen—a format in which viewers can spend time with the visual—may benefit from more detail that allows the viewer to reference individual values and explore the chart in depth. But for a chart broadcast in a presentation—when you want the audience to understand the visual in seconds—fewer structural elements will reduce distractions and make it easier to focus on the broad ideas.

Ask yourself, *What do I want viewers to do with this chart?* If the overall shape of the trend is what matters, be more aggressive taking away reference points such as grid lines and axis labels. Communicating the idea that "The price of gold is going down" probably doesn't need detailed stratification on the y-axis. But if you're hoping to have a conversation about monthly gold price trends, more reference points may be helpful. Imagine, for example, using the chart on the right above and saying to your audience, "Look what happened to prices in November." That's much harder to see here than on the middle chart. Then again, the prototype at left has so many dollar values on the y-axis that it's hard to follow them across the grid.

Back to the sales performance chart on page 122: the x-axis is unique and necessary—each pair of bars needs a label. But do we need more or fewer values on the y-axis? If we reduced it to just low, middle, and high values, would that adversely affect its ability to convey the idea? Probably not. The manager's statement of purpose shows that comparing the relative value between two time periods matters more than specific dollar values. The y-axis can be simplified.

In general, though, labels present another challenge to simplicity. A common technique for many managers is to label every visual element on the page with its specific value:

TIME SPENT ON SCREENS BY ORIENTATION, U.S.

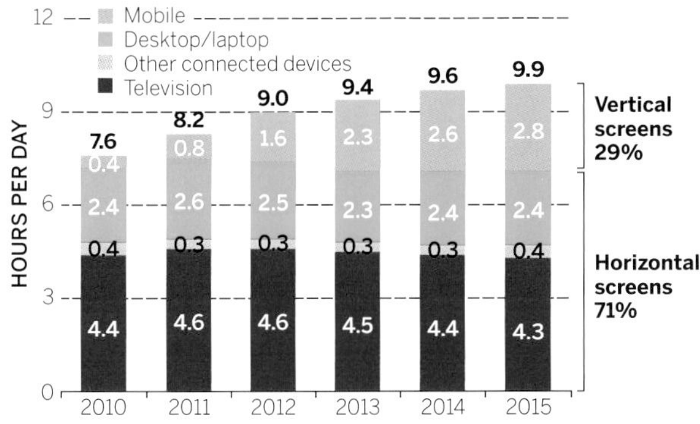

SOURCE: MARY MEEKER'S INTERNET TRENDS REPORT

As the number of values charted increases, the labels begin to overtake the visual. But why are they there? Are we meant to focus on the specific values, or on the overall shape of the thing we're looking at? A visualization is an abstraction. Labeling every value is a concretization. If you feel that it's necessary to show every value, a table may be a better option:

TIME SPENT ON SCREENS BY ORIENTATION, U.S.

HOURS PER DAY SPENT ON SCREENS, U.S.

	2010	2011	2012	2013	2014	2015
Television	4.4	4.6	4.6	4.5	4.4	4.3
Desktop/laptop/other	2.8	2.9	2.8	2.6	2.7	2.8
Mobile	0.4	0.8	1.6	2.3	2.6	2.8
Total	**7.6**	**8.3**	**9.0**	**9.4**	**9.7**	**9.9**
% Horizontal screens	95	90	82	76	73	71
% Vertical screens	5	10	18	24	27	29

The manager who made the chart to the left may argue that the table isn't as effective because it doesn't provide instant recognition of an upward trend and the growing share of mobile screen use. That manager is correct, and has unwittingly argued against her labeling every value in the chart: If the trend and the growing share are most important, the specific values shouldn't be put there to steal our attention from the overall trend.

The manager needs to ask, *Is each individual value important to expressing my idea?* and *Do specific data points have to be available to discuss the idea?* If the answer to either question is yes, a table should be made available. The manager can provide a visual as well, but he's now free to make the chart much simpler. Compare the original chart with the suite of three below, which make every value available and give viewers at-a-glance trends:

HOURS SPENT ON SCREENS

HOURS PER DAY SPENT ON SCREENS, U.S.

	2010	2015
Television	4.4	4.3
Desktop/laptop/other	2.8	2.8
Mobile	0.4	2.8
Total	**7.6**	**9.9**
% Horizontal screens	95	71
% Vertical screens	5	29

SCREEN TIME IN THE U.S.

NUMBER OF HOURS PER DAY

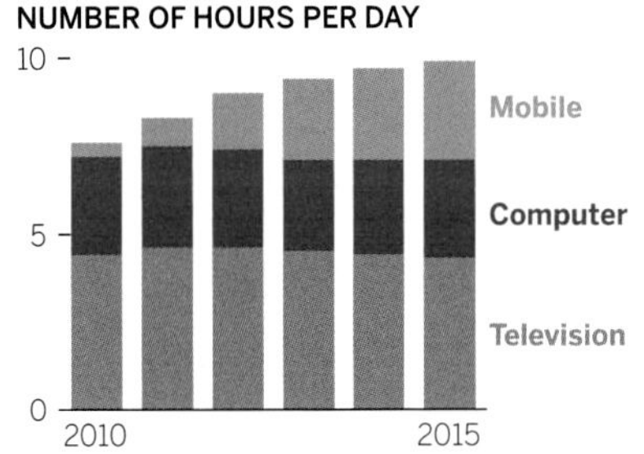

TIME BY ORIENTATION

PERCENTAGE SHARE

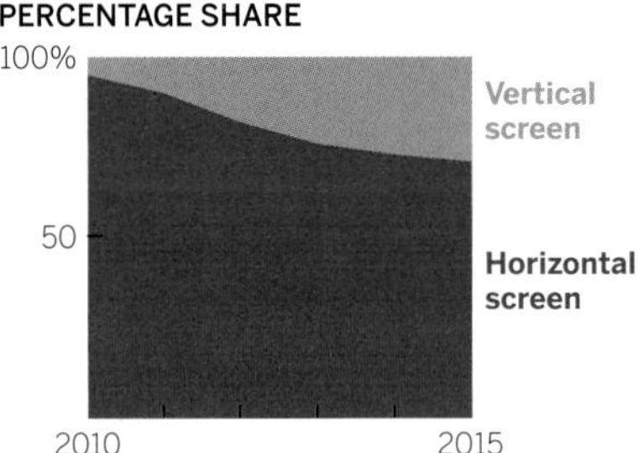

There's no right answer here without knowing the context. But it's true that more labels will reduce simplicity and demand that the viewer make decisions about what's important. Overall, be aggressive. You can almost always take away more than you think—and more than you want to. Test very sparse versions of your chart on colleagues; you may be surprised at how little you need to include to convey your idea.

The chart's elements are not redundant. Removing repetitive elements, as we just did, helps simplify, but so does removing redundant design within elements. Here are a title and subtitle for a chart:

WHAT IS MIDDLE CLASS?

Family income by city, 2013

This is clear and crisp text. But design-wise, the title is highly redundant. In order to make it stand out, it's been given *five* special treatments: size, boldface, underline, color, and all caps. Does it catch your eye? Yes. Does it need so many signals that it's special? No.

The subtitle has two distinguishing elements: size and italics. But if the text is smaller and appears right below the title, it must be the subtitle. Italics are superfluous here.

This is called belt-and-suspenders design. You don't need both to hold up your pants, so pick one. In general, a design will feel simpler if you apply as few unique attributes as possible. Here's the same title and subtitle but with only one difference assigned in each case—size, weight, or color:

What Is Middle Class? Family income by city, 2013	**What Is Middle Class?** Family income by city, 2013	What Is Middle Class? Family income by city, 2013

You might even argue that the line space between the two levels of information is redundant. If you want more space for your visual, you could put the title and subtitle on the same line and still achieve the proper relationship between them:

What Is Middle Class? Family income by city, 2013

Most of the charts in this book use both size and weight to distinguish titles. Two distinguishing characteristics are quite common with titles. As a design choice, it's fine. We present the examples with only one distinguishing characteristic to drive home the point that you don't need to overemphasize elements to get them to do their job. This kind of discipline becomes even more important when applied to axis labels, captions, pointers, and other elements. Instead of giving each its own unique attributes, create classes of information: Captions, legends, and labels can share a text style, for example. Lines, arrows, boxes, and other marks used to connect or group elements often are redundant, too. Usually, simple alignment achieves the same end without any marks at all on the page.

The chart's use of color is restrained. Simplicity suffers when you make charts too colorful because you want them to be eye-catching or you have lots of data categories to plot. In an effort to make meaning from a chart, viewers will note color differences and wonder what they mean. The more color differences they see, the more they have to work to figure out what the distinctions represent. Challenge each addition of a color to a chart: *Why do I need to make this distinction? Can it be combined with other information as a group with a single color?*

Think of color in your charts as a fraction that you need to reduce. A colorful chart is like the fraction four-sixteenths. That ratio is more clearly expressed as two-eighths, and most simply expressed as one-fourth. Find the lowest common denominator that still preserves the distinctions you need to convey your idea. For example, the first chart in this chapter, on page 110, included eight distinct three-hour time periods. We've shown iterations on that chart below to show how color reduction increases effectiveness. Giving each a unique color results in a complicated looking chart with many elements fighting for our attention. Reducing the number of colors from eight to four in six-hour chunks—enough categories to convey the idea well—helps, but the colors still fight with one another. But we can push it even further. Clustering the data as two color families: yellow for before noon and blue for afternoon, with the less common nonworking hours in paler hues, creates an obvious improvement in clarity.

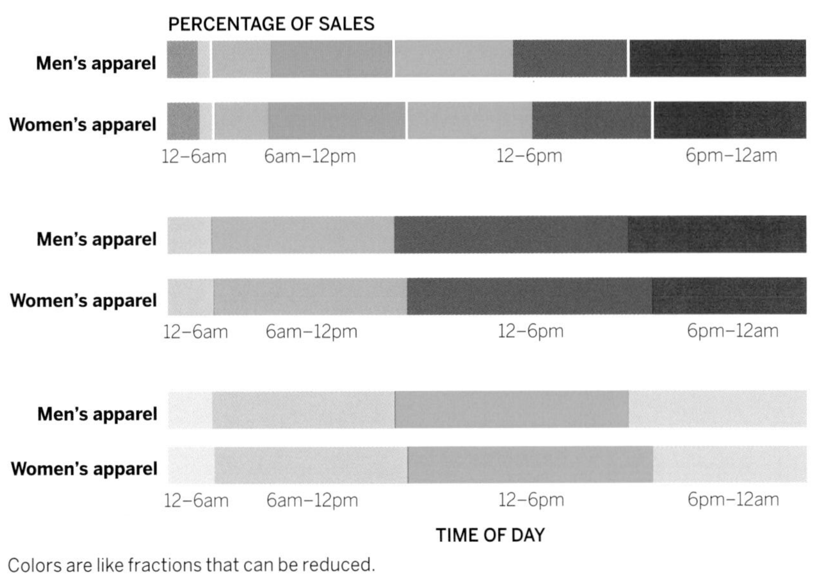

Colors are like fractions that can be reduced.

Another note: Gray is your friend. It creates an information hierarchy. We typically think of gray information as background or secondary by comparison with information presented in color. It provides context without disrupting the main idea by fighting for too much attention.[5] Retaining axis lines but making them gray preserves their usefulness but lets them recede *behind* the important visual information. Background data that provides context also benefits from being made gray. The Snow Depth on Mt. Mansfield chart earlier in this chapter is a masterly example of using color and gray to represent foreground and background information.

Color choice, too, should follow convention.[6] Contrasting data? Contrasting colors. Complementary data? Complementary colors. Groups of data? Same or similar colors. Data ranges? "Empty" colors (low saturation, paler, whiter) for lower values and "full" colors (higher saturation, richer, darker) for higher values.

COURAGE

You've already heard most of the wisdom about simplicity: It's the ultimate sophistication (Da Vinci); style depends on it (Plato); less is more (Robert Browning via Ludwig Mies van der Rohe); simple is hard (variations attributed to hundreds of people). All that is true, of course. But for managers, here's a new aphorism: Simplicity is courageous.

A manager's impulse is to show everything, which often leads to dense, difficult-to-read charts that don't so much convey an idea as turn hundreds or thousands of spreadsheet cells into a visual. In part, this is the curse of knowledge—we think it's important to represent all the data that we know about and that we've produced. Dense, complex charts, we think, convey something about the person who created them: "I know my stuff. Look how hard I'm working."

This deep-seated belief that more is better, that complex equals smart, must be eradicated. That's not what makes charts good.

Standing up at an important meeting to present a few clear, simple charts probably seems scary. Andrew Abela hears this when he's working with executives on their presentation skills. "When it comes to simplicity and clarity, there's a correct fear and a false fear," he says. "The correct fear is you do need to convey the right information, the right detail." That's what this book wants to help you do. "But then there's the false fear that if you don't show everything, they won't understand or they won't think you're working hard." In some ways, the first fear leads to the second: I'm scared I might not show the right information, so I'll show *all* the information. "I've been doing this a long time," Abela says, "and I will tell you now, nothing makes an executive happier than seeing someone show up with just a couple of excellent charts. They tell me, 'Finally, someone confident enough to just show me what I need and not bombard me with 60 slides.'"

"Once," he continues, "I helped a manager prepare for a presentation to the CEO, and even though he was nervous about it, we decided he should make the entire presentation based on one great chart that he had created. The CEO was so impressed. They spent three hours talking about that one visualization."

RECAP

REFINE TO IMPRESS

The goal of good chart design isn't to make visualizations more attractive; it's to make them more effective and easier to understand. While most of us sense good design when we see it, we don't always know why. Here are some techniques to create that sense of good design in your charts:

1. **To make charts feel neat or clean, focus on design *structure and hierarchy*:**
   - Include four elements in all charts: title, subtitle, visual field, and source line. Within the visual field include axes, labels, and sometimes captions and legends.
   - Give each element a consistent weight: title (about 12% of your visualization); subtitle (8%); visual field (75%); source line (5%).
   - Align elements: place them along as few horizontal and vertical lines as possible.

2. **For charts that just make sense or feel instantly understood, focus on design *clarity*.**
   - Remove extraneous elements. Be aggressive. Take away as much as possible while maintaining the meaning.
   - Make all the elements support the visual. Use them to highlight the idea, not to describe the chart's structure.
   - Remove ambiguity. Make sure each element has a single purpose that can't be misinterpreted.
   - Use conventions and metaphors. Take advantage of ideas we don't need to think about to understand, such as red is "hot" and blue is "cold."

3. **To make charts that look elegant or beautiful, focus on design *simplicity*.**
   - Show only what's needed. Every element should be necessary, unique, and rendered as simply as possible.
   - Avoid belt-and-suspenders design. One form of emphasis per element is enough.
   - Minimize the number of colors you use. Gray works for contextual and second-level information and for structural elements such as grid lines.
   - Limit eye travel. Place labels and legends in close proximity to what they describe.

CHAPTER 6

REFINE TO PERSUADE

THREE STEPS TO MORE-PERSUASIVE CHARTS

A MANAGER AT A NOT-FOR-PROFIT is preparing to stand in front of 20 potential donors with deep pockets and many options for where to take their philanthropy. She's launching a program to fight suburban poverty, which she will tell them is a significant, growing problem. But she knows her audience will need more than that to be persuaded to back her initiative. She's already anticipating skeptical questions, such as "Why suburban poverty? It can't be as bad as urban poverty, can it?" These people will want to see evidence. She looks at a chart that will provide it:

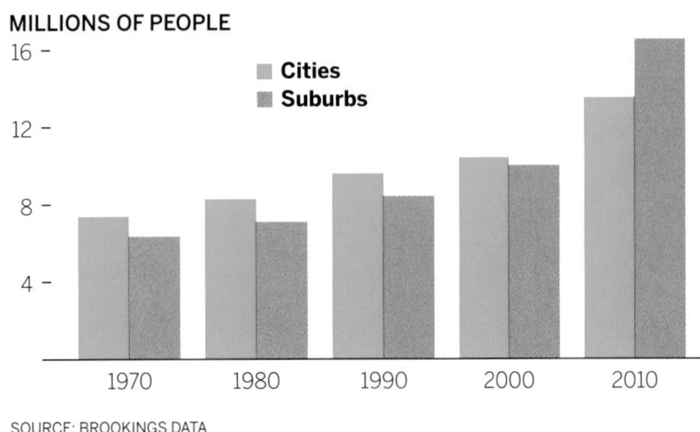

A good effort. It's simple and well designed. All the information is there. Although poverty is growing in both cities and suburbs, it has grown more in the suburbs. Still, she's unsatisfied by her effort. The first thing she sees is that poverty is growing; it takes a minute to find the suburban poverty story.

So she tries to build a more persuasive visualization and comes up with this:

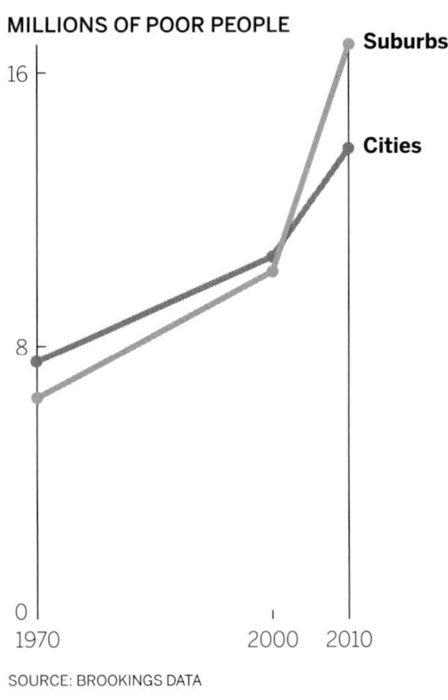

She's thrilled with this version, which is more accessible and far more convincing. The surge in suburban poverty comes through immediately, and almost directly after that, so does the idea that more poor people now live in suburbs than in cities. This will surprise and move her audience.

How did she get from her original, perfectly accurate but unsatisfying bar chart to something she's certain will help her line up donors for the program?

MAKING A CASE

For managers, it's often not enough to make a chart that's simply accurate. You're trying to reveal truths dormant in the data; to make a case; compete for attention, resources, and money; make a pitch to clients; recruit new customers; sway an opinion or help to form one. You don't just want people to believe the chart is true—you want it to lead to action, suggest a way forward.

Persuasion science defines three strategies we use to influence behavior or thinking: *economic* (carrots and sticks), *social* (everybody else is doing it), and *environmental* (relaxing music at the dentist). Visualization falls for the most part into the third category. Steve J. Martin, a heavyweight in the field and a coauthor of several books on influence and persuasion, provides a legion of examples from his and others' research of how environmental persuasion strategies work.[1] For example, a professor doubled the number of people who were willing to participate in a survey by attaching a handwritten note to the request.[2] Hotels increased the reuse of towels by 25% when they changed the wording of placards next to the towels.[3] People serve themselves less food when the color of a plate contrasts with the color of the food.[4]

The mechanisms by which information visualizations persuade us are similarly subtle and equally powerful. "Whilst we'd like to think that our decisions are the result of effortful cognition, the reality is somewhat different," Martin writes. "Much of our behaviour is driven by unconscious cues present in our environment."

We're veering away from the data scientists now. It's often their job to *show all the data*—to be as objective as possible and present everything that's available for analysis. This makes sense for them and for us when we're doing exploratory visualization. It's for fact-finding, hypothesis-testing, and analysis. This chapter focuses on those times when visual communication needs to sway an audience and effect change.

Even if we don't think much about it, we recognize the distinction between conveying information and persuading, and we allow for both types of communication. A play-by-play announcer calls the action, describing mostly what's actually happening on the field; a color commentator influences our sense of the game's narrative. A house for sale can be accurately described as "2,400 square feet with 4 bedrooms and 2 baths on 1.2 acres" or, to make you want it more, as "a huge, open-concept Colonial with a brand-new modern kitchen, on a secluded, wooded lot with spectacular views." What you may call a used car, the person hoping you'll buy it calls pre-owned. Newspapers publish both reported stories and op-eds about the same topic. Compare the sentences on the following page.

Reported story	Op-ed
The budget again seeks to retire the popular A-10 "Warthog" close air support aircraft for savings of $382 million, a move sure to anger Congress, which rejected a similar proposal last year.[5]	I appreciate the budget pressures that the Pentagon faces these days. But those arguments have serious flaws—and if we retire the A-10 before a replacement is developed, American troops will die.[6]

Is the reported story *better* than the op-ed? No, a qualitative comparison is impossible. One is informative, the other persuasive, and they use different rhetorical techniques.[7] The reported story describes facts, and speculation (Congress will get angry) is bolstered by evidence (it was rejected before). The editorial, though, uses the first person, joins the audience ("we") and feels more personal and conversational ("these days"). A significant claim ("troops will die") is stated without evidence. Neither text is better or worse than the other; each is good in its context (and, conversely, not good in the other's).

The same holds true for infoviz. When you have a point of view, you can employ techniques—manipulations—to heighten the effect. The unconscious cues—color, contrast, space, words, what you show and, as crucially, what you leave out—all work to make the idea more accessible and increase the chart's persuasiveness. Here's a dataviz equivalent of the news story/op-ed comparison above:

COST OF ONE SMALL BEER AT EVERY MLB STADIUM

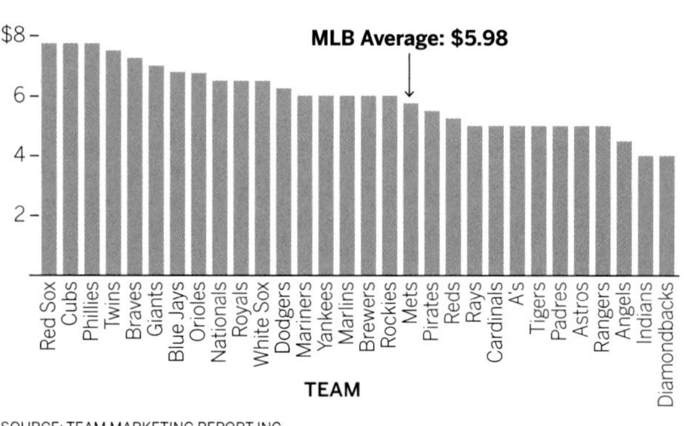

Liquor store case: $20

Ballpark average: $115

$0 — $150

IF YOU BOUGHT A CASE OF BEER AT A BALLPARK

Fans know they're getting robbed, but converting the cost of beer at all the MLB parks into a measure they can easily relate to shows just how bad it is.

Expensive
$81–$99/case
Pirates
Indians
Dodgers
Rangers
Angels
Diamondbacks

Exorbitant
$103–$131/case
Braves
Reds
Orioles
Rays
Cardinals
A's
Tigers
Nationals
Royals
White Sox
Twins
Brewers
Rockies
Phillies
Padres
Astros

Outrageous
$138–$144/case
Giants
Mariners
Yankees
Marlins
Blue Jays
Cubs
Mets

Unconscionable
$186/case
Red Sox

SOURCE: TEAM MARKETING REPORT INC.

If you wanted to persuade someone that beer is too expensive at baseball games, it's clear which chart you'd use. But if the commissioner of baseball wanted to understand the costs associated with attending games then such persuasion would be inappropriate. Admittedly, this example is extreme. Persuasion doesn't need to veer into blatant editorializing. Most of the time, managers just want to make a point more clearly and forcefully than an accurate, well-designed, but passive chart does.

THREE STEPS TO MORE-PERSUASIVE CHARTS

What often makes a chart persuasive is how easily you draw people's attention to the main idea so that they can process it.[8] Persuasion scientists refer to this as the *availability* of salient information. If you make an idea easy to access, viewers will often find it more appealing and persuasive.[9]

Which chart does a better job of persuading you that the West Coast sales team is a problem?

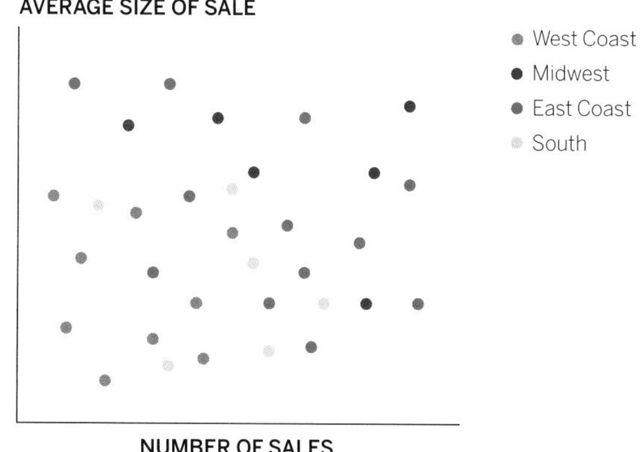

NATHAN SHETTERLEY

CHANGING BEHAVIOR WITH VISUALIZATION

"How do you get someone to do *anything* with mundane information?"

Nathan Shetterley's question is neither rhetorical nor academic. As a consultant at Accenture, he was working with a large utility client trying to find ways to change the behavior of its customers—to persuade them to be more energy-efficient. The usual suggestions were floated: awareness programs and technology that automatically turns lights on and off. But Shetterley had a different idea. He wanted to change how information was presented on customers' bills.

The idea came from his time as a student at Laval University, in Québec City. He got involved with a start-up there that was trying to change consumers' energy-use behaviors. The company made an app for monitoring energy consumption. If the software helped achieve savings of 15%, the company would split the savings with the utility. "They struggled early on," Shetterley recalls. "It was so engineering-focused. We switched out the software to something that was more graphical and user-friendly. That really helped the business."

Eventually, Shetterley saw an opportunity at the foundering start-up. "I said to the bosses, 'If I can sell X dollars by the end of the year, let me run the thing.' I hit the target and became *directeur général*—effectively the CEO."

So there he was, a few years later, with a similar challenge at Accenture. Shetterley believed that by incorporating easy-to-understand dataviz into customers' bills, he could change their habits. He found a vendor that put "about 100 times more" effort into designing its bills than other vendors. "They weren't the cheapest or the safest choice, by a long shot," he recalls. "But the team—and me in particular—were convinced that focusing on visualization in this very boring industry would make a difference."

And it did. Adding simple charts to the bills seemed to affect people's energy-use choices. The vendor Shetterley chose, OPower, became one of the success stories of the so-called green tech bubble of the mid-2000s.

His bold choice and the results it earned got noticed. From then on, when people in Accenture's tech labs needed someone to work on visualization, they'd call him. Gradually he moved into working on big data projects full-time, and he concentrated on the visualization aspect because "it was getting the least love." The focus was still on building massive databases and increasing data science muscle without necessarily thinking about how to express parts of what was being collected.

"Big data projects are a similar challenge to the utility bills, just on a much bigger scale," Shetterley says. "If you start with the data and point it at a person, you'll get only so far. You need a lens to view data through. You have to think about what the user needs. In consultant speak, you have to ask the classic question *What's the outcome we're trying to drive?*" Data scientists don't always think that way, he says. They think more passively about outcomes. For many, amassing and crunching the data is the end in itself. Shetterley knows that clients don't need to see data in charts; they need to see ideas. Consultants aren't passively showing data; they're trying to persuade clients and generate smart discussion around ideas.

The data visualization process at Accenture has been formalized in a "visual literacy curriculum," or VLC—a series of workshops that teach data scientists and other nondesigners the basics of visualization. "We've made the decision that architecture, analytics, *and* viz are all equal players. They're interconnected, and if you take one out, the others become less valuable."

Shetterley's visualization process starts with his asking questions that create context: *What objective are we trying to achieve? Who's the audience? What delights and frustrates this audience? What data is available to us?* "Not just what data do we have," he notes, "but what else could we bring in?"

Then the team starts sketching. "We don't see most engineers do it, so we incorporated it." The process is iterative and meant to get the visualizers and the data scientists on the same page, or to discover quickly—before too much work has been done—whether they need to change course. Shetterley, who often frames his process in consultants' language, calls it "expectation management with design iteration." He says, "Sketching helps you find the edges of the playground. It's really useful."

It's not always an easy sell, though. "For folks with 30 years in IT, this idea of a series of unfinished sketches is atrocious. They hate it at first. They want requirements and then some final thing. It's just how they're used to working." Still, they work together on it, and Shetterley says that once the engineers have done it a few times, they fall in love with the process.

One surprising outcome of instituting a visualization process is that the engineers have asked to do the same, but in reverse. "You're asking us to become more visually literate," Shetterley says they told him. "We want the design-driven folks to become more data-literate." So now, in addition to the VLC, Accenture is teaching Data 101 to designers.

Shetterley has expertise in both data and visualization. But he says that increasingly, the smart way for companies to organize visualization efforts is to stop looking for people with a unique combination of visualization and data skills and instead to focus on creating multidisciplinary teams.

"Get an artist, an analyst, a software engineer, an architect, and a manager. That's a five-node team. Maybe it's five people, maybe it's three, or six. But it's a scalable way to make dataviz a core competency. If you're looking for a unicorn, for one person to do visualization, you're looking at the problem the wrong way.

"It seems obvious when you think about it, but for a while we were getting ahead of ourselves with visualization. Especially here in Silicon Valley, we get excited about ideas and talk about how they're going to change the world. Then, after that, we sit down and say, 'Okay, how can we do this in reality?'"

The left chart may seem more informative because it includes more-detailed information. But as persuasion science shows, it's not about how detailed and precise you are; it's about how easy you make it to see the most important thing. That's why the chart on the right is more persuasive.

The manager who made this chart employed many of the same techniques used by the manager at the not-for profit who charted the growth of suburban poverty. When you're trying to increase persuasiveness, focus on these three things:

1. Hone the main idea.
2. Make it stand out.
3. Adjust what's around it.

Hone the main idea. The process outlined in chapter 4 for arriving at your defining statement will put you on the path to persuasion. Look again at the two urban/suburban poverty charts on page 134 and try to imagine what statements might have been made during the talk and listen phase to inform the creation of those charts. They might be something like this:

Nonpersuasive	Persuasive
I want to compare suburban and urban poverty populations, decade by decade.	I need to convince people that suburban poverty is a huge and growing problem that has rapidly overtaken urban poverty.

Sometimes, though, you won't be as fortunate as that manager in arriving at a statement that naturally leads to a persuasive chart design. To get there, you can go through a mini round of talk and listen with a counterpart. (If you're already at the talk and listen stage, add this in.) Change your prompt. Instead of asking *What am I trying to say or show?* try *I need to convince them that . . .* The former is still the best first prompt for your conversations (and for more-objective visualization projects). You may arrive at a more persuasive approach from that question alone. But if you don't, and your charts aren't having the persuasive effect you hoped for, the statement may help. Examples:

What am I trying to say or show?	I need to convince them that . . .
I am trying to show the distribution of costs of buying a beer at baseball stadiums.	I need to convince them that beer is unreasonably expensive at every single baseball stadium.
I am trying to show the relationship between increased automation in manufacturing and fewer jobs being available. Automation increases profits but creates a need for new jobs that are hard to fill.	I need to convince them that although profits are higher, robots are killing manufacturing jobs and creating a massive skills gap that offsets those short-term gains.
I am trying to show how increasing hours spent on work isn't increasing productivity and may be decreasing it.	I need to convince them that all this extra work we do is backfiring. It's hurting the company's productivity, not helping.
I am trying to show the relationship between unbundling products and declining revenue.	I need to convince them that unbundling our software suite will devastate revenue streams.
I am trying to show that the gardening population is a large, growing, diverse, and underserved market.	I need to convince them that growth in the gardening market is coming from gardeners who are hungry for apps, younger, and more technically savvy than they think.

Notice how the second prompt gives rise to more-emotional language. You've shifted from visualizing an idea (I want you to know something) to trying to persuade someone that the idea is good (I need you to believe something). Words that describe statistical trends (*increasing, declining, underserved*) naturally give way to words that describe feelings (*hurting, helping, hungry*).

One caveat: It's easy to slip into unhelpful editorializing when you prompt yourself with *I need to convince them that . . .* The manager looking at the gardening market, for example, may have arrived at *I need to convince them that they're wrong about gardeners and they're missing a major opportunity.* That's not a useful starting place for sketching and prototyping. It reflects his feelings about his audience and the results he foresees if he fails—not the ideas he wants to communicate in his charts.

Still, talking through his frustration with a colleague might help steer him toward a more useful statement of persuasion, especially if the colleague asks that pesky question "Why?"

I need to convince them that they're wrong about gardeners and they're missing a major opportunity.

Okay, why are they wrong?

Because gardeners use apps and shop online. They're not these Luddites who can't work an iPad. Hell, 7 out of 10 gardeners are under 55.

That's the missed opportunity?

Yes. Most of the growth in gardening is with people under 35. Obviously they use apps. Even older gardeners are more tech-savvy than people assume. They shop online more than the average person. That's what I need to show.

Now he has documented some usable information and found a revised, persuasive statement that he can begin to sketch.

Make it stand out. With a sharper statement, sketching and prototyping will naturally veer toward more-persuasive forms. But you can amplify the persuasive effect even further with a couple of design decisions and techniques. Specifically, you can emphasize and isolate your main idea.

Emphasize. There, I just did it. Boldface and color are a form of visual emphasis. Did you say to yourself, *This word is important; I should pay attention to it*? Probably not. But you did assign meaning to it. You treated it differently from the words you're reading now. You're more likely to remember it because I emphasized it.

Just as text allows for multiple forms of emphasis, such as **boldface,** *italics,* ALL CAPS, underline, color, and highlights, visuals use a variety of techniques to emphasize key information and ideas: Color. Highlights. Pointers. Labels. Tell me what I'm supposed to see. Make it easy for me to get it.

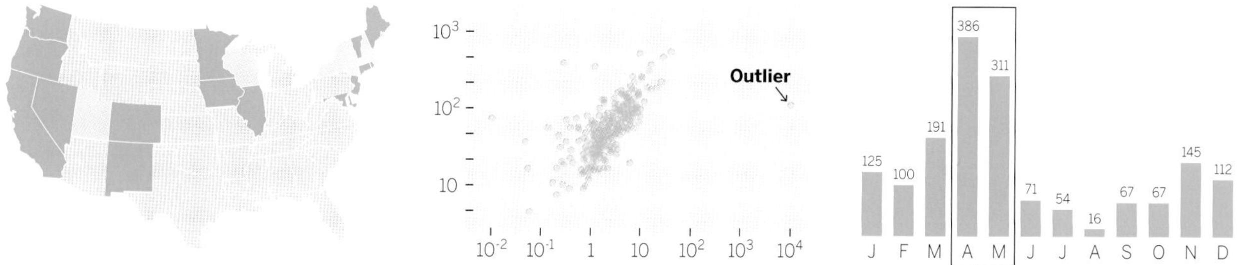

The most obvious and common form of emphasis is color. No need to overthink this: Use rich color to make important ideas come forward, and diminish other information with lighter or contrasting colors. The not-for-profit manager went through several color iterations in trying to make her main idea the most accessible one.

It doesn't take much to emphasize an idea. Color, simple pointers, or demarcations will draw the eye.

Each iteration attempts to make the surging suburban poverty trend the first thing we see and to use the comparative information, urban poverty, to support rather than

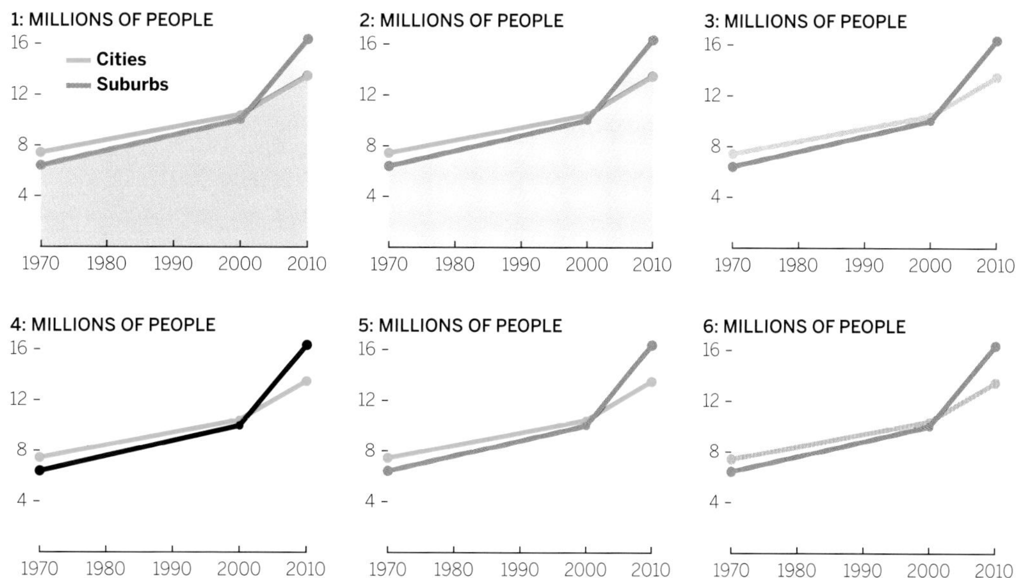

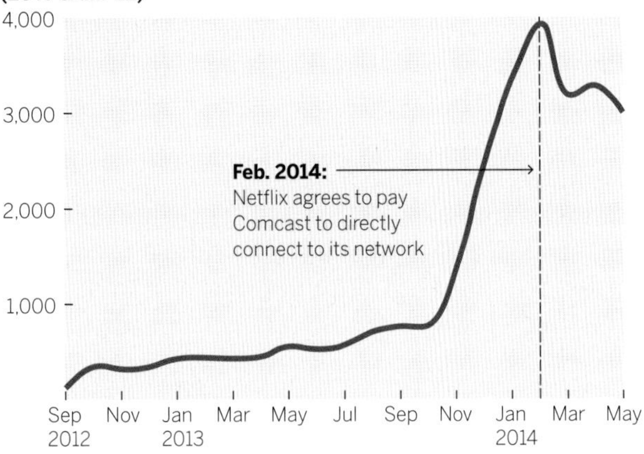

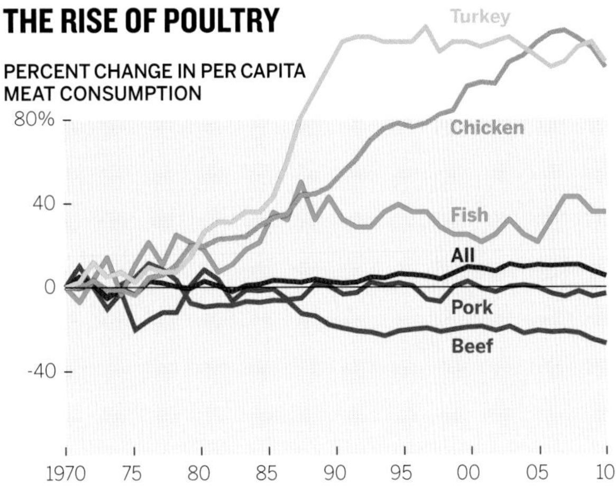

compete with that idea. Here's why the manager rejected each previous iteration:

1. The overlay of semitransparent colors creates a third color that dominates the chart and draws attention to the filled area, not the lines.
2. This clearly highlights suburban poverty more, but why is one shaded and one not? The shaded area is still distracting.
3. Darker and lighter hues of the same color suggest two variables in a group, not a comparison. She wants to contrast, not complement.
4. Black on white provides the most contrast, but black and blue don't contrast so much that the black line pops.
5. Better! But the blue is still fighting for attention.
6. Final color choice.

Demarcations may seem almost unnecessarily simple, but they can be extremely influential. The curved gray line of demarcation on the chart that maps West Coast sales performance on page 137 makes it impossible to see the team as anything other than performing below expectations. Pointers can also nudge an audience toward the narrative we want to convey. Without the dotted line and label, it would be hard to understand what was happening in the Netflix Customers chart.

Demarcations can also be used to editorialize. By exceeding the border of the visual field, the author of the Rise of Poultry chart is making a value judgment about the reasonable limits within which the data should fall. The two lines that flout convention by going outside the border draw our eye immediately—they are meant to persuade us that the values represented by these lines are *too much*. (Similarly, in the editorial chart showing the cost of beer at MLB stadiums, the axis stops before it reaches the highest value: this suggests that the cost of beer at a Red Sox game is off the charts.)

The West Coast sales-reps scatter plot uses another, less obvious way to make an idea more accessible. When charts are meant to represent some number of people or individual units, it's useful to show those units (or multiples of them) rather than a more abstract statistical representation of the whole set. In that chart, each dot represents a person. The same information could be conveyed more abstractly but would be less persuasive:

SALES REP PERFORMANCE BY REGION

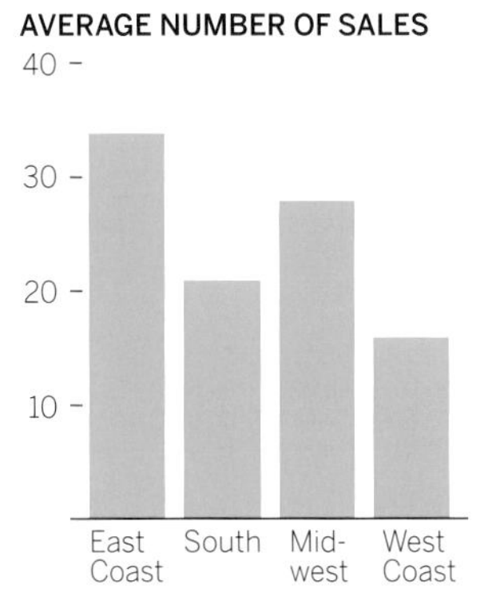

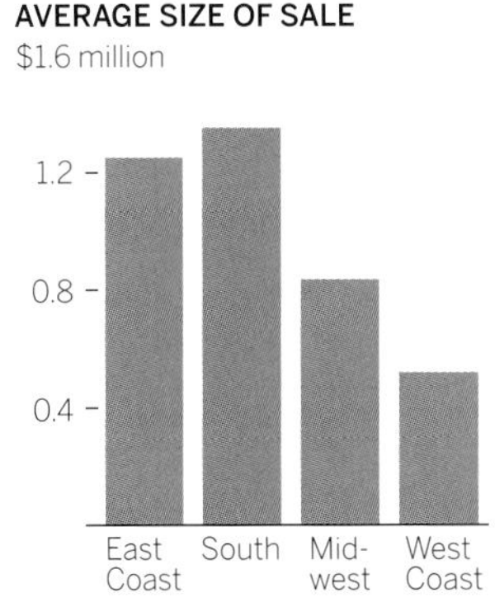

SOURCE: COMPANY RESEARCH

Even if the relative smallness of the West Coast bars were emphasized, this chart would be less persuasive than the chart that plots individuals' performance. That's because statistics are abstract things, and our minds would prefer to focus on more relatable things.[10] For example, which of these more convincingly shows the extreme unlikeliness that a high school basketball player will make it to the NBA, the pie or the unit chart?

HIGH SCHOOL BASKETBALL PLAYERS TO THE NBA

PERCENTAGE OF HIGH SCHOOL BASKETBALL PLAYERS

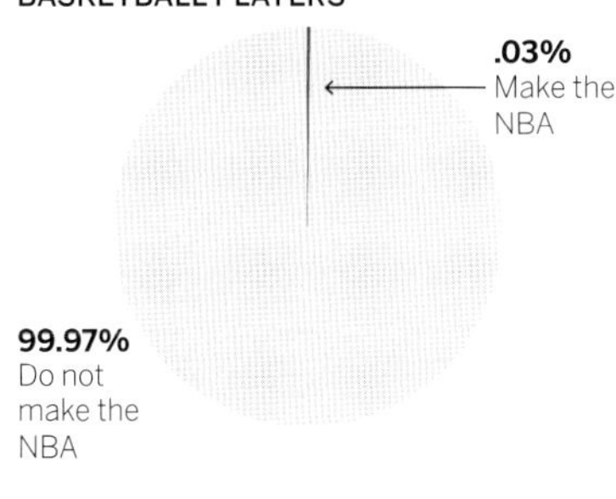

SOURCE: NCAA RESEARCH

FOR EVERY 10,000 HIGH SCHOOL BASKETBALL PLAYERS, HOW MANY MAKE IT TO THE NBA?

SOURCE: NCAA RESEARCH

The dots turn data into units that we can relate to—people—better than we can relate to a number like 0.03%. (It probably took you a moment to locate the three red dots. In this case, the *lack* of accessibility actually helps, illustrating as it does that those individuals are so rare that you must work to find them in the crowd.)

The way unit charts convey a sense of individuality have made them a popular way to communicate ideas about people. They're also effective when visualizing risk and probability (as in the NBA example, or in some other celebrated examples, death rates).[11] Another potentially powerful use of unit charts is to represent money. We often show budgets and spending as proportional breakdowns. Showing individual units of money allocated to various groups might persuade us to think more carefully about where we put those dollars.

High-resolution displays have also helped popularize unit charts, because they can display tiny points as clearly as print can. How such a chart will play on a large screen in a presentation is worth considering beforehand.

Isolate. As much as we can emphasize the main idea, we can also isolate it by de-emphasizing other aspects of the visual. De-emphasis comes from grouping elements and eliminating them. Every element that earns a unique attribute, such as color, is fighting for attention with the main idea to which we want to draw people's eyes. The fewer the unique elements, the easier it is for viewers to know where to look and to understand what they see.

Software programs that generate charts don't automatically create influential emphasis. They tend to assign colors to every variable without taking into account which ones you want your audience to focus on first, or how color and categorization can be used to create primary and complementary information.

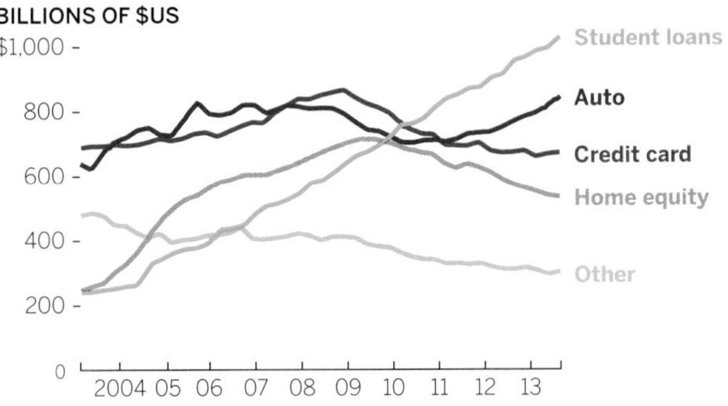

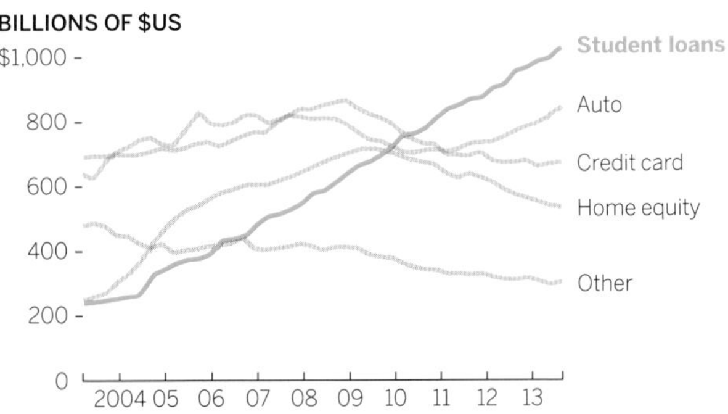

When every variable gets a bright color; no one variable stands out. Which idea is most available in the first Non-Mortgage Debt Outstanding chart? Many people first see the green line, because it's somewhat separate from the others. But this chart is in fact meant to persuade us that there's a student debt crisis. Now you may see it, but that idea was less available than it should have been. Isolating that variable creates a more persuasive chart.

For all the power of software programs and online services to generate reasonably good looking visualizations, they're not yet capable of injecting such cues. That makes sense: software renders data, but good visualization is about presenting ideas. It's still up to us to intervene with decisions and techniques that bring our ideas into high relief. The writing program I'm using right now can't anticipate which words I want bolded or italicized. It's up to me to decide which need emphasis and then apply the right kind at the right time.

Adjust what's around it. The most aggressive way to make the main idea pop is to change the reference points—the variables that complement or contrast with the main point. We can remove, add, or shift them.

Remove reference points. A chart similar to the one above right was tweeted recently with the message "The age divide in what people want from products."[12]

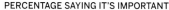

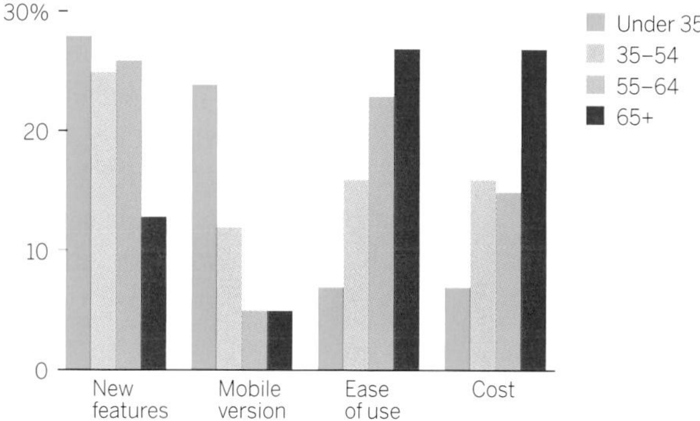

How available is the age divide in this chart? Do you see it? Are you persuaded there *is* an age divide? What about with this chart?

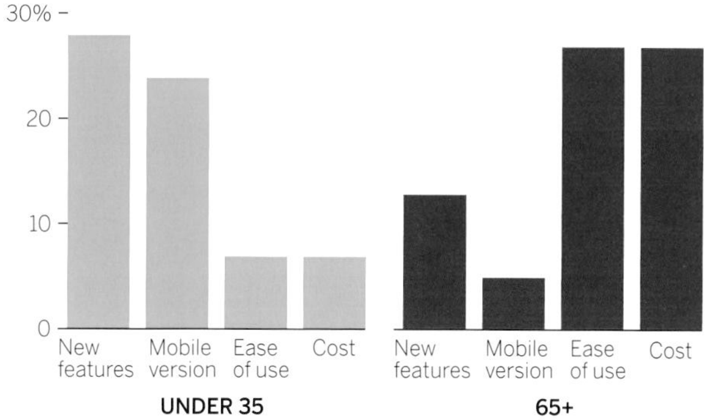

Removing reference points made the idea pop. Think of this as a more aggressive form of isolation. Instead of diminishing color or grouping elements together, you eliminate some information altogether. In the Opposing Desires chart on the previous page, the middle two age groups have been removed because they don't help illustrate the idea of an age divide. This chart also groups bars by age rather than by feature requests. That makes sense because the main idea is an age divide; those are the categories we want to compare.

Add reference points. It may seem that removing information will always make the main idea more available because it has less visual information fighting with it. But sometimes adding reference points works too. For example, a case can be made that vinyl LPs are making a major comeback:

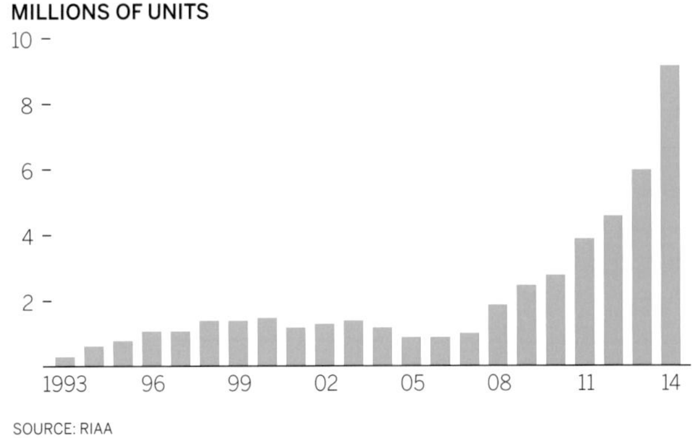

There's also a persuasive case to be made that vinyl LPs are *not* making a major comeback:

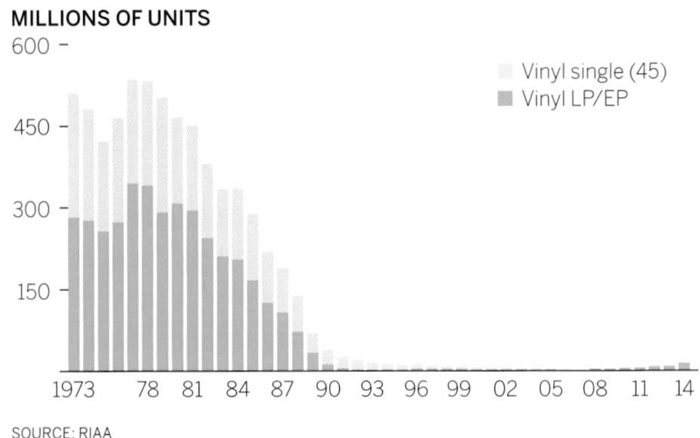

New reference points incontrovertibly alter the persuasive message—in this case from one story to its opposite.

Shift reference points. Another way to change the narrative, and therefore the persuasive direction of the idea, is to shift a comparison entirely:

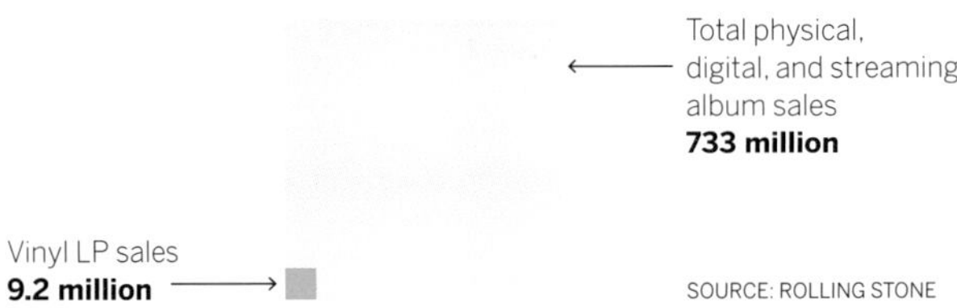

It may be true that vinyl is experiencing a minor resurgence within the context of vinyl albums. But when that trend is compared with a new reference point—total album sales in all formats—we can see right away that it's still only a tiny piece (1.2%) of the business.

This strategy is especially effective when the new reference points are familiar ones. The beer prices at MLB stadiums charts on page 136 compared the costs of one small beer at each ballpark. Unfortunately, a small beer is not the same size at all stadiums. To compare prices fairly, you'd have to calculate the cost per ounce. But how much is an ounce of beer? One sip? Two? The reference point is not easily accessible. We don't typically think about (or pay for) beer by the ounce. We do, however, pay for cases of beer. By shifting to roughly the amount we expect to pay for a case, the chart makes a faster, deeper connection with the audience about the costs.

Here's another example: A manager wants to make the case that the tech team should automate two menial processes. Each task takes only a few seconds, but both must be done constantly. He wants to show that performing the task dozens of times a day adds up over time. So he simply adds up all the time and plots it, as shown on the left.

TASK 1 AND TASK 2

HOURS LOST PER YEAR

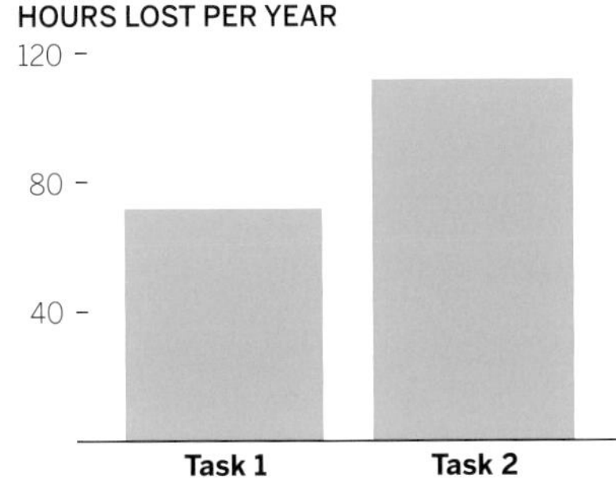

SOURCE: COMPANY RESEARCH

Hours per year is a respectable reference point, but it's not terribly dramatic—there are thousands and thousands of hours in a year, so about a hundred doesn't seem like that many. But if the manager shifts the reference point as on the right, his boss may be persuaded to take action.

Workdays—now that's something the boss gets right away. What's more, rather than focusing on hours lost to the tasks, the manager is focusing on who loses the hours. A new narrative forms: *Susan spends almost three weeks a year just on these menial tasks.* (Notice, too, that the manager changed the bars into a unit chart, with five-day blocks composing a week. This creates another easily accessible unit—a workweek—to help persuade.)

DAYS LOST TO TASK 1 AND TASK 2: TIME SINK

WORK DAYS LOST PER YEAR

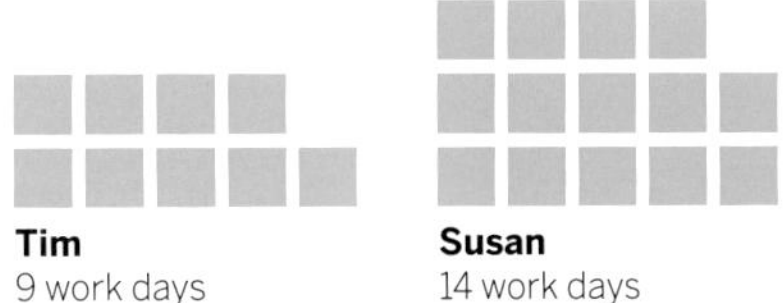

SOURCE: COMPANY RESEARCH

YOU'RE NEVER NOT PERSUADING

We like to think that we're most persuasive when we provide comprehensive information and then lay out a detailed, accurate argument for our point of view. More content is more convincing.

But as should be clear from these examples, that's often not the case. Persuasion doesn't necessarily increase in lockstep with the volume of evidence or the breadth and depth of the data. In fact, some evidence suggests that providing too many supporting claims for your idea can have the opposite effect.[13] Persuasive charts tend to be simpler and to convey one or two ideas powerfully rather than many ideas equally—depending, as always, on context.

Although this chapter focuses on conceiving and building charts to persuade, which sometimes veer into editorializing, you should understand that no matter what kind of chart you need to create, you are never *not* persuading. A chart itself is a persuasion strategy—a manipulation that exploits the overwhelming power of the visual perception system in order to communicate something more convincingly than text can. Even a basic declarative chart is a form of persuasion, in that it's deliberately not taking a stance. Dispassion can demonstrate that an idea is authentic or credible.

Perfectly objective visualizations don't exist, because perfectly objective brains don't exist. People don't particularly like the idea that they're being persuaded all the time; they think that happens to others but not to them. Not true. That experiential part of the brain that relies on heuristics, metaphors, and experience to color interpretations of the world is a powerful influence, even when we look at information visualizations. Consider these two curves. They tell different stories. With the first, you notice the upward trend followed by a plateau: a rise and a hold, almost like

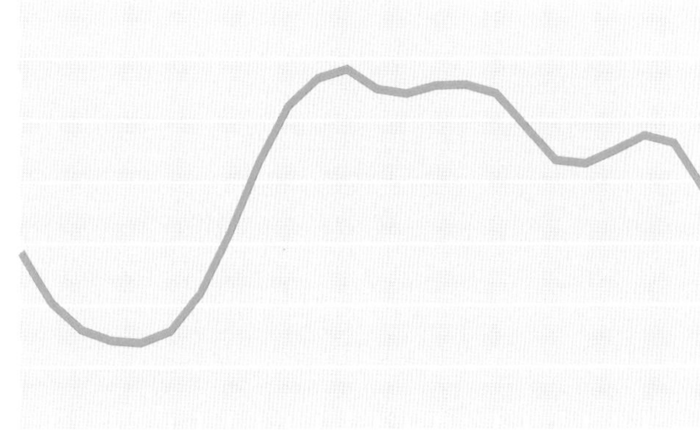

a plane's trajectory. In the second, it's hard to miss the sheer climb followed by an almost equally steep but shorter, bumpier drop—more like a ride on a rocket ship.

In fact these two curves plot the exact same data on the same scale. The only differences are the stretching of the y-axis and the compression of the x-axis. So which chart is more "objective"? More "correct"? What's the proper width for a chart if the x-axis plots, say, time? Of course, there's no right answer. Width is arbitrary and often dictated by the medium. The chart on the facing page was designed for a computer screen. The chart on this page responsively re-formed to fit on a smartphone.

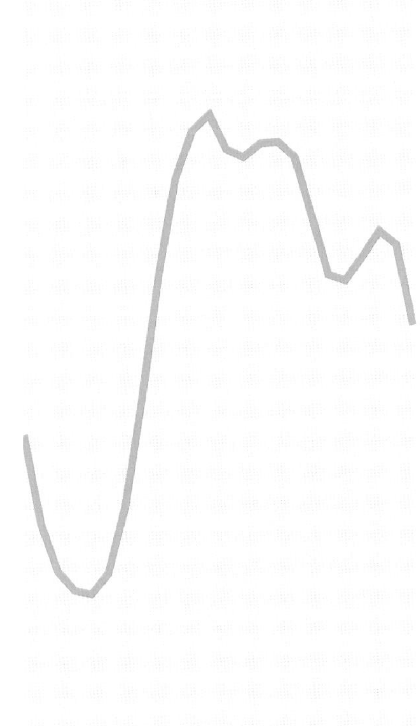

Same data, completely different experiences for the eye and the brain, which may lead to different interpretations. The persuasive power of this chart could be a function of something as capricious as how wide it is. If I needed to show an active trend with a steep rise, I might be tempted to create a narrower chart to exaggerate that part of the curve. If I knew my boss liked to think of this trend as relatively stable, I could stretch it out.

Every chart is a manipulation. If I'm going to proffer persuasive techniques, as I have, I need to talk about the ethics of using them.

RECAP

REFINE TO PERSUADE

It's often not enough to make a chart that's simply accurate. Managers may need to reveal truths that are dormant in the data to help make a case—to compete for attention, resources, and money; to pitch clients; to recruit new customers; to sway an opinion or help form one. To make charts more persuasive, use these three techniques:

1. Hone the main idea.
Adjust your prompt. Instead of asking *What am I trying to say or show?* start by saying *I need to convince them that . . .* This will expose where and how you can focus your energy on persuading an audience. For example:

What am I trying to say or show?	I need to convince them that . . .
I am trying to show the relationship between unbundling products and declining revenue.	I need to convince them that unbundling our software suite will devastate revenue streams.

2. Make it stand out.
Use simple design techniques to reinforce your main idea.

- **Emphasize** the main idea by adding visual information that calls attention to it. For example, use unique colors, pointers, labels, and markers to draw the audience's focus.
- **Isolate** the main idea by reducing the number of unique attributes for all other elements. For example, group them together, make them gray, or otherwise de-emphasize them to bring the main idea into high relief.

3. Adjust what's around it.
Manipulate the variables that complement or contrast with the main point to make it pop.

- **Remove reference points.** Eliminate plotted data that distracts or dilutes the main idea.
- **Add reference points.** Add plotted data to the chart to expose otherwise hidden context.
- **Shift reference points.** Change the plotted data used in comparison with the main idea to create new context.

CHAPTER 7

PERSUASION OR MANIPULATION?

THE BLURRED EDGE OF TRUTH

"THAT'S NOT WHAT I sent and not what I requested," Tamar's e-mail read. "Let's meet to discuss." Colette's spirits sank. Her boss, the head of HR, was rejecting the visualization Colette had created for her. Colette knew why. Tamar had sent her a chart she'd spit out of Excel while analyzing her data, along with a note:

Colette—Data and rough visual attached. For the board presentation, want to show the big change, the U-curve for current satisfaction and the huge gap in current vs. expected for young employees, which closes and flips in midcareer. Important for presentation to show where we need to address employee satisfaction issues before we propose funding for engagement programs.—T

Colette knew that employees were asked to rate their current job satisfaction and their expected satisfaction in five years, on a 1-to-10 scale. She saw that Tamar's chart plotted only the area where the average scores fell, from 6.4 to 7.8—it was truncated. She had reproduced her boss's chart and then created her own version, using the full 1-to-10 scale for the y-axis:

JOB SATISFACTION

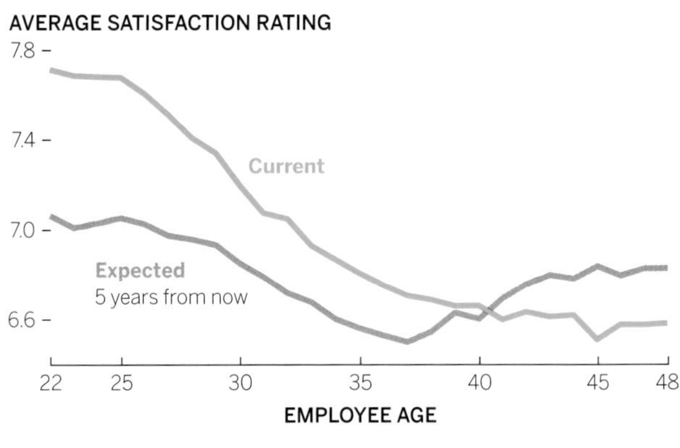

SOURCE: COMPANY RESEARCH

JOB SATISFACTION

AVERAGE SATISFACTION RATING

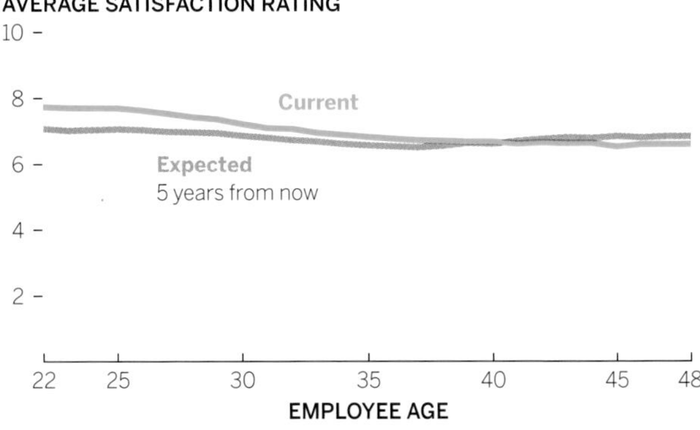

SOURCE: COMPANY RESEARCH

As she looked at her revised plot, Colette thought about the keywords from Tamar's e-mail: *big change, U-curve, huge gap, flips*. Those were clear in the original version of the chart, but her version looked almost changeless—a small gap separated flat lines that slowly converged in an unremarkable crossover.

Colette felt that her version more accurately depicted the data and the idea. Tamar thought it robbed her message of its persuasive power. When they met, Colette explained that the truncated axis made the separation and the changes in satisfaction look more dramatic than they actually were. Tamar shot back that it was accepted practice to "zoom in" like this. Academic journal articles and news articles did the same; she even showed Colette a few examples. All the colleagues Tamar had spoken to had said they'd do the same thing. And anyway, the change *was* dramatic. "In this case, that gap between current and expected satisfaction for young employees is significant," Tamar insisted. "And that dip and rebound in current satisfaction for workers in their thirties is hugely significant. We need to stress that. We're competing for resources here. If we show the board members your chart, they're not going to fund our engagement programs. I'll be saying, 'Look at this major issue we have to address,' and they'll be looking at a couple of flat lines."

THE BLURRED EDGE OF TRUTH

Who's right? Some will side (and empathize) with Colette. You don't have to be a "y-axis fundamentalist" to see how cutting off the top and bottom of the satisfaction scale exaggerates the shape of the curve so dramatically that it alters the idea that emerges from the data.[1] Others will back Tamar, who is fighting for money and who knows that although the changes look small on a full-axis chart, they *matter*, so they should be made to look that way. For her, the truncated axis doesn't alter the idea—the full axis does.

There's no easy answer here. Would that a clear line existed between visual persuasion and visual dishonesty. Even if it were a fine line, at least we could see it and stay on the ethical side of it. But in fact, and of course, no such line exists. Instead we have to negotiate a blurred and shifting borderland between truthfulness and unfair manipulation.

MARK JACKSON

STAKING A CAREER ON VISUALIZATION

"After six years, I wasn't sure what I wanted to do, and I was getting worried."

Mark Jackson was a consultant at KPMG. Analytics was part of his job; building charts and graphs wasn't. But he did it anyway, spending lots of time bending Excel to his will to create charts that he thought might help in his work. But he was burning out. "I could become a manager or director without any deep experience in one area, but that's not usually a good approach—plus, I had to get off the road," he says, past exhaustions creeping into his voice.

Jackson signed on as a project manager at Piedmont Healthcare, where he continued his visual analysis in Excel for projects such as process improvements, scheduling, even where to locate offices. He also started following dataviz blogs and reading up on the topic. It still wasn't officially part of his job, but visualization work continued to command more of his time, and it was getting him noticed.

"The light went on for me," he says, "when we looked at a project on throughput in catheterization labs, and I built all this data out in charts in Excel. I had discovered Tufte at that point. I made these visualizations very Tufte-ish, and people found those charts so helpful." Jackson also created a visual way to explore changes in physicians' schedules to improve the patient experience. "We needed to show doctors that how they worked was inefficient, that if they focused on one thing at a time, they'd actually be more productive." That was difficult but necessary. Doctors' compensation is tied in part to their productivity, so they're not going to change how they work unless they know it will make them more productive. "We used dataviz to show them that it would all be okay."

Eventually, the corporate team asked Jackson to design 40 pages of charts for a report, just when he felt ready to devote himself to the visual part of data analysis. "I said to them, 'I'm willing to stake my career on this. This is the future.' Basically, 'Can I make this my job?'"

They said yes. Jackson is now the director of business intelligence and management reporting and the go-to dataviz guy at Piedmont.

Explaining how he visualizes doesn't come easy. "It's like explaining how you walk," he says. "You just know how to do it." Jackson spends a lot of time reading about visualization, paying attention to other people's work and mimicking it. He will try what they try and then twist it to his needs.

"A really big part of being successful with visualization is asking people why they want to do something," he says, echoing that crucial question you're meant to ask over and over again during the talk and listen phase outlined in chapter 4: "Why?" "If someone says to me, 'I need a report that gives me a trend for each month of sales,' that's not going to work. You don't have answers yet. There are too many assumptions there. So I'll force us to take a step back. I ask, 'What do you really want to know? Why do you want to know that?' You have to dig deep with them."

Jackson also likes to focus on use cases with his visual output.

He often creates three versions of a chart that move from simplest to most complicated according to how much time he expects people have to explore it: twenty seconds for executives, two minutes for managers, and twenty minutes for analysts.

"I also pay attention to how they want to use it on their own," he says. "We're still a paper-driven culture here. Clinical managers want something they can print out and walk around with, show to others in person. So I'm not burying their visuals in a toolset—I'm creating something that will look good printed out. At the same time, there's the interactive version for people who have the skill and want to explore the visualizations that way."

Jackson now experiments with dataviz as a way to improve his skills. He's become one of the community members he once read and mimicked. He created an interactive visualization of controversial Wikipedia articles that garnered significant attention online for its eye-catching form and, ultimately, the analysis it provides.

"Looking at it initially, it's beautiful," Jackson says. "But what I like better than that is that after you see how nice it looks, you realize the patterns are telling you something."

In this chart Jackson is expressing what he sees as the value of entertainment and engagement. "Sometimes you can probably learn something quicker with a bar chart, but people want to enjoy visualizations. Admittedly, in business you have to be careful. People just want answers. But I'd argue there are still ways that you can incorporate that entertainment value, by making charts beautiful, or at least not harsh to look at. I've been in meetings when we bored the audience to tears getting to the answer. If they're not interested by the time you get there, what's the point?"

Top 100 articles for deletion discussions on Wikipedia

Click a line to view the article name and see a running sum of the votes.

Articles that were ultimately
○ Deleted
◉ Kept

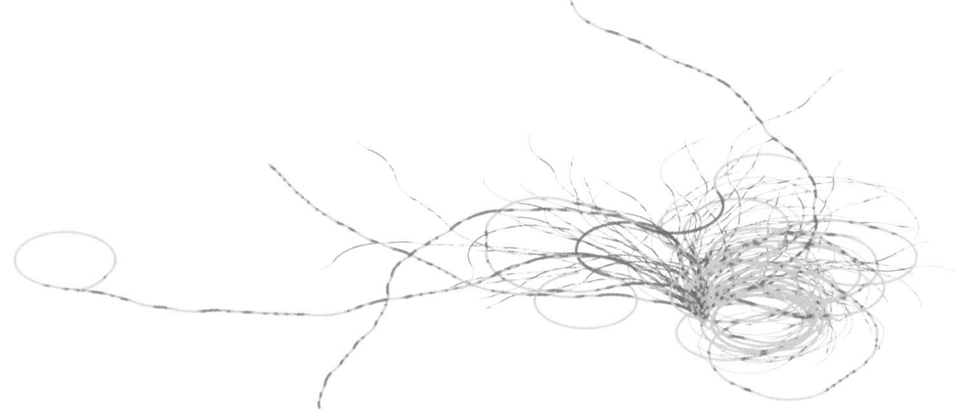

Line length indicates the duration of the discussion.

Controversial

Controversial discussions have a lot of alternating keep and delete posts resulting in a relatively straight line.

Ric Romero

Unanimous

Discussions that are fairly unaminous will curl. In this instance, there was initial controversy, but led to a high degree of consensus in the end.

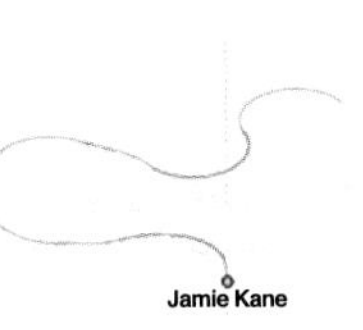

Swinging

Swinging discussions have an S-shaped trajectory. They have alternating series of keep and delete arguments.

Inspired by the work of Moritz Stefaner at http://notabilia.net

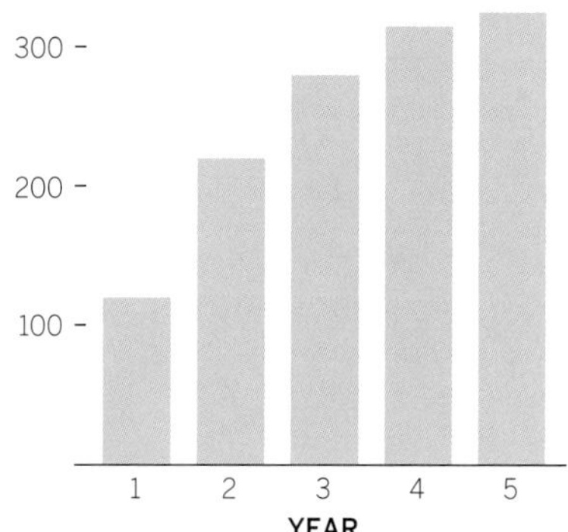

On one side of this indefinite border are the persuasion techniques outlined in chapter 6: emphasis, isolation, adding or removing reference points. On the other side are the four types of deception: falsification, exaggeration, omission, and equivocation. One person's isolation—removing distracting visual information—is another's omission. It's easy to see how emphasis, applied too forcefully, might slip into exaggeration.

I won't dwell on falsification; the commandments should be obvious: Don't lie. Don't deliberately mislead. Don't create a chart like the one on the left.

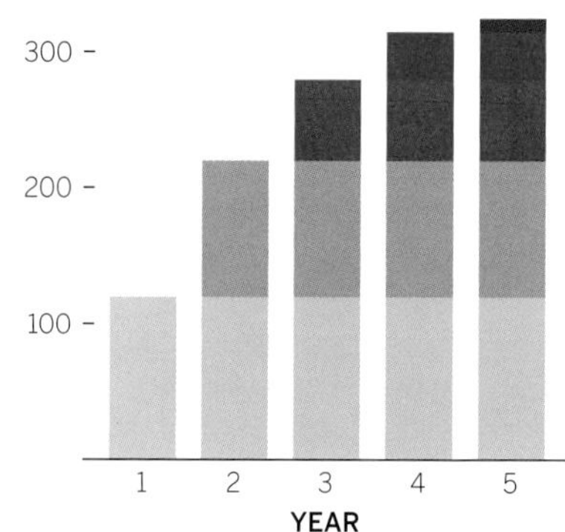

It looks like a positive revenue trend, but here each bar is *cumulative*, accounting for all previous years' revenue as well as new revenue. Year 1 is counted five times (see the chart top right), although that revenue was earned only once. This is continuous data, a trend line, hiding in a categorical form: we expect each bar to represent a distinct value. The breakdown shown bottom right is the more honest depiction of the revenue trend.

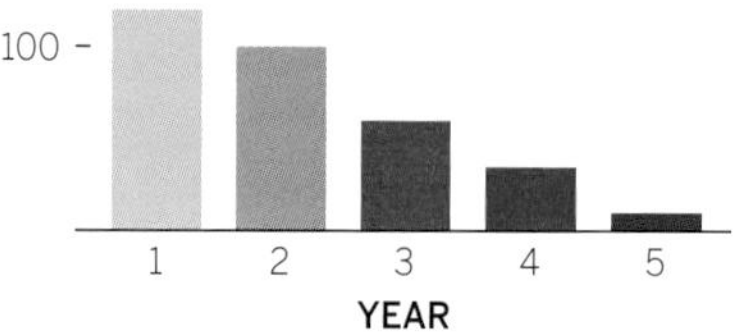

EXPLORING THE GRAY AREA

Arrant deception of this sort is uncommon.[2] More frequently, managers find themselves looking at—and creating—graphics like Tamar's job satisfaction chart—not so much intentional efforts to mislead as extraordinary efforts to persuade, which may drift into that blurred borderland between honest and deceptive.

Persuasion is a knife, and knives can be used in any number of ways: skillfully, carelessly, recklessly, even illicitly. Unpacking the ways in which charts slip into deception is like learning to handle a knife so that you don't accidentally cut yourself or others.

Rather than trying to create a doctrinaire list of dos and don'ts, I'll deconstruct three of the most common techniques that put charts in this gray area, explain why you might want to use them, and lay out why they may not be okay.

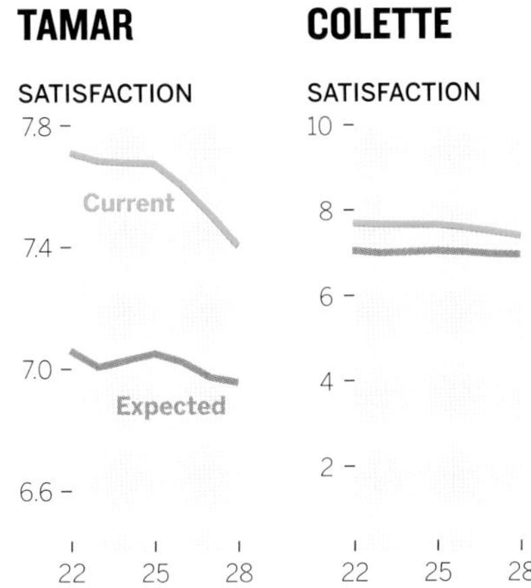

The truncated y-axis: exaggerating trends. The debate over the y-axis is visualization's version of grammarians arguing over whether or not it's okay to end a sentence with a preposition. Even if we think it's wrong, we do it because the proper alternative often feels awkward.

Why it may be effective. It emphasizes an idea. Cutting empty ranges out of an axis increases the physical distance between values, revealing texture and making change look more dramatic, as shown in the slices of Tamar's and Colette's charts to the left.

Tamar's argument for truncating her y-axis was that not doing so makes it harder to see important differences, and that's clearly true. Colette uses about 7% of the y-axis to show the 7% gap. Tamar uses almost 50% of the chart's vertical space to represent the 7% gap. Truncation is a way of zooming in and isolating the main idea. It's not unlike looking through a magnifying glass.

It's also true that if a range of data is consistently far from zero, you'll need much more space to effectively unflatten the visual while maintaining a full y-axis.[3] You'll have to manipulate the height and width of the chart. This quickly becomes an impractical exercise: it yields strangely formatted charts that, although they preserve some detail of the curves, ultimately distract the viewer, like the chart to the right.

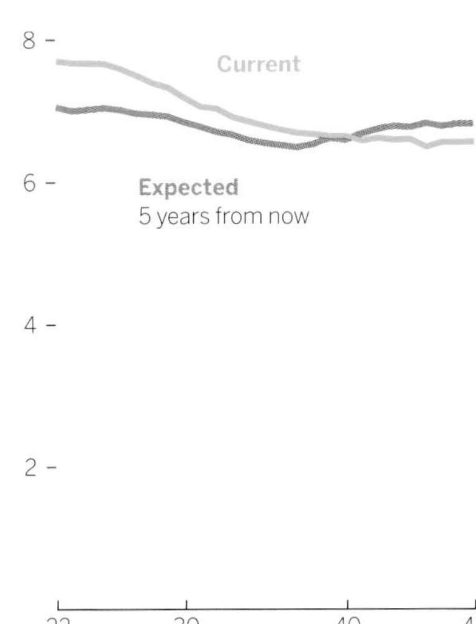

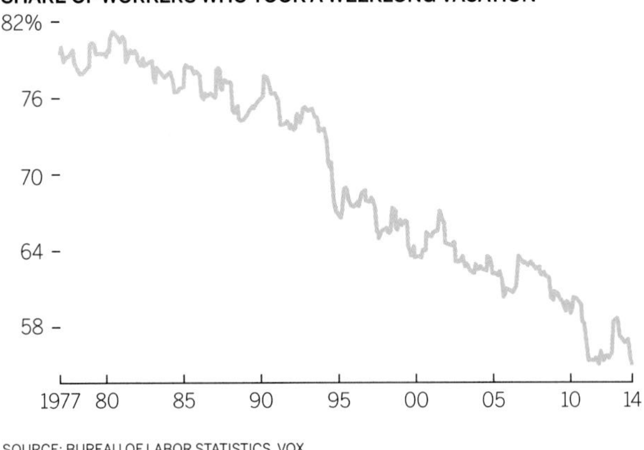

Why it may be deceptive. Some will argue that truncation acts less like a magnifying glass than like a fun house mirror, distorting reality by exaggerating select parts of it. The line on the Taking a Vacation chart to the left represents a drop of 25 percentage points, from 80% to 55%. But its physical descent covers almost the entire y-axis. In other words, the line descends 100% of the y-axis to represent a 25% decline. Truncation also hides representative space. The line here divides space that represents vacationers (below) and nonvacationers (above), but neither space accurately represents the proportions at any given point. Charting the *space* very roughly below shows how those proportions in the truncated chart are simply inaccurate.

A note: Sometimes people equate truncating the y-axis with not starting at zero. But lopping off the top of an axis's range also produces a distortionary effect, even if the axis starts at zero. That kind of truncation is less often noticed and produces fewer outbursts

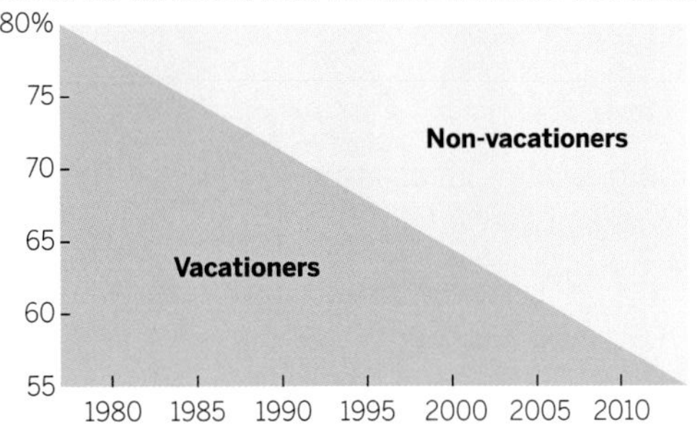

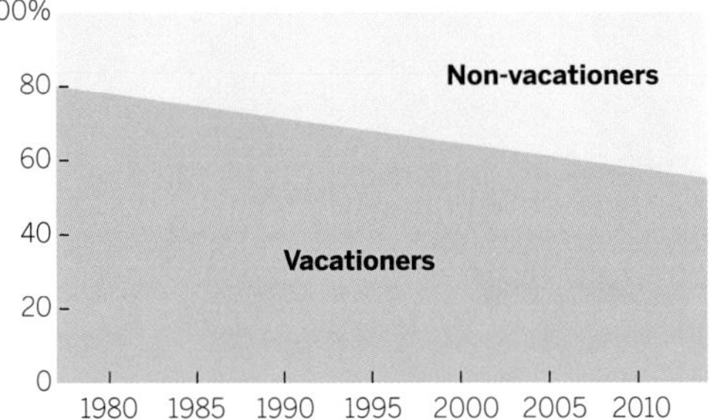

from y-axis fundamentalists, but it can hide representative space in the same way, especially with a finite range of y-axis values, like percentages.

Another good way to understand the effect of truncation is to pluck three points from the data set and turn them into stacked bars, one group with a truncated y-axis and one that spans from zero to one hundred.

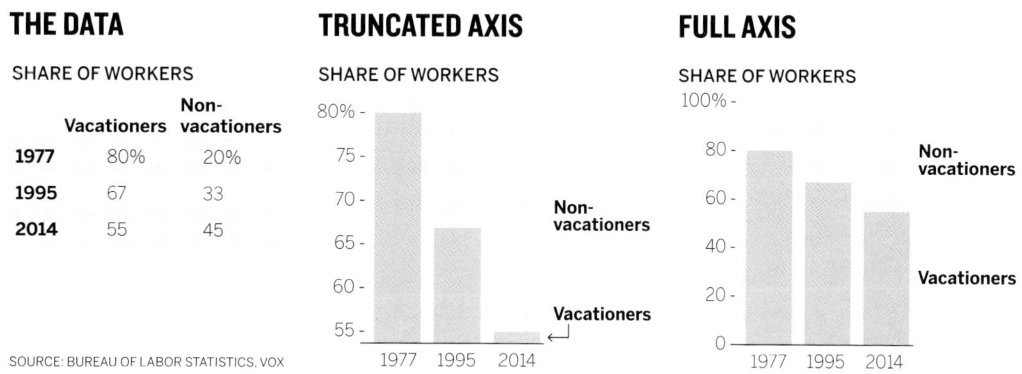

Rather than persuasive or even deceptive, the truncated-axis chart looks plain wrong, and it is. Its 1995 bar, for example, at 67%, should be 2/3 dark orange and 1/3 pale orange, but it's split about 50/50. Truncation with categorical data doesn't work. We see it used like this mostly when deception is the goal.[4] And yet the original line chart represents a similar dividing of space, except with many more data points along a continuum.

Truncation presents another problem. We know that the experiential part of the brain relies on experience, expectation, and convention to assign meaning and form narratives. It uses heuristics to rapidly grab meaning so that we don't have to think much about something we see all the time. And research shows that we assign metaphorical value to certain visual cues. Up is positive, down is negative.[5]

In our minds, expectation trumps raw data. When a line approaches the bottom—the "end" or the "floor"—of a chart, we take that as a cue that it's approaching zero, or

SHARE OF WORKERS WHO TOOK A WEEKLONG VACATION

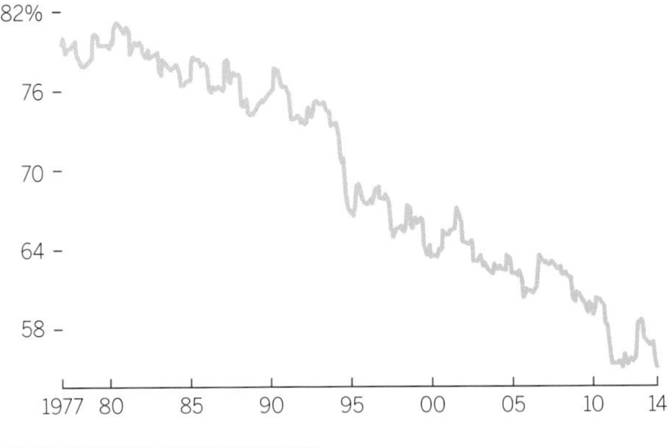

SOURCE: BUREAU OF LABOR STATISTICS, VOX

TAKING A VACATION

SHARE OF WORKERS WHO TOOK A WEEKLONG VACATION

100%

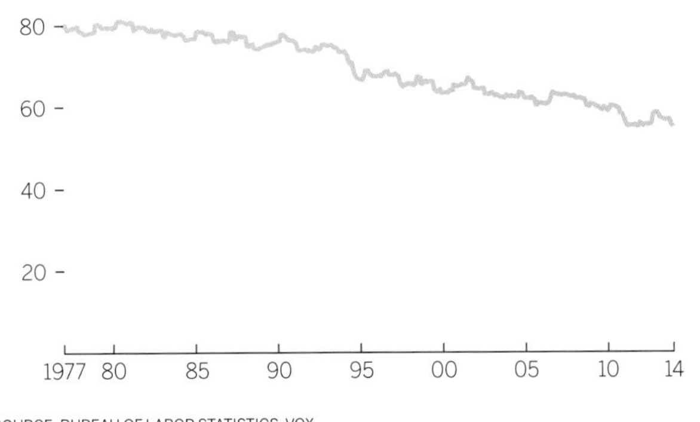

SOURCE: BUREAU OF LABOR STATISTICS, VOX

nothing. This creates a false sense of termination. We *expect* the bottom to be zero, and our brains want to process it that way. When we realize it's not zero, we have to expend more mental energy trying to understand what we're actually looking at. Conversely, we see the top of the chart as the maximum, pinnacle, or ceiling. The truncated-axis vacation chart leads us toward the idea that *everybody used to go on vacation and now no one does*. But compare it to the full y-axis version below it.

Okay, the number of vacationers is indeed declining, *but more people than not still take a vacation*. Did that idea come through from the truncated version? Did you see it first? Was it an accessible idea? Did you get the sense that on average, over nearly four decades, a vast majority of people took vacations and a majority still do?

This is why Colette grimaced when she compared Tamar's truncated y-axis plot to her own version. She believed it was overdramatic and accidentally deceptive. For her part, Tamar asserted that the 7% gap between current and expected happiness for young employees was huge and that the 10% fluctuation in reported satisfaction was a big change that the visual should show prominently. That's a value judgment. It's her context. To justify persuading through truncation, she must trust her expertise, and her audience must trust her credibility.

The double y-axis: comparing apples and oranges. Compared with truncation, double-y-axis charts provoke little agitation. An internet search for "truncated y-axis" returns top results about lying with charts, but a search for "secondary y-axis" turns

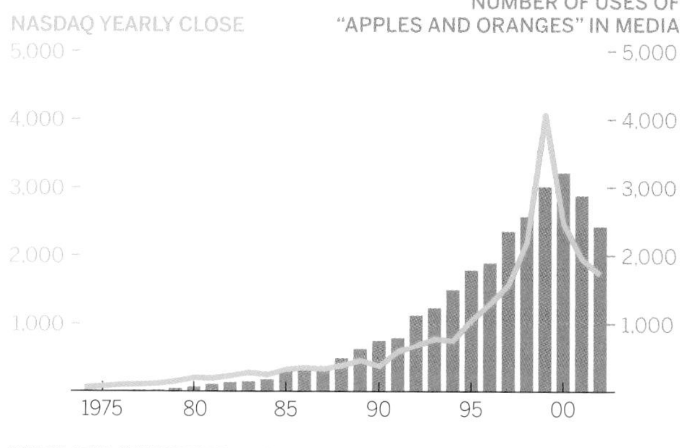

SOURCE: LEXIS-NEXIS RESEARCH, NASDAQ

up mostly sites that teach you how to add one in Excel. Still, charts with two y-axes deserve similar scrutiny.

Why it may be effective. It compels an audience to make comparisons. Instead of trying to convince people that there's a relationship between two variables, it creates a relationship by fiat. Above is an example I created for a humorous essay on the use of the term "apples and oranges" in the media.

You can't look at this chart and consider each plot on its own merits. The fact that they're together forces you to think about them as *something*, not two things that happen to share a space. What does this chart say? More than likely you formed the narrative I wanted you to: *Stock market gains lead to more people using the term "apples and oranges."*

Of course, that idea is absurd on its face—but it's almost impossible not to make the connection. I knew that (or at least I sensed it; this was created long before I thought about the mechanics of chart making) and leveraged it to send you down a path of trying to figure out *why* this relationship exists and to make a funny point. Two y-axes can shape a narrative that goes in the direction you want it to.

Why it may be deceptive. The relative sameness or difference in the shapes of lines or the heights of bars being measured on two different scales is much less meaningful than it appears to be. The simplest illustration is a chart that uses two axes representing the same type of value but in different ranges.

In the top chart to the right, it appears that gold and silver are roughly the same price and their prices move together. But the range of the secondary y-axis is two orders of magnitude lower than that of the primary y-axis. (In addition, they're truncated, so the closeness of the lines is artificial.) That means we're seeing lines that interact in fake

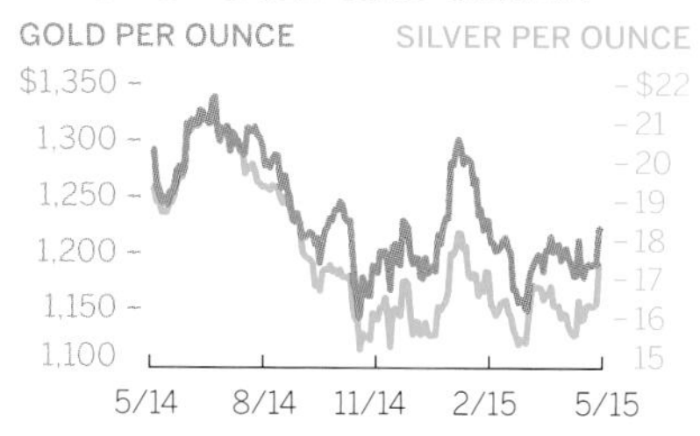

SOURCE: BULLIONVAULT.COM

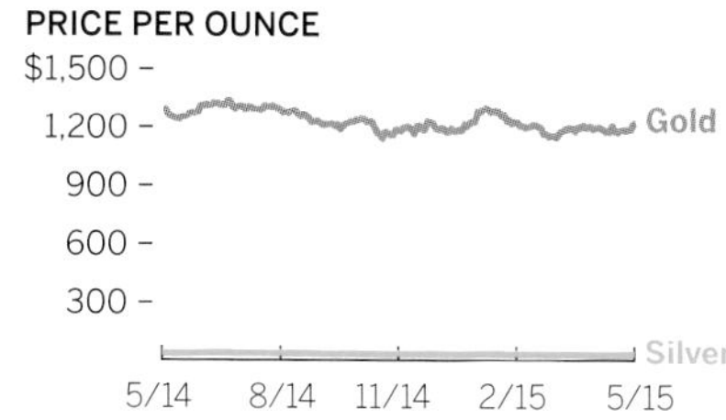

SOURCE: BULLIONVAULT.COM

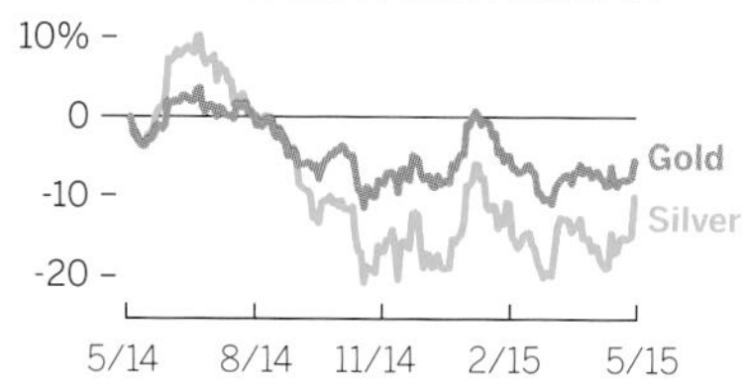

SOURCE: BULLIONVAULT.COM

ways. When the blue line is higher on the chart, the price of silver isn't actually higher than the price of gold. When the lines cross over, prices aren't crossing over. Both axes measure US dollars, so why not use just one y-axis?

That's what the middle gold and silver chart on the previous page shows, and it's simply less useful. We can't see what's happening to silver prices. One solution to this dilemma would be to show relative change in price rather than raw price, as the bottom chart in the series shows.

The price of silver, a flat line in the previous chart, is actually more volatile than the price of gold—an idea we don't see in the first chart. If anything, the price of gold looks more dynamic in that first chart, but the relative change from $1,300 to $1,200 is smaller than the change from $21 to $18, even though the slopes match when we use separate y-axes in the same space. Still, this new version creates new challenges. It shifts the main idea from the price of precious metals to the change in price—from value to volatility. Knowing the actual price of gold and silver at any given time is not possible in a percentage change chart.

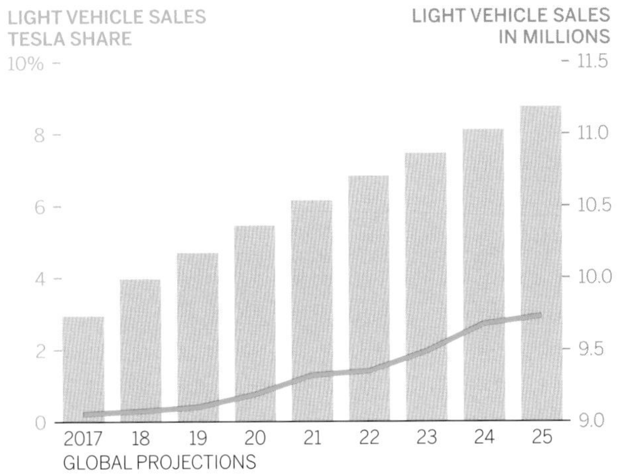

Things get even murkier when the second y-axis uses a different value altogether. A version of the chart to the left was published online.

Here it's hard to miss the narrative that Tesla's market share is going to come on strong in light vehicle sales. Its line reaches higher and higher into the bars that represent all light vehicle sales.

Unfortunately, that narrative is illusory. Although in 2025 the line reaches about 33% of the height of total light vehicle sales bar, its y-axis is measured in percentage, not raw numbers. In 2025 it would have just a 3% market share—only 1/33rd of that year's plotted bar. The top chart on the facing page is an accurate portrayal of the scenario.

GLOBAL LIGHT VEHICLE PENETRATION—ONE SCENARIO

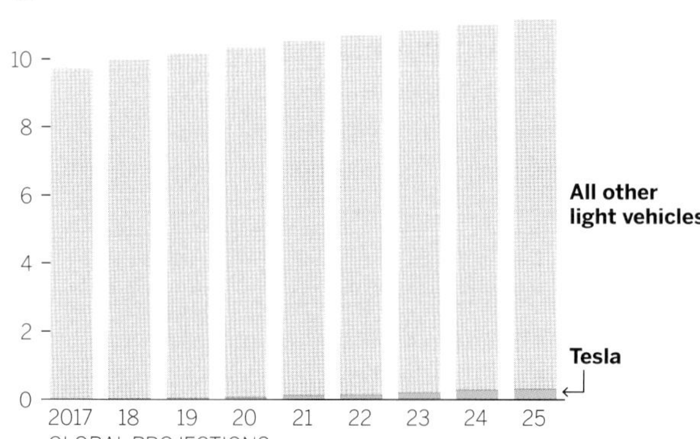

SOURCE: GOLDMAN SACHS GLOBAL INVESTMENT RESEARCH

PAGE VIEWS AND TIME ON PAGE

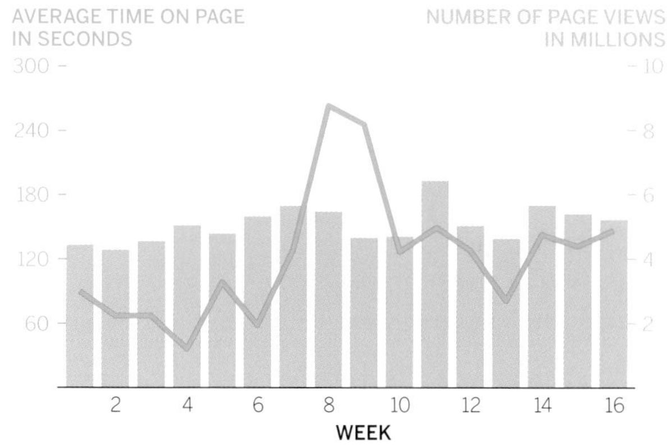

SOURCE: COMPANY RESEARCH

When two measures bear no relationship at all, things get truly weird, as with the chart bottom left on this page.

We see events in physical space—crossovers, meeting points, divergences, convergences—that suggest a relationship that doesn't exist. Time on page didn't *cross over* or *go higher than* page views between the seventh and eighth weeks—and what would it even mean for seconds to be higher than page views? It's as if soccer and football are being played on the same field and we're trying to make sense of both as one game.

Nevertheless, when we see data charted together, our minds want to form a narrative around what we see. Charts can be concocted that combine truncation with dual-y-axes to manipulate the curves into similar shapes to encourage that narrative-seeking, such as the chart to the right. The two variables here are statistically correlated. The tempting if unlikely narrative is that the increase in falling down stairs is caused by the fact that more of us are staring down at smartphone screens.[6] What happens when this visual parlor trick is applied to less silly examples? In an age of very big data sets and sophisticated tools for mining them, it

CORRELATION DOES NOT IMPLY CAUSATION

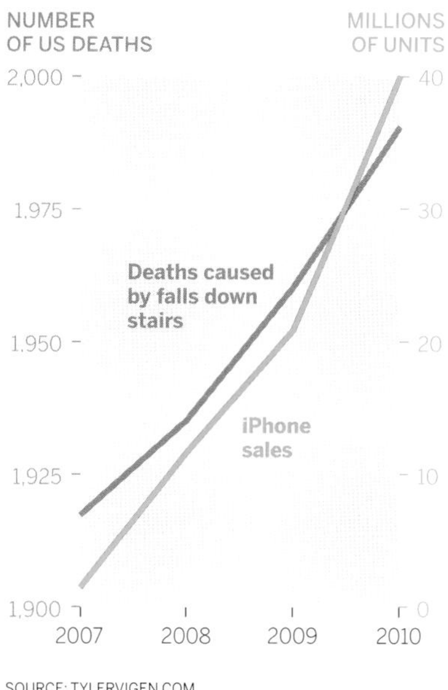

SOURCE: TYLERVIGEN.COM

becomes easy, as the Stanford professor of medicine John Ioannidis puts it, to "confer spurious precision status to noise."[7] Chart 1 in the series below is a good example.

The relationship we see here is unmistakable. Sales and customer service calls map closely over the course of the day. The tight link might make a manager think that customer service should be staffed according to how much money the company expects to be bringing in at that time of day. More money, more reps. But the way these lines stick together, as much as we might want to believe it means something, is artificial. First, the lines stick together in part because they use separate grids.

Chart 2 in the series exposes the grid lines to show the tight connection between lines is artificial. It's almost as if each chart were on a semitransparent piece of paper and we slid one over the other until the curves aligned. In chart 3, when the axes are lined up to share a single grid, the picture changes.

Similarity remains, but now calls are *always* lower than sales (keep in mind this is all still nonsensical since the values are completely different). Even so, we get the sense that

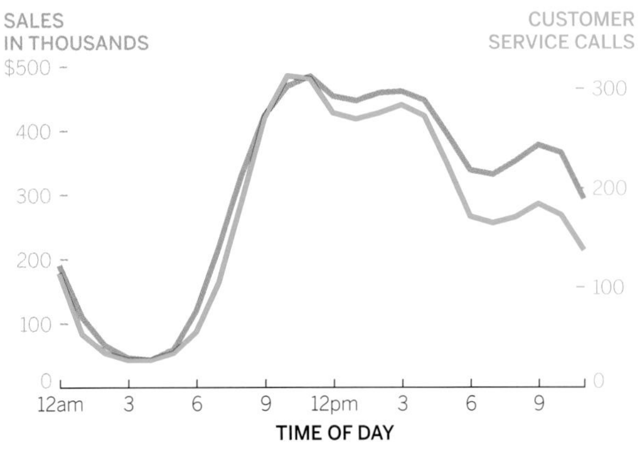

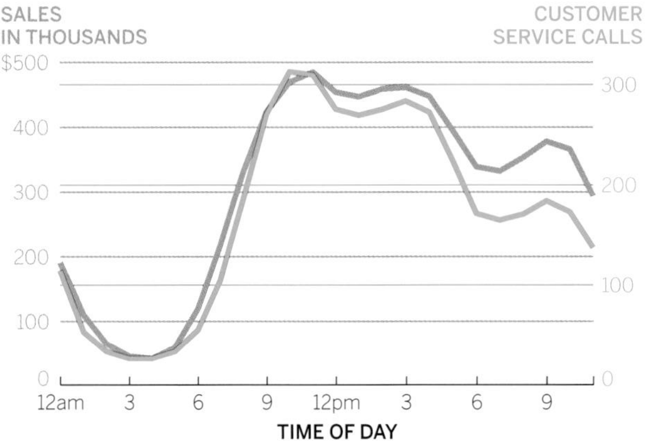

sales and calls go up and down together. This chart still might persuade us that staffing should follow the day's sales trends.

But what if we take a view of the data that doesn't rely on an artificial similarity in the shape of curves? Using the same data, let's compare sales per customer service call each hour as a ratio, shown in chart 4 in the series.

If sales and customer service calls really were as closely linked as the original chart suggests, this line would be essentially flat—as sales rise, calls rise. But this view tells a different, somewhat more nuanced story: The customer service team is handling many more calls for every $100,000 earned in the early morning than at other times of day. And the ratio bounces up and down all morning. In the first chart in this series, that time period was when the lines were almost perfectly in sync, but that's when there's the most change in how many calls are being handled for the amount of sales coming in.

Comparisons are one of the most basic and useful things we do with charts. They form a narrative, and narrative is persuasive. But it should be obvious by now that there are no easy ways to handle different ranges and measures in a single space. Pushing down

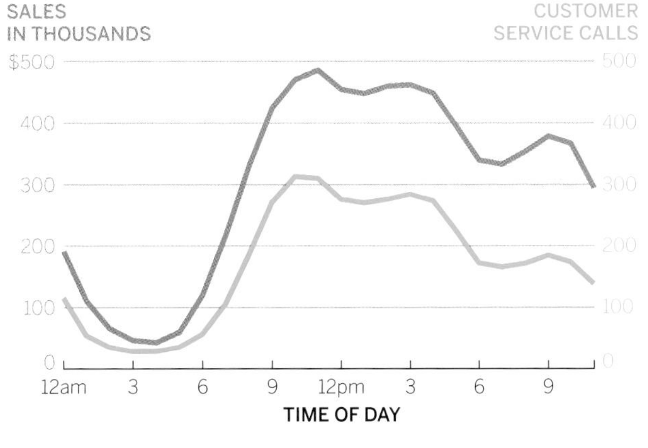

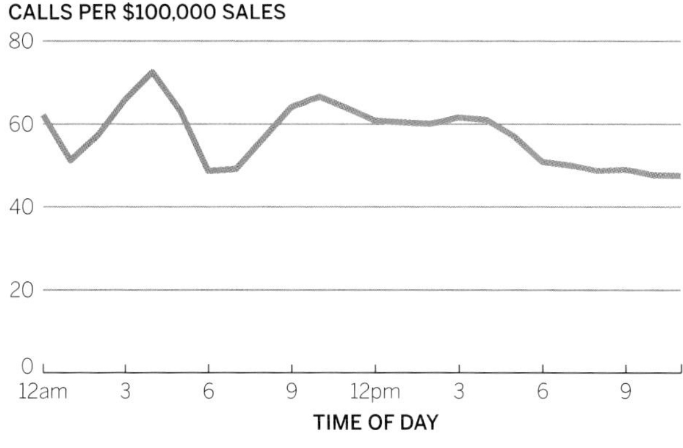

one misleading problem can cause another to pop up. More-accurate portrayals, such as percentage change, may also be less accessible, or even alter the idea being conveyed.

The simplest way to fix this is to avoid it. Placing charts side by side rather than on top of each other, and using presentation techniques that we'll talk about in chapter 8, can help create comparisons without creating false narratives.

The map: misrepresenting Montana and Manhattan. Maps are themselves information visualizations, but they're also popular containers for dataviz. Tools such as Tableau and Infogr.am have made it much easier to assign values from spreadsheets to geographic spaces. The rise in popularity of color-coded maps, or "chloropleths," has spawned one of the toughest dataviz challenges in terms of toeing the line between effectiveness and deceptiveness.

Why it may be effective. Maps make data based on geography much more accessible by making it simple to find and compare reference points, because we are generally familiar with where places are. Comparing country data, for example, is easier when we embed values in maps, especially as the number of locations being measured increases. Looking at the Solar Capacity map and bar chart, see how long it takes you to complete the reasonably simple task of comparing the United States with Japan, then Spain with France, and finally Germany with Australia.

Chloropleths also help us see regional trends that other forms of charts cannot. It's difficult, for example, to look at the bar chart and form ideas about, say, the European versus the Asian deployment of solar capacity, but in the map we can make those assessments almost without thinking.

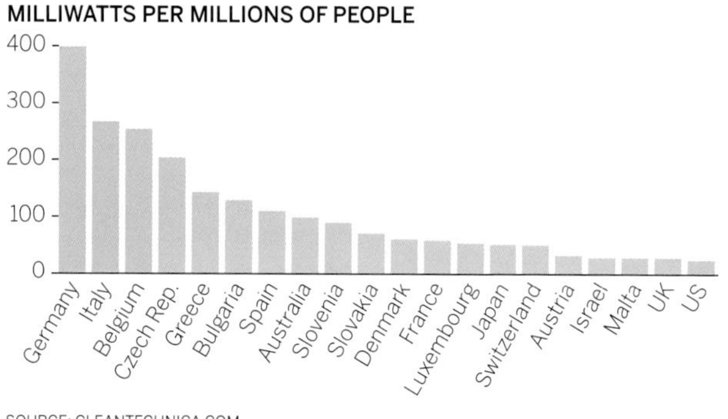

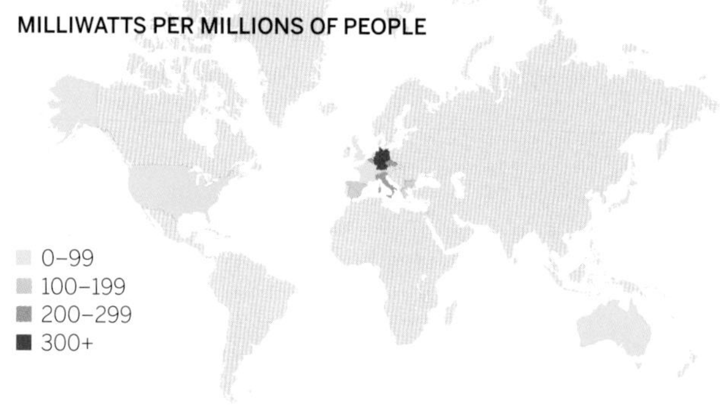

Why it may be deceptive. The size of geographical space usually over- or under-represents the variable encoded within it. This is especially true with maps that represent populations, as we see during elections. You might call this the Montana-Manhattan problem:

THE MONTANA-MANHATTAN PROBLEM

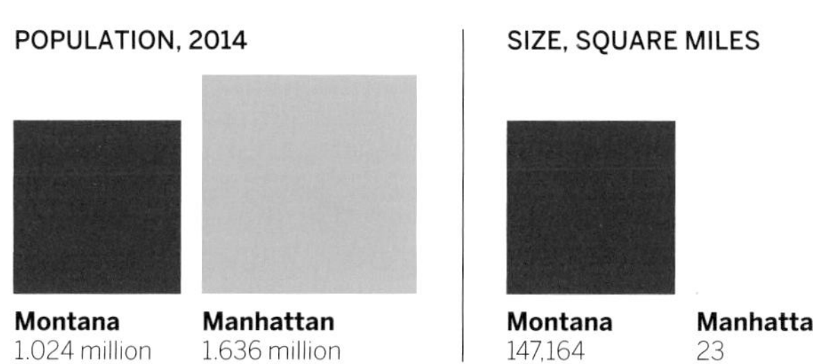

SOURCE: U.S. CENSUS

More people live in Manhattan, even though Montana is almost 6,400 times its size. Another way to express this is to show how many people live in one square mile of each place. Each dot here represents seven people:

POPULATION DENSITY: MONTANA VS. MANHATTAN

Montana
1.024 million people reside in 147,164 square miles

Manhattan
1.636 million people reside in 23 square miles

SOURCE: U.S. CENSUS

It may be hard to see, but Montana's square mile contains one dot. So when Montana votes one way during an election, the visual representation is of a colored-in area that's more than 6,400 times the size of the one for Manhattan, even though 60% more people live in Manhattan. This happens all over the world. To the right are the election results for Scotland's referendum on independence plotted on a map and as a simple proportional bar chart.

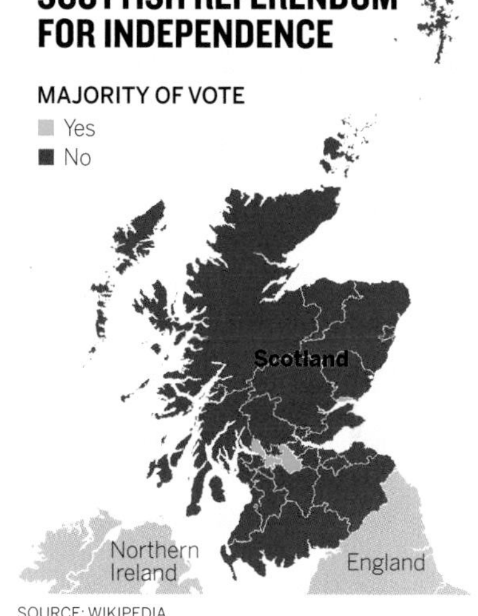

SOURCE: WIKIPEDIA

What looks geographically like an overwhelming victory isn't actually so one-sided. It's a solid victory for "no," true. But less than 5% of the landmass on the map represents a "yes" vote, whereas 38% of eligible voters voted "yes." Consider that in Highland, that massive northernmost red region on Scotland's mainland, only about 166,000 people voted in total—fewer than the 195,000 who voted "yes" in Glasgow, one of the small blue wedges.

But moving away from maps reintroduces the problems that maps are meant to solve by using our knowledge of spaces to to make values

SCOTTISH REFERENDUM RESULTS

PERCENTAGE OF VOTES

SOURCE: WIKIPEDIA

more accessible. The proportional bar chart below makes it nearly impossible to connect places to values quickly or to make regional estimations.

More-accurate representations of data lead to less accessible geographic information. Conversely, good maps tend to misrepresent data values. This paradox has vexed designers, cartographers, and data scientists for some time. For a while, cartograms—which use algorithms to distort geography so that the area of a region matches the value it represents—found favor as a possible solution.

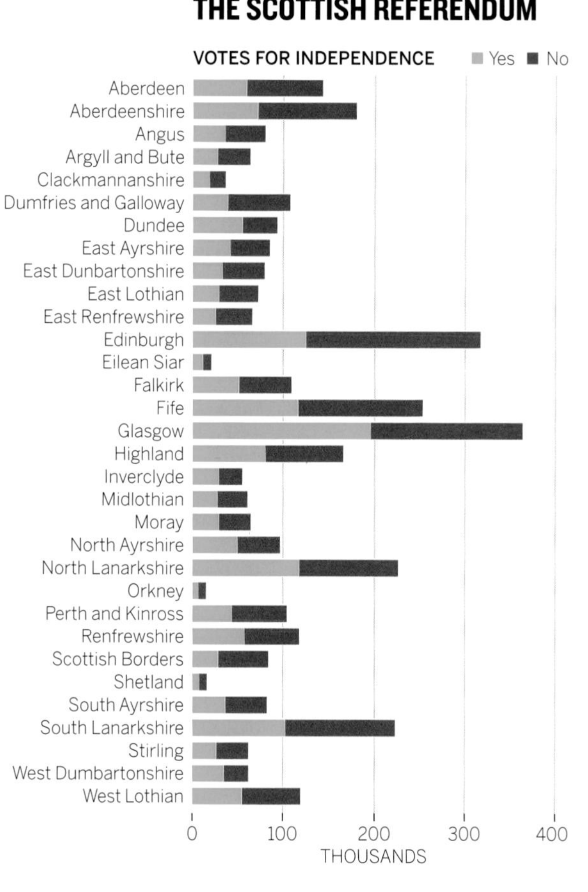

Above is the Scottish referendum as a cartogram.

Cartograms like this tend to look like wads of chewed bubble gum, and the more extreme the difference between geographic area and the value represented in that area, the more distorted the map, making it nearly impossible to reconcile the geography. In this cartogram, for example, that massive region in the north, Highland, is a squashed pink smear.

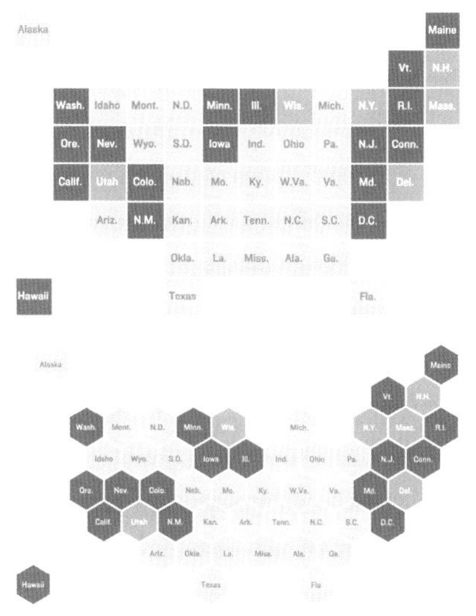

Equal State Area, Sample Choropleth

Grid maps provide an alternative solution. In a grid map, every region is of equal size and placed roughly where we imagine it belongs on a regular geographical map. Values are represented by color and color saturation. Multiple types of grid maps are being created and experimented with, as shown on this page.[8]

These are not perfect; it still takes more work to grab locations in these grids than it would in a regular map. Rhode Island is oddly east of Massachusetts in the hexagonal version, and Washington, DC, nearly borders Florida in the square version. When I think of a map of the United States, I think of Kansas as being roughly in the middle; so when I look for Kansas in the square version, I'm thrown off by finding Kentucky there. The four-hex version solves some of those issues; but then again, Louisiana and Texas look strangely similar and off-kilter. Grid maps also rely on color gradations to show differences in value between regions, which, if the data includes many values, may make it hard to discern differences from one level of saturation to the next.

These efforts are less misrepresentative than the ones that use area to encode other variables, but they also flout a deeply ingrained convention—the shape of the world—and make us work a little harder to find what we're looking for. That can be frustrating and therefore less persuasive.

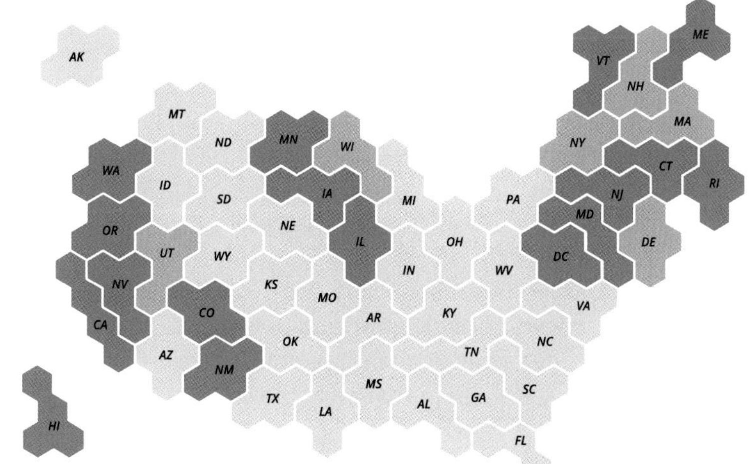

J. Emory Parker :: @jaspar
The Post and Courier

KNIFE SKILLS

I described the borderland between persuasion and deception as blurred. It should be obvious why. Most of the examples deconstructed here feel not perfectly right or wrong but, rather, endlessly debatable.

I also described the borderland as shifting, and in some ways that's the more difficult characteristic of persuasion techniques to reconcile. Tamar's truncated y-axis chart may be fine in one setting and violative in another. Even two colleagues in the same meeting might disagree about whether it's convincing or spurious.

Judging whether your visualization crosses that indefinite line will, like any other ethical consideration, come down to one of those difficult, honest conversations with yourself. Ask:

- Does my chart make it easier to see the idea, or is it actively changing the idea?
- If it's changing the idea, does the new idea contradict or fight with the one in the less persuasive chart?
- Does eliminating information hide something that would rightfully challenge the idea I'm showing?
- Would I feel duped if someone else presented me with a chart like this?

If you find yourself answering yes to questions like these, you've probably entered deceptive territory. Another way to check yourself is to imagine someone challenging your chart as you present it. You might even recruit a colleague to practice. Do you have the supporting evidence to counter a challenge? Could you defend your chart and yourself against attacks on its and your credibility?

Tamar was trying to do that when she gave Colette reasons why her truncated-axis chart was valid. If Colette pushed back, she might compel Tamar to produce supporting information—or even new visuals—to demonstrate the significance of the change, such as a chart showing how even a half-point gain in job satisfaction positively affects the bottom line.

At the very least, Tamar should point out the truncated y-axis whenever she shows the chart and be prepared for someone to challenge her. She needs to be able to explain why what looks flat and changeless on the full scale actually means something.

Like all of us, Tamar should focus less on whether the persuasion techniques she's using are right or wrong and more on making sure that the idea those techniques help her convey is defensible.

RECAP

PERSUASION OR MANIPULATION?

Used too aggressively or recklessly, persuasion techniques—emphasis, isolation, adding or removing reference points—can become deceptive techniques: exaggeration, omission, equivocation. The line between persuasive and deceptive isn't always clear. The best way to negotiate it is to understand the most common techniques that put charts in the gray area, understand why you'd be tempted to use them, and realize why they might not be okay. Here are three:

1. THE TRUNCATED Y-AXIS

What it is:
A chart that removes valid value ranges from the y-axis, thereby removing data from the visual field. Most often it doesn't start the y-axis at zero.

Why it may be effective:
It emphasizes change, making curves curvier and distance from one point to another bigger. It acts as a magnifying glass, zooming in on the space where data occurs and avoiding empty space where data isn't plotted.

Why it may be deceptive:
It can exaggerate or misrepresent change, making modest increases or declines look "steep." It disrupts our expectation that the y-axis starts at zero, making it possible or even likely that the chart will be misread.

2. THE DOUBLE Y-AXIS

What it is:
A chart that includes two vertical scales for different data sets in the visual field—for example, one for a line that tracks revenues and one for a line that tracks share price.

Why it may be effective:
It compels the viewer to make a comparison between data sets that may not naturally go together. Plotting different values in the same space establishes a relationship between the two.

Why it may be deceptive:
Relationships between different values are artificial. Plotting those values in the same space creates crossovers, matching curves, or gaps that don't actually mean anything.

3. THE MAP

What it is:
A map that uses geographical boundaries to encode values related to that location, such as voting results by region.

Why it may be effective:
Geography is a convention that allows us to find data quickly on the basis of location rather than searching through a list of locations to match data. It also allows us to see trends at local, regional, and global levels simultaneously.

Why it may be deceptive:
The size of a region doesn't necessarily reflect the data encoded within it. A voting map, for example, may be 80% red but represent only 40% of the vote, because fewer people live in some larger spaces.

Judging whether your visualization crosses that indefinite line between persuasion and manipulation will, like all other ethical considerations, come down to a difficult, honest conversation with yourself. Ask:

- Does my chart make it easier to see the idea, or is it actively changing the idea?
- If it's changing the idea, does the new idea contradict or fight with the one in the less persuasive chart?
- Does eliminating information hide something that would rightfully challenge the idea I'm showing?
- Would I feel duped if someone else presented me with a chart like this?

PART FOUR

PRESENT AND PRACTICE

CHAPTER 8

PRESENT TO PERSUADE

GETTING A GOOD CHART TO THEIR EYES AND INTO THEIR MINDS

BY NOW YOU'RE CONCEIVING of and building smart, persuasive visualizations—good charts. So far all your energy has gone into working out ways to develop and manipulate the charts themselves. Now, you can focus on taking that well-conceived object and helping people to connect to it.

Typically, we aren't terribly good at that. We build a smart viz and hope that the chart itself—this clear, self-sufficient, persuasive little object of visual communication—will engage an audience. But the text of a brilliant speech doesn't compel an audience to action; the orator does. The score of a symphony doesn't move people; its performance does.

How you get a good chart to people's eyes and into their minds is what matters most. Effective presentation marks the difference between information visualizations that are merely adequate exposition and ones that move people.

Getting charts to eyes and into minds may sound figurative, but I mean these things literally. The twin challenges here are to help people when they first see the visual—how you present it to them—and to help them process it: how you get them to engage with it. I'll take these in turn.

GETTING IT TO THEIR EYES: PRESENTATION

At some point most managers learn how to give a presentation. They read books about it, take a class, or hire a coach.[1] The skills those tools offer are useful in presenting charts, but those learning methods may not cover more-specific techniques for presenting visualizations that can help make them easier to understand and more persuasive.

First show the chart and stop talking. Researchers estimate that about 55% of our brain activity is devoted to processing visual information. The visual system, crudely explained, includes a high road that handles spatial information and navigation and a low road that recognizes and processes objects and shapes. No matter what the visual input, both roads teem with activity. Put a chart on a screen, and the entire ventral section of the brain fires up to suss out some meaning. As George Alvarez, a visual perceptions researcher at Harvard, puts it, "Mostly, vision is what the mind does."

So if you present a chart and immediately start talking over it, you'll make it harder for your viewers to understand the chart. Their brains really want to *look*, and you're asking them to *listen*, too. It distracts. Visual processing is so intense that once we see something salient such as a color or a shape, we start to tune out other visual information—never mind sounds—in order to make sense of what we see.

Instead, display the visual and don't talk for several seconds. If it helps, count five beats in your head. Let the viewers' brains dial in on this new thing to look at. You've done the hard work of making the visualization clear and persuasive. You've made the salient information highly accessible. You've used the title and subtitle as confirming cues about the idea you want to convey. Don't undercut your own hard work. Let the chart do what it was built to do.

The urge to start talking over a visualization is noble enough: You want to make sure people *get it*, and silence can be unnerving. But inevitably, what happens during this initial pause is more useful than anything you might preemptively say. In education, such an extended silence is a well-established tactic called "wait time" or "think time."[2] Teachers who allow three seconds or more to pass after they ask a question tend to have classes that are more engaged, think more critically, and come up with more-sophisticated answers to problems.

That's what will happen if you pause after showing a chart. Eventually, someone in the audience will puncture the silence with a question, or offer analysis or an opinion. You may find that the chart spurs discussion without your having said a word. If you let people arrive at their own insights, the idea in the visual will be talked about more, and more deeply, than if you immediately tell them what they should see. Paradoxically, the silence creates a deeply interactive moment.

When it's time to talk, don't read the picture. The easiest way to lose your audience in any presentation is to read bullet points verbatim from a slide. Explaining the structure of a chart that you're presenting will disengage an audience just as badly.

Imagine presenting this map with the following script:

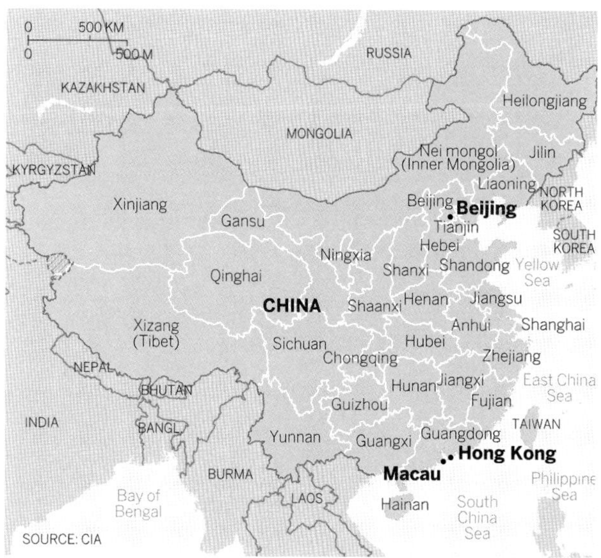

So, here's a map of China divided into its provinces. North is at the top of the map, and each province is distinguished by a light yellow border outline and labeled with its name. Surrounding countries are labeled as gray, and the East and South China seas are shown, which are lighter gray. As you can see, distance is measured according to a key in the upper left corner.

Explaining how a map works toes the line of condescension. Yet we present dataviz with the same descriptive approach. Here's a typical presentation of a chart and the script that might accompany it:

AIR TRAVEL TRIP COMFORT VS. TICKET COST

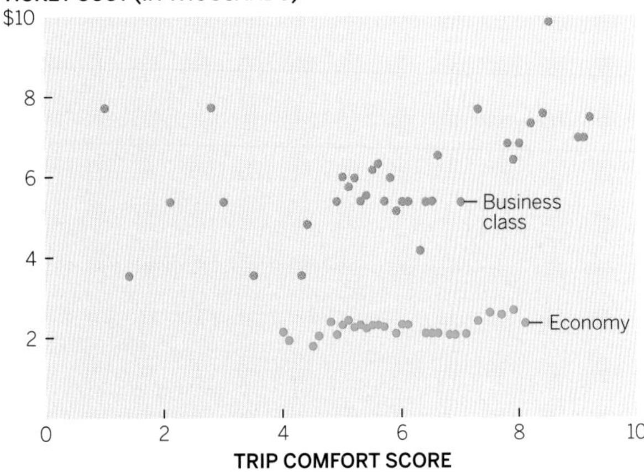

SOURCE: CARLSON WAGONLIT TRAVEL (CWT) SOLUTIONS GROUP, TRAVEL STRESS INDEX RESEARCH (2013)

So, here we are showing trip comfort versus how much a plane ticket costs. Comfort is 0 to 10 on the x-axis, and the cost of the ticket is on the y-axis. As you can see, economy class tickets—the blue dots—don't vary much in cost, but comfort does. There seems to be a little more correlation between comfort and cost for business class tickets, but only at the very high end, and even then, it's not a very strong effect.

Everything this presenter has said we can already see; he even says "as you can see," which is a clear tip-off that he's wasting time declaring the obvious. If they can see it, why say it?

You don't need to say what the axes are—they're labeled. You don't need to point out color coding—it's labeled. Once it's time to talk, discuss *the idea*, not the object that shows the idea. Here's a new script for the presenter:

[After five beats] Money doesn't seem to buy much comfort on plane trips, unless we pay the very top prices in both economy and business class. For most trips, comfort is average—in the middle—whether we pay $5,500 for a business class ticket or $2,200 for an economy ticket. This suggests that only the most expensive business class tickets are worth the cost to help our employees have comfortable trips. Since we know it's not cost that determines comfort, we should explore what does so that we can ensure productive business trips at the best cost.

There's no talk here of axes or color or how dots are clustered. Everything the presenter says is about the idea (money doesn't buy comfort), analysis of the idea (most business class tickets aren't worth the cost), prompts for discussion (if cost doesn't affect comfort, what does?), and a reminder of the value of discussing the idea (happier employees at a reasonable cost).[3] Notice how discussing ideas instead of explaining the data and structure naturally leads to more human-centered language. Rather than a price-to-comfort ratio, he's talking about comfortable employees and successful business trips. That's good. As the presentation guru Nancy Duarte put it to me, "Don't project the idea that you're showing a chart. Project that you're showing a reflection of human activity, of things people did to make a line go up or down. It's not 'Here's our Q3 financial results,' it's 'Here's where we missed our targets.'"

Reading a chart's structure during a presentation is often a sign that you lack confidence in the visualization. If you aren't sure the audience will get it, you probably haven't highlighted the main idea well enough. If you find yourself explaining the salient information, maybe you haven't emphasized and isolated it the way you should. Resist the urge to just read the chart, let those five beats of silence go by, and the questions and comments that come back will be a referendum on the chart's effectiveness. If people are asking about axes and labels and what they should be looking at, the visualization needs improvement.

With unusual forms and for added context, guide the audience. Mostly you should avoid talking about the chart itself, but there are exceptions. Unusual or complicated forms may require brief explanation prior to discussing ideas. Familiarity with forms does affect the ability to understand visualizations: you can't, for example, drop an alluvial diagram like the one below on an audience without at least some explanation of how it works.

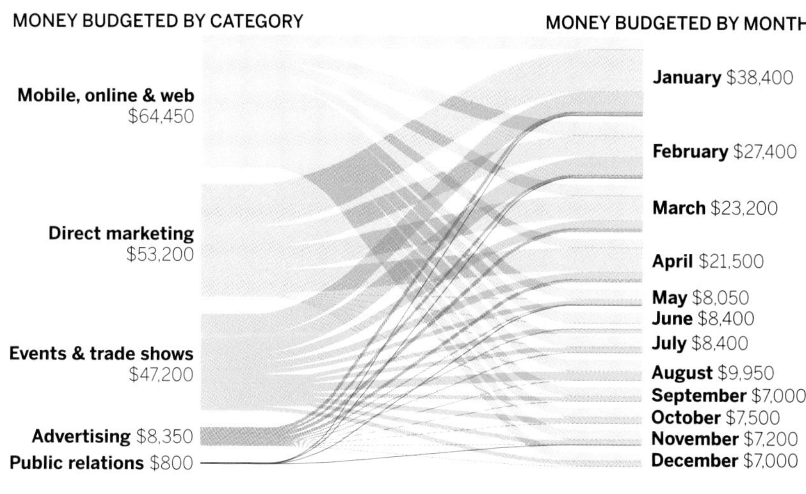

A diagram like this may elicit *oohs* and *aahs*, but if the viewers can't find meaning in it, they'll quickly write it off as a pretty picture or, worse, an attempt to show off that favors eye candy over insight.

That doesn't mean you should avoid unusual and complex forms: if they help frame ideas well, they can be powerful ways to engage people. But the time from *Gee whiz!* to *I see!* must be short. To make the transition, describe the function of the chart form before focusing on the idea:

This alluvial diagram shows how our marketing communications dollars flow throughout the year. It helps us see three things: One, how our budget is distributed by program, represented by the thickness of the bars on the left. Two, how our budget is allocated by month, represented by the thickness of the bars on the right. And three, how each program's money flows over the course of the year, represented by how the lines move from left to right. Take a look. [Wait five beats] We seem to have two seasons for marketing communications: January to April, a shorter season of heavy, heavy spending. And May to December, a long season of spending a little bit on a lot of programs. Big direct marketing investments fall into that first time frame, which also happens to be when our events business needs heavy investment. Is this distribution okay? Do we need to rethink this?

Notice that even in this case, while the speaker rightly explained the function and mechanics of an alluvial chart, she didn't fall into the trap of describing this particular example. She didn't say:

The events business, in green here, represents a little more than 25% of our budget, and the spending skews slightly toward the beginning of the year, as you can see by the thicker bars flowing into January and February.

Keep explanations of forms brief, clear, and general, not specific to the data encoded in your chart.

Use reference charts. Prototypical examples can also guide the audience, providing cognitive nudges toward clearer meaning. Presenting average, ideal, and other reference points works well even with basic charts, but it can be especially effective when presenting unusual forms. If you wanted to assess Tom's sales skills on seven different measures, you could use a dot plot like the one on the facing page. Or you could try the spider graph (also called a radar chart) next to it, which gives shape to multiple data points. It's more difficult to assess Tom's *overall* performance in the Skills Rating dot plot, because we have to evaluate seven discrete data points and then intuit what they combine to mean. But with the spider graph, we see a whole thing: one shape.[4]

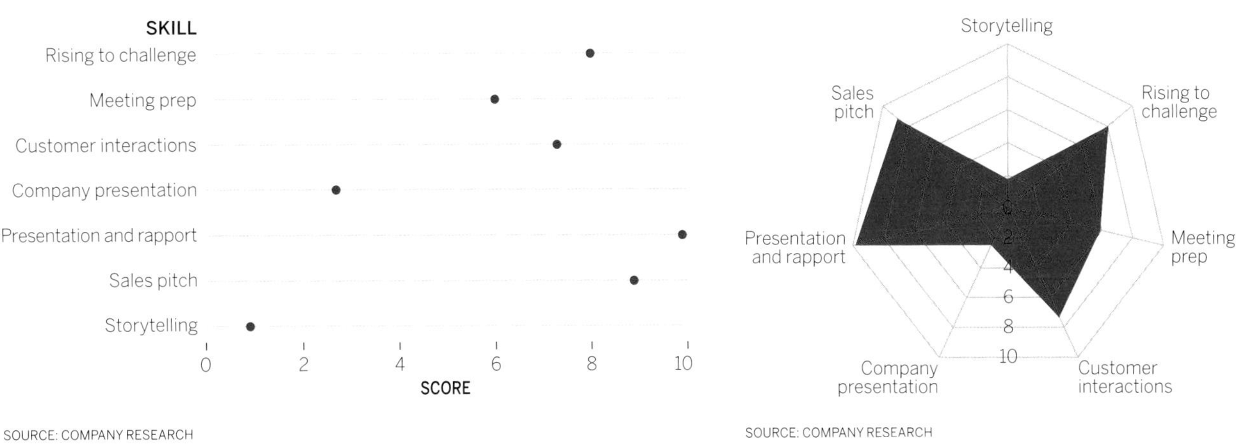

Okay, but the shape is meaningless in itself. Presenting this chart on its own would create questions that aren't easily answered. Is this a *typical* shape? Is it *good*? The data, Tom's overall *score*, is clear. The main idea, Tom's overall *performance*, isn't nearly as accessible. Let's add two prototypical references, *average performance* and *desired performance*, along with an accompanying script for the spider graphs:

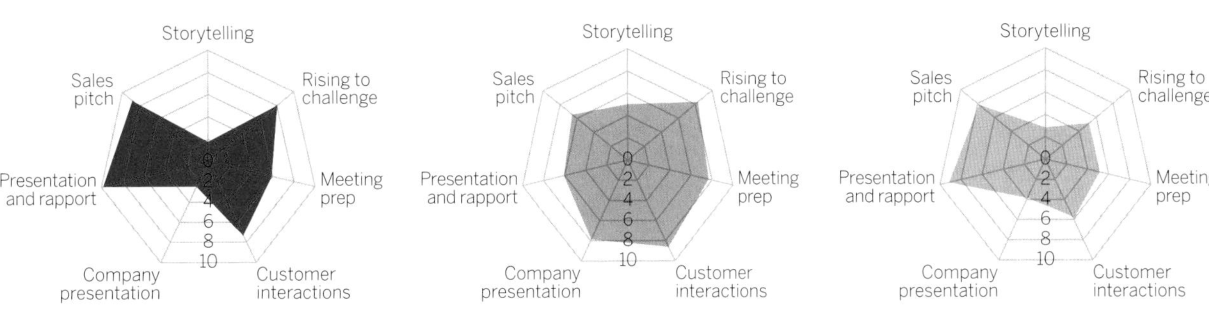

The shape we're looking for skews to the right side of the chart. Those skills on are more closely linked to sales success. But on average our sales team is strong on the left. Is that at the expense of developing the skills on the right? Tom's performance skews more right than average, but notice his bowtie shape. Those pinched points at the top and bottom are even below average. Storytelling skills and company presentation skills have got to improve, but especially company presentation. We need to invest there.

Notice how the reference charts inject meaning into Tom's chart. They help us set expectations and make sense of an otherwise arbitrary visual. Also, since we're now evaluating a reasonably simple shape, the charts don't require much detail and can be scaled down. The entire sales staff could be presented in multiple small charts, with little additional explanation required. A team that had grown accustomed to these visualizations might not even need labeling. (Remember, we get better at extracting meaning from charts as we gain experience using them.) Imagine a sales dashboard in which a sales manager could see the shape of team performance at a glance, such as the set shown above right.

Now, without labels, and having looked at just one example previously, you can spot the best- and worst-performing salespeople.

COMPARING MULTIPLE SALESPEOPLE

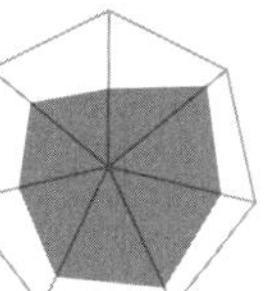

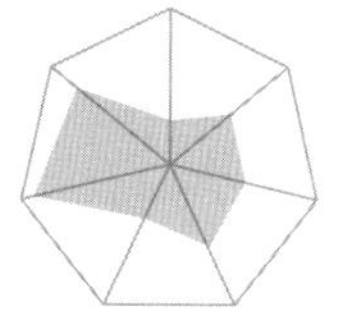

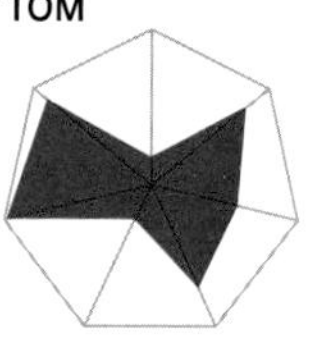

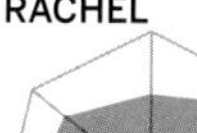

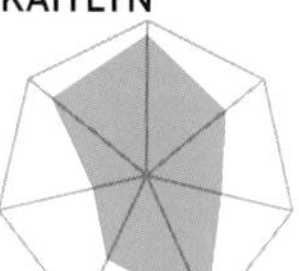

SOURCE: COMPANY RESEARCH

When you have something important to say, turn off your chart. This presentation technique comes from George Alvarez, who had noticed in his Harvard lectures that as long as he kept a dataviz on the screen during class, students' eyes would be fixed on it. Even when Alvarez had moved on to another subject, he sensed that his students weren't fully with him as he tried to make important points.

One day in class he showed his visualization and then, when he was ready to say something that the students needed to hear, he shut off the screen entirely. The effect was stunning. Eyes that had been fixed on the picture darted to him and locked in. With nothing else to look at, the students listened intently.

This is an unusual technique that requires practice. (Since Alvarez suggested the idea, I've tried it. The effect is uncomfortably immediate and takes getting used to, but it has worked for me.) There's a moment in every presentation, however, when you want the audience to focus on what you have to say. It could be when you raise an alarm about performance, or explain the reason for a strategy shift, or ask for money. At those crucial times, the best thing to do with your visualizations is to put them away. Give the audience no choice about where to focus.

Show something simple. Leave behind something detailed. A good chart depends on context—we know this. The context of a presentation requires disciplined simplicity—you have a few seconds for the audience to get it. But nothing precludes your producing more-detailed versions of the visualization to leave behind with your audience so that they can explore the visual in more detail in their own time and at their own pace.

Compare the spider graphs of sales team performance—a good choice for a presentation or a dashboard—with a leave-behind chart that combines all that data in one space:

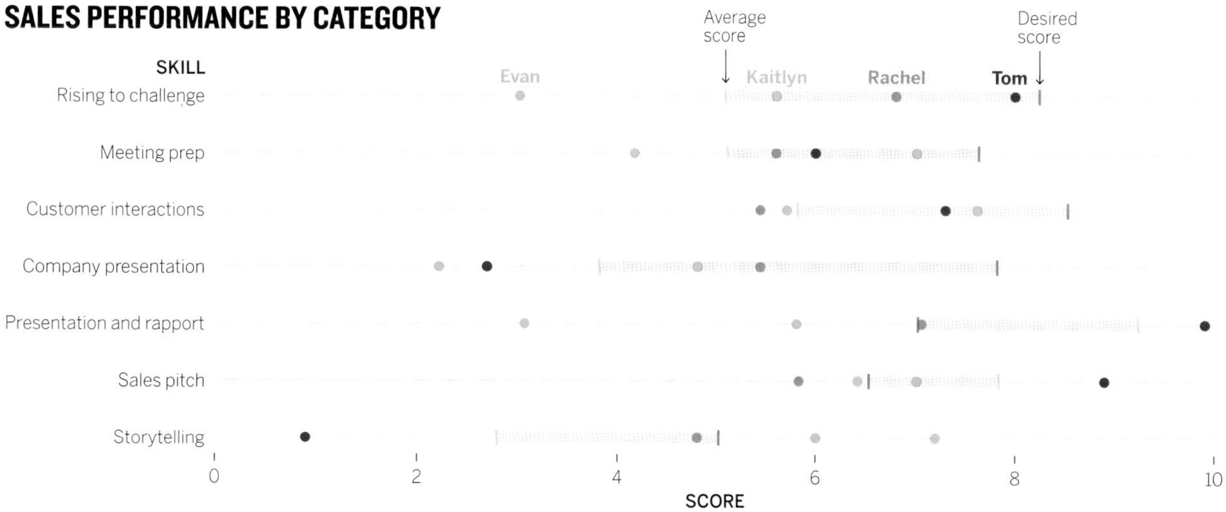

This plot wouldn't play well projected on a screen. It contains too many data points and offers too many places to focus. It doesn't steer us to any particular idea. It can be used vertically (comparing, say, average with desired scores across all seven categories) or horizontally (comparing everyone within one category).

The spider graphs gave an at-a-glance sense of how individual salespeople were performing. This leave-behind visualization would allow a sales manager to spend time on his own more deeply absorbing the information. Think of it as a bit of visual discovery—a category of dataviz in which we tolerate additional complexity for the sake of finding new things. The sales manager may want to confirm or refute a hypothesis he has about what skills his team needs to improve on. He may make notes about courses of action to take on the basis of what he finds. He may notice, for example, the lack of dots near the desired score for "company presentation"; the sales team as a whole isn't even close to where it needs to be in that skill.

Finally, it's good practice to make data tables available as leave-behinds too. This mini-system of visualizations—the presentation version that requires a few seconds to understand, and the personal version that an individual can spend time looking at and thinking about, and a table that provides the raw material, and may allow someone to do some of their own visualizing—extends the usefulness of your presentation beyond the formal group setting.

INDIA SWEARINGEN

IN SEARCH OF AHA! MOMENTS

"I was not hired to do this."

India Swearingen, of San Francisco's United Way of the Bay Area, sounds almost defiant about her budding expertise in data visualization. "I was hired to evaluate the effectiveness of our programs," she says. "I have a statistics background. I know how to do data analysis."

Swearingen seems worried that her deftness with visualization may lead people to forget that she's a skilled data scientist. "I spent years in college learning hard, high-level statistics," she says. "I thought that's what would be most meaningful to the organization." But when she presented her statistical analyses, some of it visualized, she was met with confusion and blank stares. People weren't really getting it, and she was spending more time than she had anticipated trying to make her visualizations more effective. "What I found was that people really just needed to know what was happening. They were hungry for the basic story."

She taught herself how to use visualization software and kept improving her visuals. Swearingen recognized that as her visualizations became simpler, her audience responded better. "People were so desperate to understand the big picture, and I was providing it," she says. "I'm helping them make decisions. I'm creating those *Aha!* moments."

Before long, she was hooked.

Swearingen's visualization process echoes the talk-sketch-prototype framework laid out in chapter 4. She starts by defining her audience and then asks herself, *What is the story?* "The form comes out of that. When I'm building my story, I'm thinking about the key insights I want them to see. I'm writing, erasing. Putting stories on top of stories. I end up with a storyline."

Then she sketches—"a lot." On whiteboards. Walls. Paper. Any form she can think of that might help her create the *Aha!* moment. She calls this part the visualizing, because it's when the idea, the story, starts to take on a visual form. Creating the actual charts is less a matter of visualizing than of building what she's already visualized during the sketching process.

With sketches in hand, she solicits reactions from colleagues. "Since I don't have a data team, or training in visualization, really, I don't have the opportunity to have deep critique sessions," she says. "So I run things by people." She brings in "strong thinkers" from various teams—marketing, leadership, program development—to get their gut reactions to her charts. "I listen for their questions, see where their minds go. I don't think they truly know exactly what I'm doing, and how they're helping, but it works. It really helps me create those charts that people respond to, because what we see and think about when we create a chart may not be what others see when they look at it. We have to test their reactions."

After a few rounds, when her recruits start asking fewer questions, she knows it's time to start building the visualization.

As for the *Aha!* moments: "I've had a lot of them now. But my favorite happened recently." The United Way relies on engagement with its donors and volunteers; Swearingen saw a need to understand that engagement better statistically. "How do people view the organization's role compared with our perception of who we are? Where are we strong and weak? If we see people donating less, how do we know what's really happening?" She proposed that the organization launch a major survey to acquire some deep data on engagement. This was no small investment, and she needed approval from "basically everyone" to do it, so she knew the output from the investment had to be good. Her reputation, her perceived value to the organization, in some ways depended on it.

When she presented to the all-staff meeting, there were no doubts about her value. "It was this really neat, really awesome moment," Swearingen recalls, "really the first truly interactive session since I got here. I could see people's engagement with the visuals. They were asking good questions. They were drawing conclusions based on what they saw and discussing it. Hunches were being confirmed and denied. The questions just kept coming out of the audience."

Engagement strategies and programs were adjusted. Swearingen also benefited: Initial skepticism about investing in data analysis eroded. "Now they see the value of gathering, submitting, and tracking data," she says. "It was a good presentation, but it could have been so much better with more data." That's Swearingen the data scientist.

Swearingen is thriving. "Right now, I'm special, because so many people are intimidated by dataviz. But that's changing. Tools are making it easier. More people are trying it. I'm doing it really well and working on getting to the next level."

That next level includes more exploratory visualization and interactivity. Swearingen has already seen how tools help to bring interactive visuals to lay users. She has even seen these techniques seep into formal presentations—a development she views as exciting and possibly transformational. "To be able to have a good visualization on the screen and have someone say, "Let's see that data filtered to show only results for younger people and women," and then to be able to instantly show a good visual representation of that filtered data—that will change how presentations work, I think. It allows the audience to take more ownership. It's a shared approach."

Even though she wasn't hired to do visualization, Swearingen is happy with the turn her career has taken: "I just kind of evolved into the dataviz person here, and it has absolutely helped me in my career. Without this, I'd be behind the scenes, answering questions about data. With it, my image in the organization and beyond has really increased."

GETTING IT INTO THEIR MINDS: STORYTELLING

The presentation techniques discussesd above are specific and tactical and, frankly, somewhat defensive. Mainly they focus on preventing you from undermining your own charts and helping to keep the audience from disengaging. If you hew to those techniques, you'll get charts to your viewers' eyes effectively. Now let's focus on getting the ideas in the charts into their minds—by telling stories.

Right now nothing's trendier in visualization than storytelling. An entire genre of journalism is building up around the notion of telling stories with data. My Twitter feed is rife with links that promise to tell you "the story of [unemployment, climate change, the Roman Empire] in [one, seven, fifty] charts.[5]

Data scientists, too, are latching on to narrative as a way to communicate the complexities they pluck from big data sets, and software is trying to make it easier to string visuals together into a story.

In a way, visual storytelling is just a tributary feeding into a deeper, swifter river of business activities that use narrative as a catalyst—selling, persuading, leading. Much of it is born in design thinking and bolstered by neuroscience. As much as visual perception scientists might say that *vision* is what the mind does, many neuroscientists would argue that *stories* are what the mind does. They've shown that our brains react differently, and more positively, to stories than to a bulleted list of items or a series of data points.[6] Many more parts of our brain are active when we're engaged with a narrative. Stories increase empathy, understanding, and recall. Storytelling is persuasive. The psychologist Robyn Dawes even argues that we can't make sense of statistics very well without narrative—that our "cognitive capacity shuts down in the absence of a story."[7]

Here are two stories about two different topics. The first, on this page, is textual. The second, on the facing page, is visual.

Throughout the 1990s and into the early 2000s, the price of copper was stable, and historically low at about 65 cents per pound. But then in 2003 a landslide at a mine sent prices over $1 per pound. After a strike at a mine in Chile in 2004, prices passed $2 per pound. Because of these events and continued high demand, production fell below consumption, which caused prices to reach nearly $4 per pound by 2006.

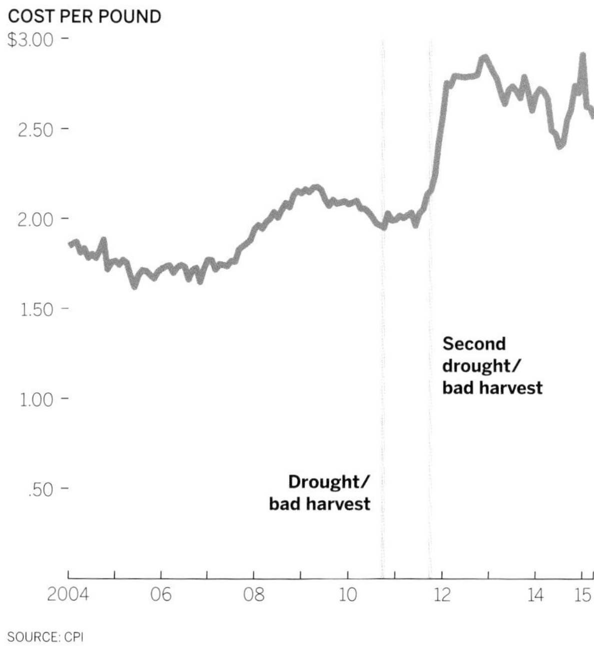

I chose different stories because if I had used the same narrative, reading the text first would have made it hard for you to evaluate the chart's merits independently. Still, you can compare your experiences with each, because their storylines are nearly identical—stable prices followed by sequential events that changed conditions and sent prices skyrocketing.

Notice how much more quickly you reach understanding when you look at the picture. The text feels like a transfer of information—something you work to understand, through reading and thinking. In the chart, you see just the price spike and the events related to it. You don't have to hold specific values—prices, dates—in your mind, or calculate time frames for the change. You see a long period of stability followed by a quick spike. Comprehension feels almost instantaneous.

So our brains grab on to narrative, and we need it to make sense of statistics. And narrative emerges much more quickly when it's visual. Thus visual storytelling is an immensely powerful way to present ideas. If we define narrative broadly, as just a sequential presentation of related events, then even a simple chart can become a visual story. Intuitively, we know this. We sometimes present charts by saying, "This chart tells the story of . . ."

But more practically, you need to know how to present visuals in a way that taps into the human need for narrative and exploits visualization's power to convey a story instantly. Here are a few techniques:

Create tension. Your boss likes to play games. He walks into a meeting and sings a familiar tune: "A-B-C-D-E-F-G. H-I-J-K . . ." He stops. And waits. Many people in the room will feel real tension. They'll feel beholden to the unresolved melody. It's captivating, in a literal sense. Nothing else can happen until it's been finished. They can't *not* finish it, and inevitably, someone will finally sing out, "L-M-N-O-P," or even all the rest of the alphabet.

If you think of a chart as having a melody—the shape of a line, or how dots are scattered on a plot—you can similarly captivate an audience. Until you reveal all the visual information, that melody is unresolved.

The easiest way to do this is exactly what your boss did with the alphabet song—pause before you get to the natural stopping point. "Here's how we scored with customers last quarter. And this quarter's scores [pause] . . ." The short, unexpected silence generates anticipation, causes people to look up from their doodles, turn away from their screens, focus on the visual, and wait for the ending.

This technique invites interaction. Viewers are forced to think about how the melody will resolve. They'll try to fill in the blank space. Encourage this. Show three versions of your revenue chart and ask them to guess which one reflects reality before revealing the answer. Withhold labels from a bar chart that shows which products generate what portion of overall revenue, and ask them to figure out what products the bars represent. Withhold key information, as with the slope graph to the right and its script below.

[Wait 5 beats] There's not a college major charted here in which women earn fewer than 40% of the degrees given out. This shows great progress. But we haven't yet added computer science and engineering to the chart. [Pause]

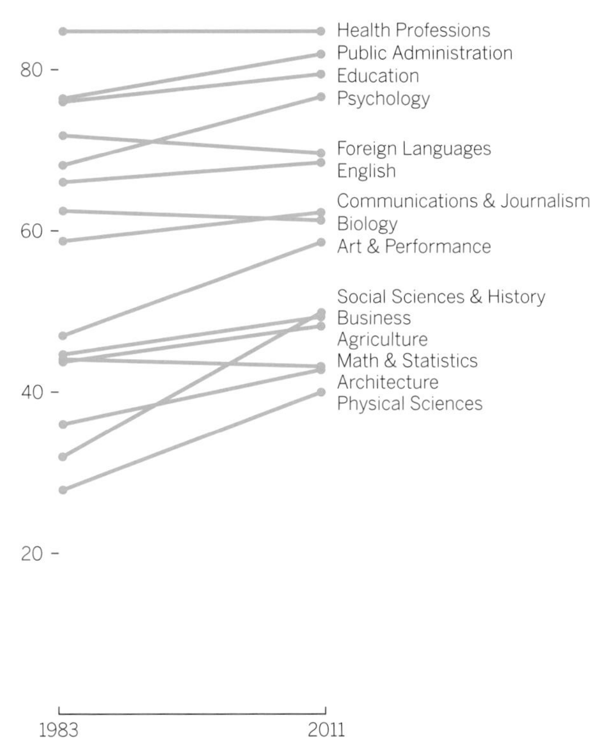

The presenter signals his intention to show more. The audience wants to know where those majors fit in. Many people (including you) are already guessing. The presenter would do well to encourage speculation. "Where do you think they'll be?" And the longer he holds the moment, the more people will need an answer—the more they will want to resolve the melody before proceeding.

There are other ways to create tension. Using time and distance can help convey a sense of vastness or large values. A simple and effective example is distancetomars.com, an animated visualization that supposes that Earth is 100 pixels wide and then "travels" through space from Earth to Mars as stars fly by. A few seconds after you leave Earth, you arrive at the moon, 3,000 pixels away. Then you take off again (moving at the equivalent of three times the speed of light). After ten seconds or so, tension rises, because it's unclear when you'll finally "arrive" at Mars. Ten seconds becomes 20. Then 30. The longer it goes on, the more a sense of uncertainty overtakes you as you watch. Even though you've already grasped the main idea—Mars is really, really, really far away—you still want to get there.

Ultimately, it takes about one minute to get to Mars. It feels like a long time, but also just short enough that you don't become annoyed and start thinking, *OK, I get the point.* That elicits the first of two caveats about creating tension: make sure you resolve it soon enough after you create it.

For example, are you annoyed that you don't yet know what percentage of computer science and engineering degrees are given to women? Did you forget about that chart? I probably ruined the effect of the tension by waiting too long to resolve it and distracting you with other things in the meantime. It won't be as effective now, but here it is below.

That would have been a powerful reveal had I timed it well. Second caveat: use the reveal technique judiciously, when its effect will be felt because

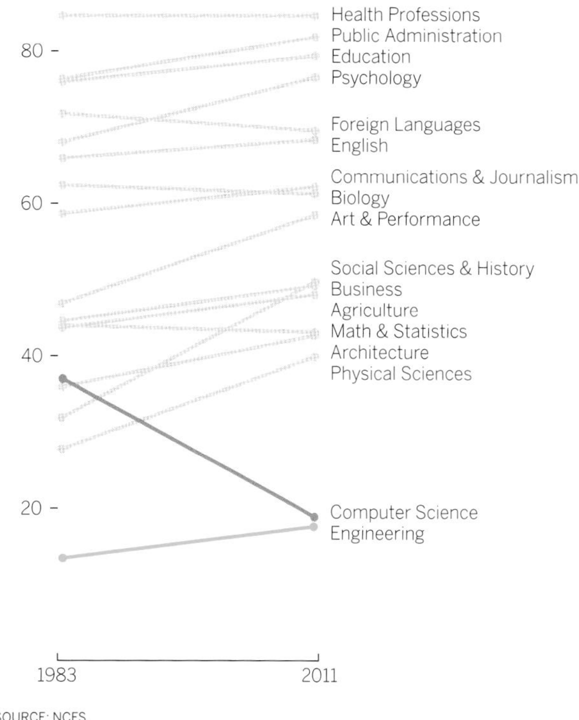

the idea being conveyed is somehow remarkable. A typical quarterly revenue chart that contains no surprises doesn't lend itself to creating tension. Pausing with every chart, inviting speculation on all visuals, would grow tiresome quickly.

Creating tension works best when the reveal is dramatic. The reveal about women's degrees is unexpected—even if you were sure that computer science degrees would be lower, did you think they would be *that much* lower? Did you expect they would have fallen by *half*?

It also works when the information is overwhelming. Christopher Ingraham, a journalist at the *Washington Post*, used this kind of tension and reveal well when he wanted his audience to understand how much water had flowed into Houston's reservoirs during a recent series of storms. The amount is hard to comprehend, so Ingraham started by comparing two things we can relate to—one acre-foot of water (a standard measure) and a person—and then walked us through increasingly large comparisons.

"Quite a bit, isn't it?" Ingraham asks after the first in the series. But you know it's going to become more overwhelming than this.

After the second he says, "We're still not at the right scale." At each step the audience's tension increases a little, but so does its understanding of the vast volume of water we're

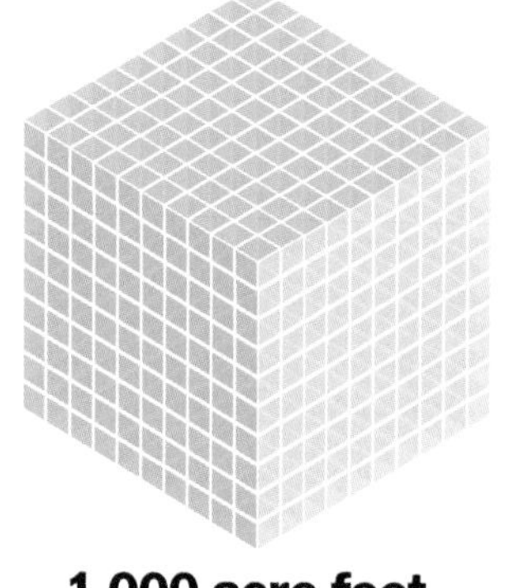

talking about.[8] These intermittent reference points make us wonder just how "insane" (Ingraham's word) the amount of water was.

"Now we're getting somewhere," he writes after the third visual, and at this point we feel that he's just playing with us. We need this melody resolved. How much water flowed into Houston's reservoirs?

Finally, the reveal. It's enough water, he explains, to serve 64 million people's water needs for one year. The scale of the disaster is better understood because of how he brought us through the story.

Before-and-after charts are also effective at creating and resolving tension. Think of home-makeover shows. We stay tuned to see a bathroom transformed from something run-down into something astonishingly attractive. A bait and switch, or what scientists sometimes delightfully refer to as a "lure procedure," is also suited to the reveal.[9]

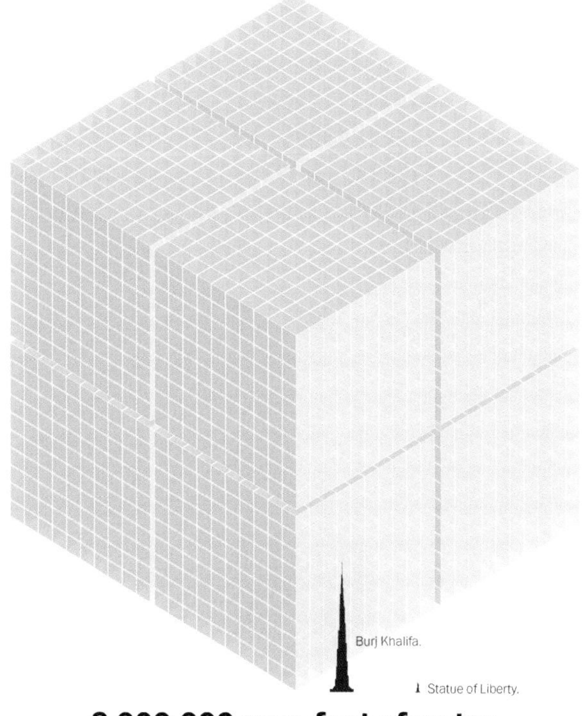

ROBOT GAINS VS. JOB LOSSES

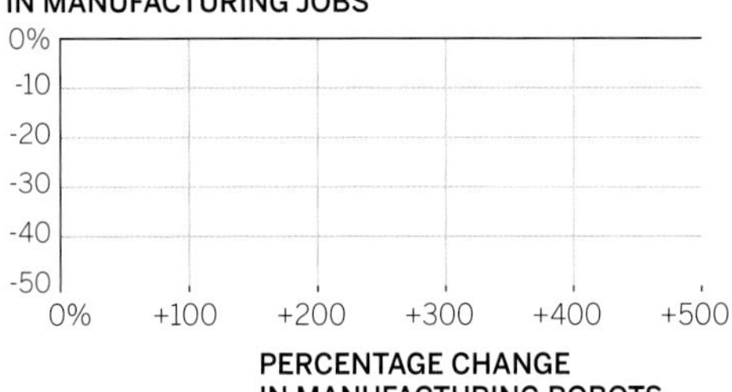

[Pause five beats] Robots are taking our jobs, right? Automated systems obviate the need for workers. We wanted to see the trend, so we decided to look at manufacturing job losses compared with the number of robots deployed over the past 15 years in 10 countries. What do we expect to see on this chart? [Pause, wait for answers] Right. As the deployment of robots increases, jobs decrease. Something like this?

ROBOT GAINS VS. JOB LOSSES

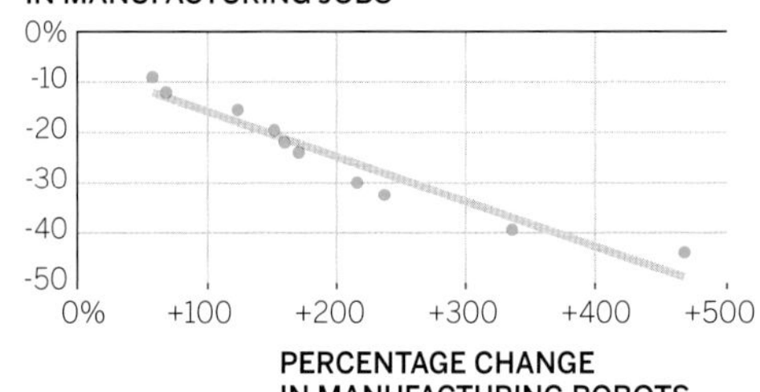

[Pause five beats, wait for agreement, and nod] That looks right. Well, when we plotted the actual data, this is what we saw: [Pause three beats]

ROBOT GAINS VS. JOB LOSSES

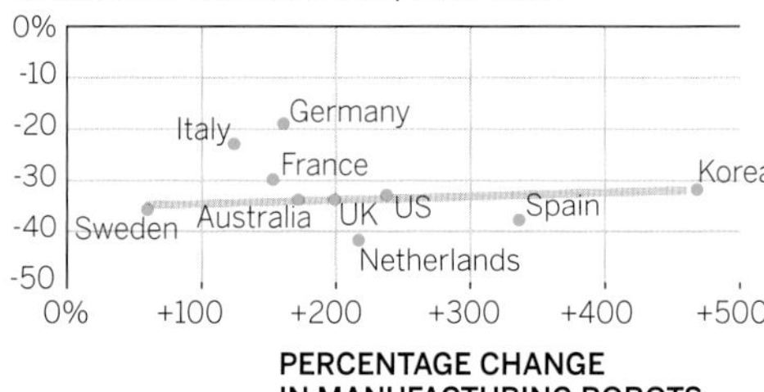

SOURCE: GRAETZ AND MICHAELS, "ROBOTS AT WORK," AND BROOKINGS INSTITUTE, MARK MURO ANALYSIS OF BUREAU OF LABOR STATISTICS DATA

We were wrong. There's no correlation at all. In fact, the UK and Sweden, two of the four countries that have lost the most manufacturing jobs, have deployed robots much more slowly than other countries.

In this series, the center chart with the expected results lures people to commit to an idea. The reveal is so completely different, however, that it compels the audience to think through what just happened. *Why* isn't it what I thought it would be? Inconsistency creates internal anxiety that we feel compelled to fix.[10] And the greater the inconsistency, the more we want to reconcile the dissonance. In the face of visual evidence like this, it's hard to hold on to assumptions or even deeply held beliefs. It's a powerfully persuasive presentation technique.

Deconstruct and reconstruct. I'm fond of this Football vs. Rugby chart that compares time use in televised American football games and rugby matches.

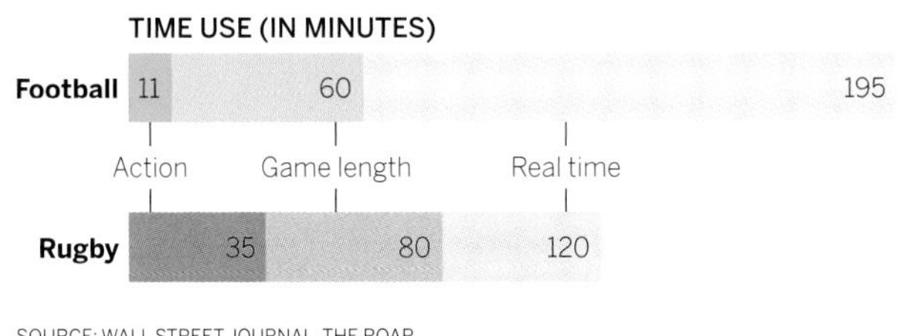

The point I want to make is that rugby is more exciting than football: it's a longer game that features more action in less real time. That idea comes through, eventually. In truth, this is not a great chart for a presentation. I've given you no fewer than 15 bits of information to look at here. The main idea, which is a fairly simple one, doesn't pop as well as it could. If I want to make it work better, I could do another simple binary comparison, first showing rugby, then football, similar to what I did with the women's degrees chart:

[Pause 5 beats] A rugby match contains a lot of action, and because there's very little stopping except for halftime, most of the time you're watching, you're watching the game itself. Compare that with American football. [Pause 3 beats before adding football chart to the screen]

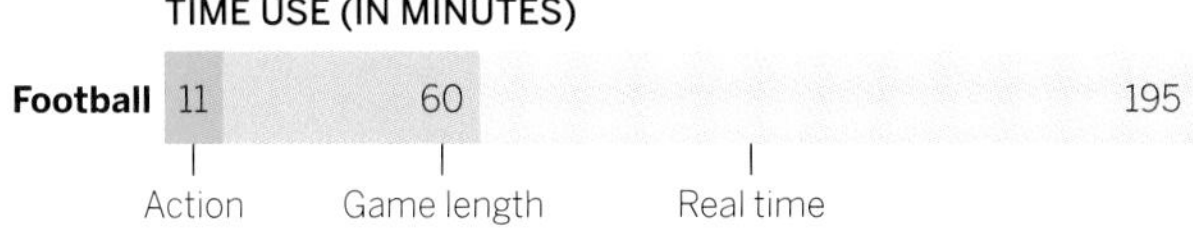

This is better; my viewers can focus on one sport at a time. But I'm still asking them to think about three things in relation to one another, then to do it again, and then to compare the two sets of relationships. In contrast, the women's degrees chart showed one thing—all other degrees—in the before state and just two new pieces of information in the reveal.

The thing about having options is that it slows us down. Here we borrow from Braess's paradox, a principle of traffic management developed by the mathematician Dietrich Braess, which states that adding route options (new roads, new lanes) to congested roadways can decrease traffic performance.[11] That's because when many people can switch routes (and switch again) for more-favorable personal outcomes, they slow the system down. Braess's paradox has been demonstrated in the real world many times when traffic improved after roads were removed. It has been applied to phenomena other than traffic, including power transmission (performance declined after systems were decentralized), protection of endangered species (the prospects for many species improve when one species goes extinct), and crowd control (multiple paths from a concourse to a seat in an arena make it take longer to get to seats).

What we experience with a complex chart isn't technically Braess's paradox, but it's similar. Think of all the places to focus on the Football vs. Rugby chart as the route options. Should you start with the orange bar or the green? Should you compare the bars overall or the pieces? Do the specific values matter enough to focus on them? Which route will get you to understanding fastest? Options require choices, and choices take time. In a presentation, different people may choose to focus on different things.

FOOTBALL VS. RUGBY

WHAT'S THE OFFICIAL LENGTH OF A GAME?

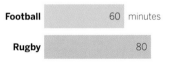

HOW MUCH ACTION OCCURS IN A GAME?

Football 11

Rugby 35

HOW LONG DOES A GAME ACTUALLY LAST?

By deconstructing a chart, you can remove all possible routes except one so that your presentation provides the fastest path to understanding. Here's the Football vs. Rugby chart deconstructed for a presentation. Each chart would be shown one by one, starting with the top one.

The top chart is unambiguous. We've eliminated all but one route here: how long a game lasts. Viewers will grasp this immediately because it's a simple comparison and it's the only one available. The subtitle further prods them, asking the question the chart answers, in case there was any doubt.

In the second chart, we've added some new information now but, crucially, we've also *removed* some of the previous labeling and the first subtitle. We feel confident removing them because they were so clear and immediately understood. The bars of lighter color remain, serving to put the new information in context. Because viewers aren't figuring out where to look, they can quickly assess that a rugby match has proportionally much more action.

One more time—add new information, remove old. Only one route. This time the reveal feels much more powerful. Viewers haven't once had to think about where to focus or decide what's important. Instead of spending mental energy figuring out the chart, viewers are free to think about and discuss the idea. It's also more unlikely that they'll disagree about the meaning of this story, because it has been presented in such a way that they can't start from different places or focus on different things. Everyone can agree on what's shown here.

Some vanguard neuroscience suggests that might be important. The neuroscientist and marketing professor Moran Cerf, with Sam Barnett, recently published a paper suggesting that what makes a story memorable or engaging or vivid is how many brains respond similarly to it.[12] Put another way, what the authors call "cross-brain correlation," or CBC, predicts whether people will remember a story as well as or better than other measures, such as how they rate the story or how long they spend with it. To the extent that we can make our visual stories concise and unambiguous, they're likely to be far more engaging and memorable.

Animate. Deconstruction and reconstruction lends itself to animation. Used skillfully—that means sparingly and functionally, not decoratively—animation can deepen understanding and engagement.

To show the massive scale of death in World War II in a way that conveys the tragic loss of human life rather than reporting statistics, for example, is difficult even with data visualization. Neil Halloran did it, though, in his interactive documentary *Fallen.io.* Halloran deftly uses movement (along with narration and sparse background music) to traverse a field of data points, zooming in and out to help viewers understand the vast scale of the war's carnage. In one powerful section he tallies deaths in the Soviet Union. The animation adds units of people killed—each icon added represents 1,000 deaths—for 45 harrowing seconds (using time to create tension), until it finally reaches 8.7 million. A fast zoom out shows the total in comparison with other countries' columns of units before redistributing all the deaths over time as a stacked area chart. One person who commented on the dataviz illuminated the effectiveness of the narrative techniques we've discussed here in communicating statistics that are too absurd, too abstract, to grasp in other forms:

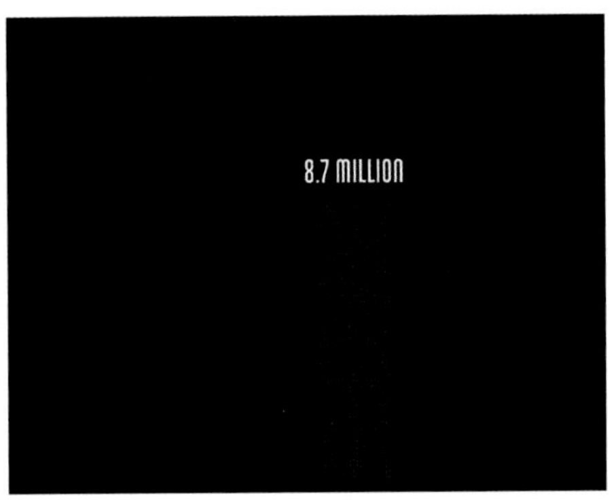

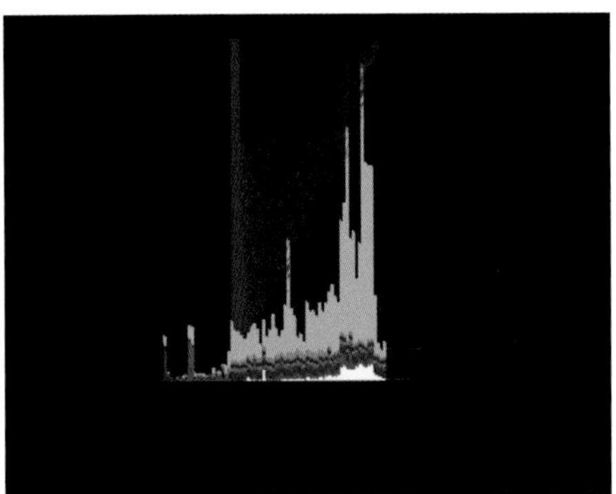

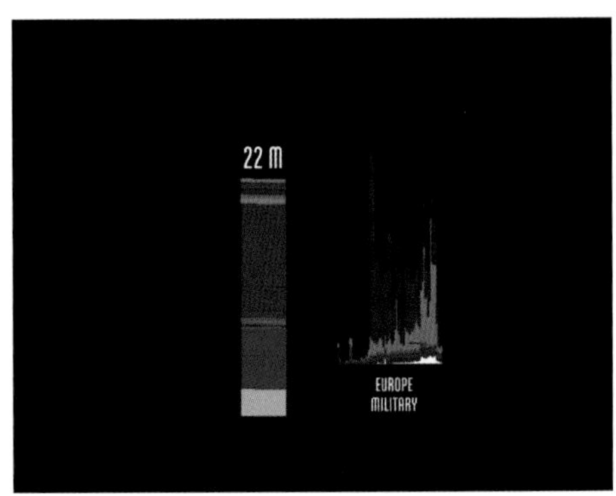

Fallen.io masterfully visualizes the harrowing death toll of World War II, using animation and multiple presentation techniques outlined in this chapter. Deaths stack up in unit charts in which each unit represents 1,000 deaths before those units are redistributed into a stacked area chart that shows how the deaths occurred over time.

One million, six million, seventy million. Spoken or written, these numbers become a buzz. Incomprehensible. Presented graphically, they hit closer to the heart. As the Soviet losses climbed, I thought my browser had frozen. Surely the top of the column must have been reached by now, I thought.[13]

Tell stories. When you want to deeply impress an audience with dataviz, your impulse may be to show them uncommon and unusually beautiful forms. "Eye candy" is the perfect moniker for charts like that, because they tend to give a quick buzz that doesn't last.

Storytelling is the best, most powerful tool for making the kind of lasting impression that can create new understanding, change minds, or even effect policy change. Halloran's animation is visual storytelling at its most captivating. It moves us in a way that the text and static charts I've used to describe it can't capture. In a world in which it's said that people can't sit still for more than a minute or two, this 18-minute dataviz went viral.

It essentially consists of three basic chart types—unit charts, bar charts, and stacked area charts—deconstructed and reconstructed over and over again. Powerful presentations that grab an audience don't have to rely on clever chart types. They can rely on your ability to craft your idea as a little drama.

Any story can be told in multiple ways, but a good way to start is to break the idea into three basic dramatic parts: setup, conflict, and resolution:

Setup: Here is some reality.
Conflict: Here is new information that complicates or changes reality.
Resolution: Here is the new reality.

In general, when we tell stories, the setup and resolution get about half of our attention. The other half is devoted to the conflict. That's where the action is. That's what makes narrative. No change, no story.

This formula is deeply entrenched in how humans experience stories; most successful narratives follow it. We can crudely map just about any story, or story archetype, onto it:

MAPPING STORIES

	MOBY-DICK	HARRY POTTER	WILE E. COYOTE AND THE ROAD RUNNER
Setup	Man goes on whaling voyage	Boy Wizard survives attack by Evil Wizard	Wile E. Coyote sets trap to catch speedy Road Runner
Conflict	Man's captain becomes unhinged seeking revenge on one whale	To defeat Evil Wizard, Boy Wizard must give up his life	Trap fails spectacularly
Resolution	Ship sinks, only man survives	Boy Wizard gives up life, Evil Wizard defeated	Road Runner escapes, Coyote injures self

This is deeply reductive, but intentionally so. Obviously, crafting a great novel or eight feature-length movies involves much, much more than a few sentence fragments outlining the structure. But it's a useful way to practice deconstructing narratives (try it with your favorite stories) that will help make your dataviz presentations more engaging.

Setup, conflict, resolution. Beginning, middle, end. You don't have to follow chronology, though usually you will; you only need to have your story proceed such that the setup makes sense on its own, the conflict affects the setup, and the resolution follows the conflict. Focus primarily on the conflict: that's what creates uncertainty, or introduces obstacles, or simply changes the status quo. It doesn't have to be negative. It could be the hiring of a star performer that changes your department's fortunes. Or it could be a new exercise regimen that positively affects your productivity.

To find this rough story structure in your visualization, break down and refine the idea statement that you came up with in the process of talking and sketching. (It should be clear by now just how important arriving at some statement of your idea is to successful visualization.) The story will be easiest to find in time-series data, which is inherently sequential. Take the idea described in the peanut butter chart on page 189. *Consecutive bad harvests due to drought have sent once-stable peanut butter prices to historical highs.* That is:

Setup: Prices are stable for years.
Conflict: Droughts create consecutive bad harvests.
Resolution: Prices spike and then stay high.

WHAT CAUSED THE HIGHER PRICE OF PEANUT BUTTER?

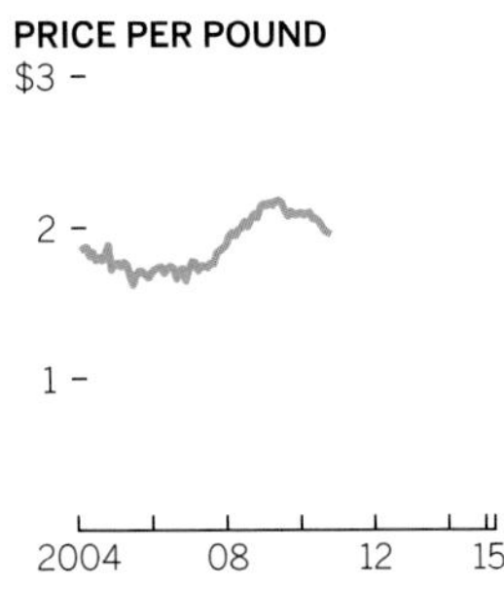

[Pause 5 beats] For nearly a decade, prices of peanut butter were smooth. Modest increases during the recession mapped to rises in most food prices.

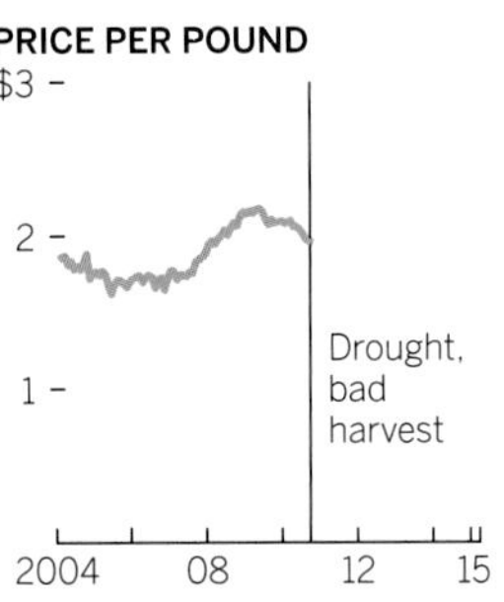

But then there was a drought and a bad peanut harvest. What happened? Where did prices go from here? [Pause, invite speculation].

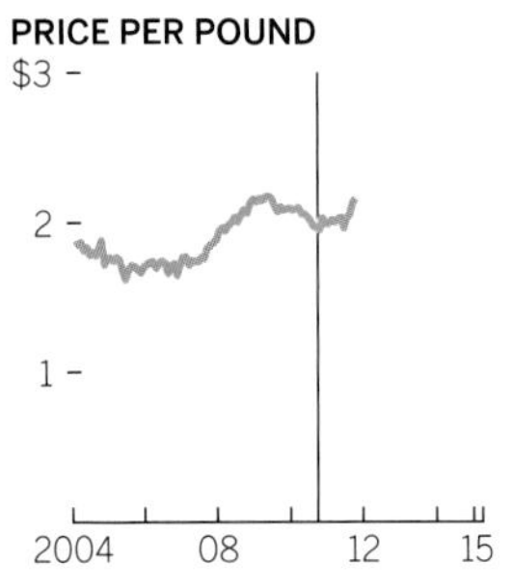

For most of the following year, prices were actually flat, until the next harvest approached, when prices started to rise as growers feared another drought.

And that's what happened: another bad harvest. Prices spiked almost 50%. And since then . . . [Pause]

Prices have remained high. One bad harvest was tolerable, but two sent prices to nearly $3 per pound, where they've remained for nearly half a decade.

SOURCE: CPI

These breakdowns demonstrate how you might turn one good chart into a series of simpler charts, as we did with the football/rugby comparison, to create little dramas. Each step becomes its own chart or adds new information to the main chart. Above is the peanut butter narrative, with presenter's script, using narrative to engage the audience.

Reserve dramas for your most complex ideas—explaining how multiple economic factors are affecting your business, for example—and your most important ideas, those for which you need to be especially convincing and persuasive.

PUTTING IT ALL TOGETHER

It can be useful to apply narrative principles to a chart, but it's far more powerful when, with multiple charts, you turn a presentation, or part of one, into a story.

Let's say you're a start-up pitching potential investors on a new type of coffee pod for single-serve coffee machines. The market for coffee pods is saturated, but yours is different. It's recyclable. You could just go in and say, "We have a recyclable pod that fixes a problem in the market." But will they understand the problem? Do they care? You want them to *feel* the problem so that when it comes time to show them your solution, they'll have no doubt

INVESTOR PRESENTATION — RECYCLABLE POD

COUPLE OF CONCEPT CHARTS → X | X BASIC CHARTS

USE MAPS/SPACE "FILL-UP"

STATEMENT: THE WASTE GENERATED BY PODS IS MASSIVE EVEN A SMALL GROWTH IN RECYCLED PODS WILL MAKE A BIG DIFFERENCE.

MAKE THEIR JAWS DROP! VISCERAL CONNECTION TO THE VOLUME OF WASTE

SET UP: SINGLE SERVE IS HUGE!
CONFLICT: WASTE PRODUCED. HUGE!
RESOLUTION: WE HAVE A RECYCLING OPPORTUNITY. HUGE!

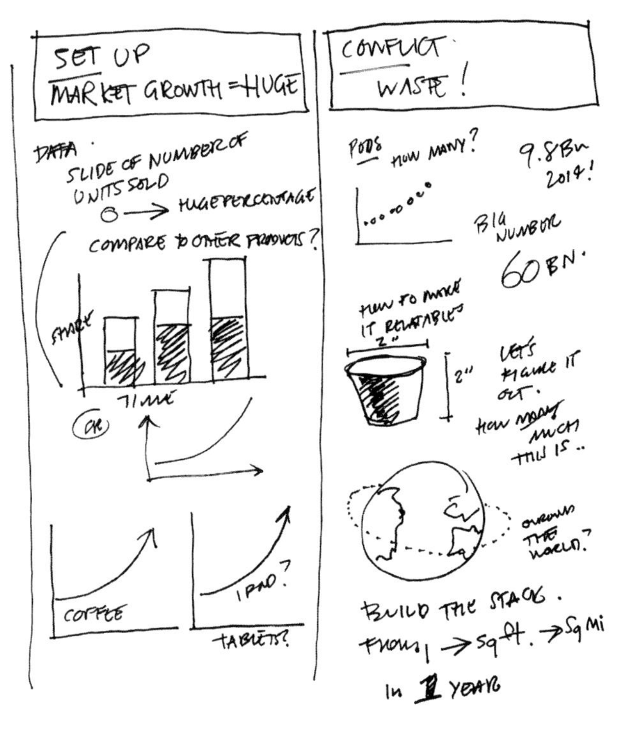
SET UP
MARKET GROWTH = HUGE
DATA.
SLIDE OF NUMBER OF UNITS SOLD
→ HUGE PERCENTAGE
COMPARE TO OTHER PRODUCTS?
TIME
OR
COFFEE
IPAD?
TABLETS?
CONFLICT
WASTE!
PODS HOW MANY?
9.8Bn 2014!
BIG NUMBER
60 BN.
HOW TO MAKE IT RELATABLE?
2"
LET'S FIGURE IT OUT.
HOW MUCH THIS IS..
AROUND THE WORLD?
BUILD THE STACK.
FROM → sq ft. → sq mi
IN 1 YEAR

WOULD FILL X STADIUMS
FOOTBALL FIELDS?
IT WOULD COVER VERMONT X TIMES. TO A DEPTH OF X
THEN APPLY TO HOW MANY SOLD AND USE COMPARATIVELY
LET THIS TAKE TIME

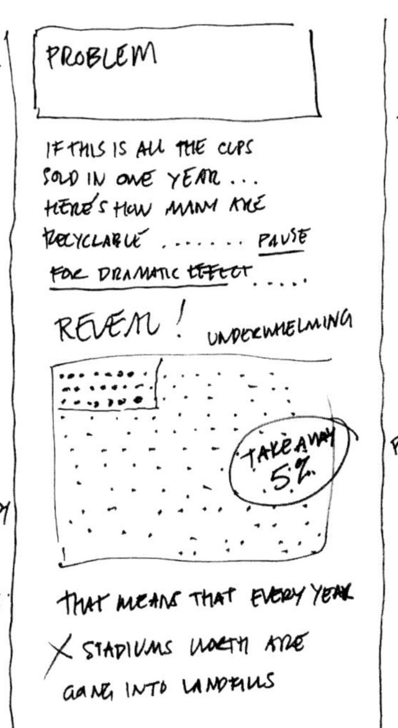
PROBLEM
IF THIS IS ALL THE CUPS SOLD IN ONE YEAR...
HERE'S HOW MANY ARE RECYCLABLE .... PAUSE FOR DRAMATIC EFFECT ....
REVEAL!
UNDERWHELMING
TAKEAWAY 5%
THAT MEANS THAT EVERY YEAR X STADIUMS WORTH ARE GOING INTO LANDFILLS

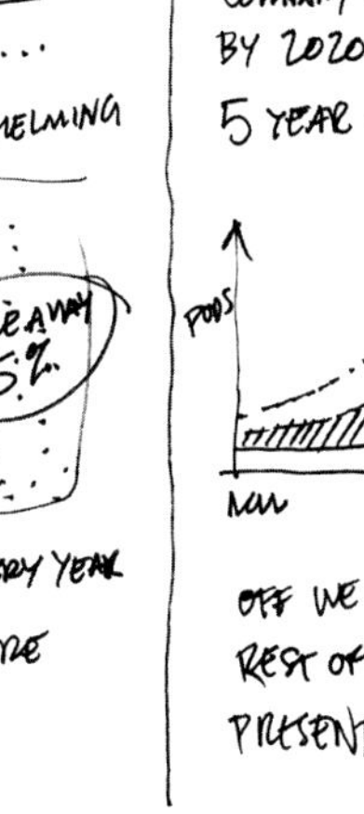

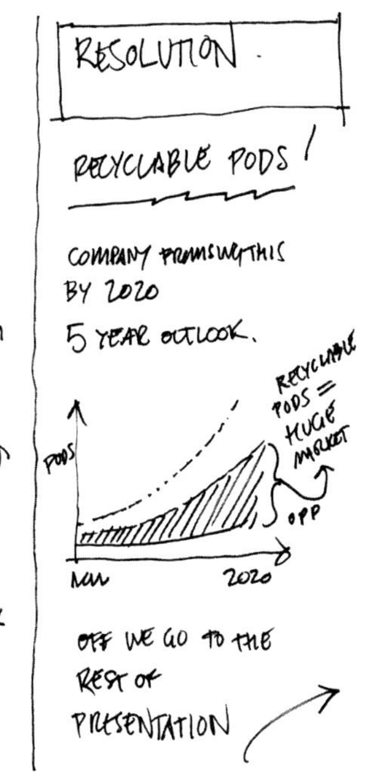
RESOLUTION.
RECYCLABLE PODS!
COMPANY PROMISING THIS BY 2020
5 YEAR OUTLOOK.
PODS
RECYCLABLE PODS = HUGE MARKET
OPP
NOW
2020
OFF WE GO TO THE REST OF PRESENTATION

that there's a need for it. Turn the beginning of your presentation into a short narrative.

First sketch out the three main parts of the drama, in words and literal sketches:

> **Setup:** Single-serve coffee machines are taking over the consumer coffee market.
> **Conflict:** The pods these machines use are nonrecyclable and have produced a staggering and growing amount of waste.
> **Resolution:** Recyclable pods will help solve this problem.

You've mapped out a story. It's a good sign that most of the time and space has gone into the conflict section, where drama has the greatest effect. Another good sign: you're already thinking about the presentation of the idea, making notes about using tension, time, and reveals to increase the persuasive effect of what you're showing.

Now you have to build those charts. Each chart will still go through the talk-sketch-prototype process; some may go through it together. But each needs to be well conceived and convey its idea effectively so that the audience can focus on the story rather than on making sense of the visuals. For brevity's sake, I'll skip to final charts and presenter's notes. Notice how they pull together everything discussed in this chapter, from not reading the picture, to using silence, to creating tension and reveals, to telling a story.

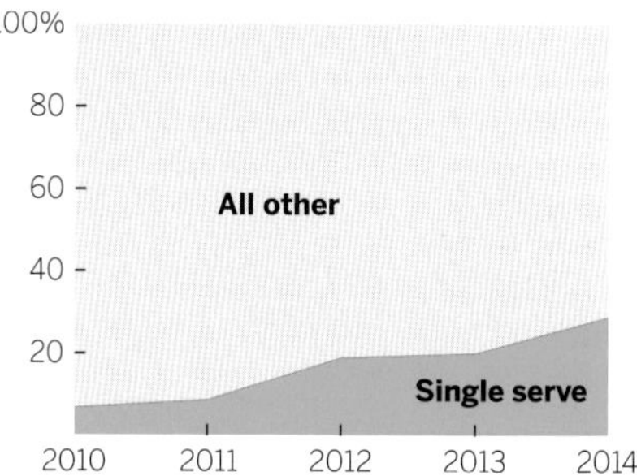

Setup:
[Show first chart, pause five beats] We all know that single-serve coffee is a growing phenomenon, but just how intense its surge is can't be understated. Its share has quadrupled in the past four years. In 2007, single serve's market share was virtually zero. Last year almost one in three people said their last cup came from a single-serve machine.

IPHONE MARKET SHARE

100%
80
60
40
20
All other
iPhone
2010 2011 2012 2013 2014

For perspective, here's the growth of the iPhone's share of the mobile market over the same period. [Display next chart next to first]

BILLIONS OF PODS SOLD

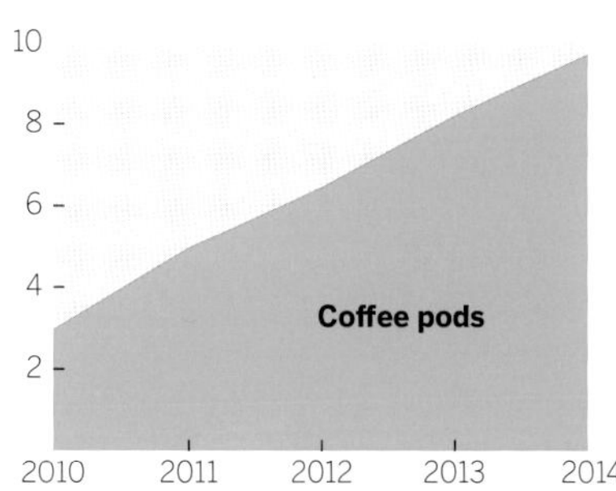

[Pause 3 beats] Every single-serve cup brewed requires a pod. Sales numbers on pods are notoriously difficult to pin down, but we know that the leading vendor alone is approaching 10 billion pods sold in one year—six times as many as five years ago. [Pause three seconds] During my pause right there almost 1,000 pods were sold.

A TYPICAL COFFEE POD

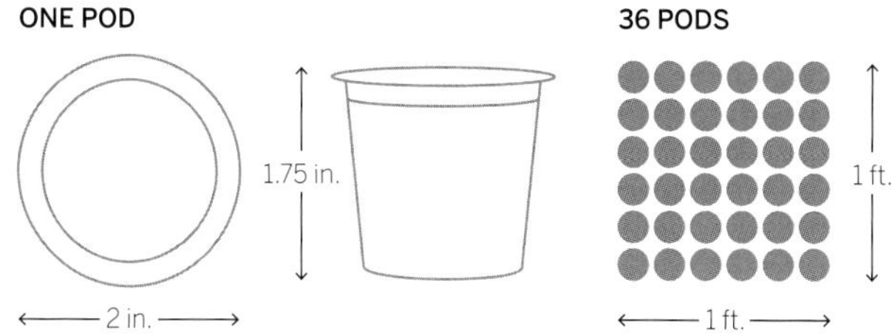

Conflict:
And most of them aren't recyclable, which has created a significant waste problem. The dominant vendor sold 18 billion pods in the past two years. But it's hard to fathom how much waste that really is, so let's try to break it down. If we lined up the pods, 36 would fill a square foot.

HOW MANY COFFEE PODS WOULD FILL AN ACRE?

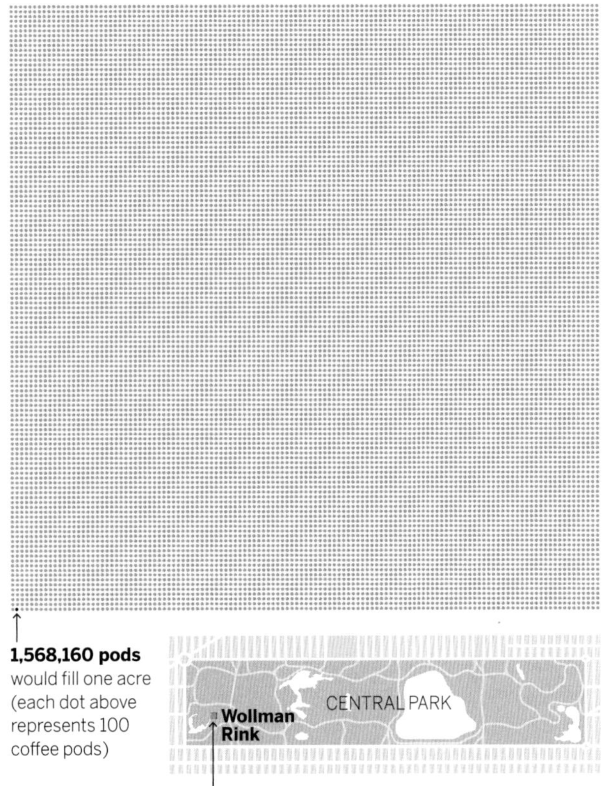

1,568,160 pods would fill one acre (each dot above represents 100 coffee pods)

One acre is about the size of New York's Central Park ice skating rink

PODS TAKE CENTRAL PARK

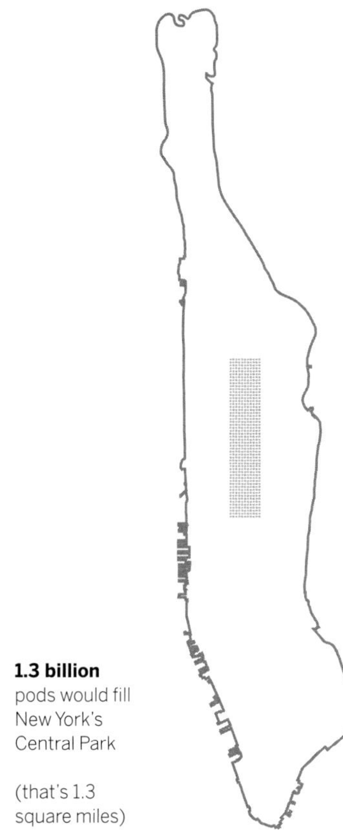

1.3 billion pods would fill New York's Central Park

(that's 1.3 square miles)

[Pause 3 beats] Think of an acre: like the skating rink in Central Park. Covering that with pods would account for eight one thousandths of one percent of the pods sold by that one vendor in the past two years.

We have to go far bigger to see how much space 18 billion pods would take up. Would covering Central Park in pods use up all those sold in the past two years? Would it at least take half the pods to cover Central Park? [Pause] No. It would take only about 7%.

We're going to have to start stacking them to account for the rest. If we did that in Central Park, the entire park would be just over two feet deep in the coffee pods sold by the leading vendor in the past two years. We'd be thigh-high in unrecyclable used coffee pods. But to be fair, we should subtract the pods that are already recyclable. If we did that, how much lower would the pile be in Central Park? [Pause, remove recyclables on same image, change label from 24 in. to 22.8 in.] About 1.2 inches lower. Not even a single pod's height.

Resolution:

The reason there are so few recyclable pods is that it's been a technically difficult design to achieve. We have a design that we believe solves that problem. And if our design can gain even 15% of the market in two years, we can reduce this pile of trash in Central Park by almost half a foot. [Again tweak image to remove pods and change label to 16.8 in.] That's a big start.

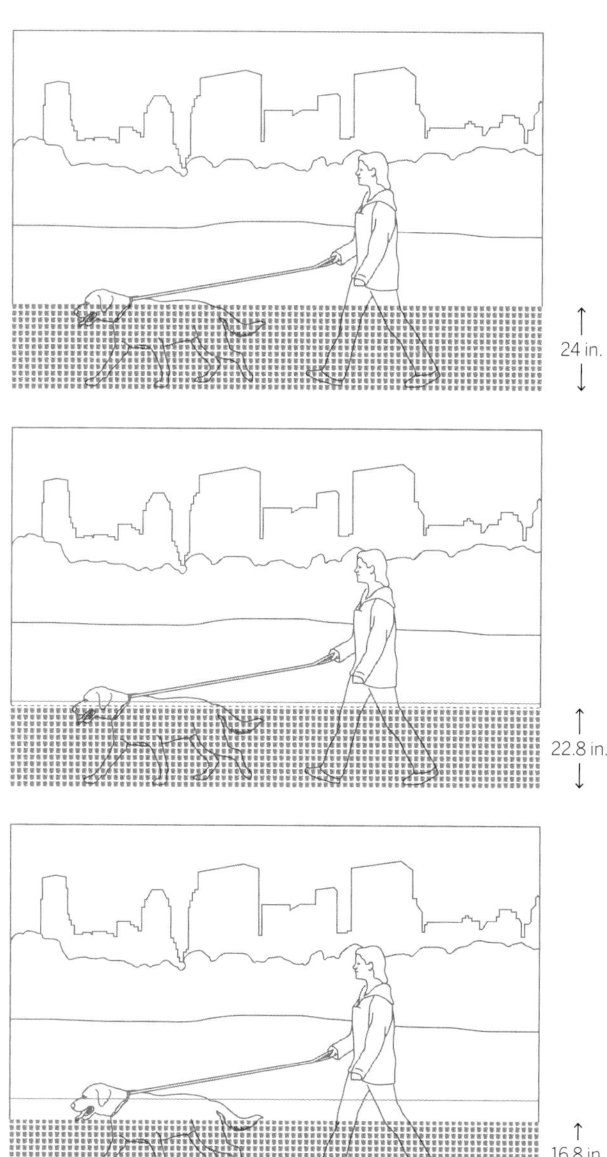

This story doesn't guarantee success, but it's a hell of a lot more engaging and impressive than projecting standard spreadsheet charts and reading the data in them—or, worse, reading bullet points verbatim. Notice how little you've said about the data itself; instead you focus incessantly on helping the audience understand the idea, which is not simply that 18 billion coffee pods were thrown away. The idea is that *the popularity of single-serve coffee creates a major waste problem that current recycling efforts can't begin to address—but we can.* The number 18 billion is big enough and abstract enough that simply stating it can't possibly convey its meaning in terms of objects. Imagery, relatable points of reference, and a narrative arc conspire to make that abstract number tangible.

You're sparking viewers' brains so that they'll understand the idea better, engage with it more, and remember it in a way they otherwise wouldn't. Even when charts are perfectly executed, to truly engage an audience, the play's the thing.

RECAP

PRESENT TO PERSUADE

Beyond manipulating charts themselves, you can make visualizations more effective by improving your presentation skills. The twin challenges here are to help viewers when they first see the visual (how you present it to them) and to help them process it (how you get them to engage with it).

PRESENTATION TIPS

- **Show the chart and stop talking.**
  A good chart will speak for itself. Let the viewers' active visual systems work without distractions.

- **Don't read the picture.**
  Talk about the ideas in the chart, not its structure.

- **For unusual visual forms, guide the audience.**
  Don't read the picture, but do provide some brief explanation of how the form works.

- **Use reference charts.**
  Companion visuals that show "ideal" or "average" cases can add context and make your chart easier to understand.

- **When you have something important to say, turn off your chart.**
  As long as a visual is displayed, viewers will look more than listen. If you want them to hear you, turn off the screen for a moment to refocus them.

- **Show something simple. Leave behind something more detailed.** Use the simplest forms possible in presentations, but create versions with more information that audience members can spend time with on their own.

ENGAGEMENT TIPS

- **Create tension.**
  Before revealing a full visual, show parts of it and ask the audience to speculate on what it will ultimately show.

- **Use time.**
  To make an audience grasp large values, reveal them gradually.

- **Zoom in or out.**
  To give viewers a sense of scale, start with a relatable value and then increase or decrease the scale step by step to show the value you want them to understand.

- **Bait and switch.**
  Lure viewers in with a visual they may expect to see and then show them the actual version, which contradicts expectations.

- **Deconstruct and reconstruct.**
  Break down a visualization into multiple, simpler charts and then put it back together for the audience.

- **Tell stories.**
  Use the dramatic structure of setup, conflict, and resolution to make a chart or several charts tell a short story.

CHAPTER 9

VISUAL CRIT

HOW TO PRACTICE LOOKING AT (AND MAKING) GOOD CHARTS

GOOD WRITERS ARE GREAT READERS. They look to others' work for ideas and borrow (okay, steal) from what inspires them. Creators in general approach their craft this way, and visualization is no exception. One of the best ways to get better at making charts is to look at, and think about, a lot of them.

Good news: there's a surplus available. It's hard to be on the internet for a hot minute without stumbling on some dataviz that's going viral. If you follow #dataviz or visit any number of visualization-heavy websites (The Upshot on the *New York Times* website, for example, or *The Economist*, which tweets many charts every day), you'll find plenty of fodder.

But don't just pick ones you like or you think look cool. Find simple ones. Boring ones. Complex, artful ones. Ones on topics you know nothing about. Look at each one with a purpose. Do you get it? What do you like? What don't you like? Deconstruct technique. Think of ways you might have approached the chart differently. Re-create it in your own way.

This doesn't have to feel like homework. It can be done casually and quickly. Here's a way to learn from others' work or to take a fresh look at your own.

1. Make a note of the first few things you see. We know we see first whatever stands out. So document the first element your eyes focus on? A "spike"? "Blue bars"? It may be more impressionistic: "A long smooth line," or "pick-up sticks crossing over each other all over the place." What you wouldn't see first is "interest rates going up in the past few fiscal quarters." That kind of content focus requires some parsing of the idea beyond what first hits the eyes. Here you want to get at that initial, instantaneous visual perception.

2. Make a note of the first idea that forms in your mind and then search for more. You've looked at the chart for a few seconds now. What is it trying to tell you? Here's where you might say, "It tells me interest rates are going up, and fast." Ask critical questions about this idea you've formed: "Does it match the chart's intent?" "Is the chart misleading or is something missing?" After your initial impression, study it; see if you can find deeper narratives, or if more questions arise the longer you look at it.

3. Make notes on likes, dislikes, and wish-I-saws. Don't focus on what you think is wrong or right. We've spent plenty of time debunking that binary thinking. Just focus on the feeling you get. "I don't like all the labels." "I like how they used gray for the background information." "I wish I saw this in comparison to last year." Sometimes these gut feelings are reactions to what makes a chart successful or signal what may be improved. If you follow this process long enough, you'll find that you react consistently to certain elements; you'll discover both common missteps and your own aesthetic. Under "dislikes," note possibly misleading or inaccurate portrayals of data and ideas: "I don't like the y-axis truncation, because it exaggerates the trend." "I don't like cutting the data off before 1990, because it hides important historical data."

4. Find three things you'd change and briefly say why. "Say why" is the crucial bit. Your reason should ultimately improve the chart's effectiveness. "Because I don't like blue" is thin reasoning. "Because the blue is hard to see with the yellow right next to it" is better. Limit yourself to three changes—that will force you to prioritize the most important ones. If you made a list of ten things you'd change, you'd end up quibbling over the pixel weight of grid lines, or whether the subtitle should occupy two lines rather than three. The aim here is to focus on what will help the main ideas shine through.

5. Sketch and/or prototype your own version, and critique yourself. Revisualizing is the most powerful way to learn. The before-and-after comparison helps you see whether what you thought would make a chart better actually does. If you have a data set, great. Otherwise, create a simple spreadsheet with estimates of the key values. (If it's a conceptual visualization, you don't need anything; just start.) Value speed over precision here, as you do when you sketch and prototype your own dataviz. The self-critique will attach what you've learned about what works and what doesn't work to your effort. Try to include both positives and negatives in your self-critique.

CRIT I

Here's an example showing this process in action. I found this chart online:

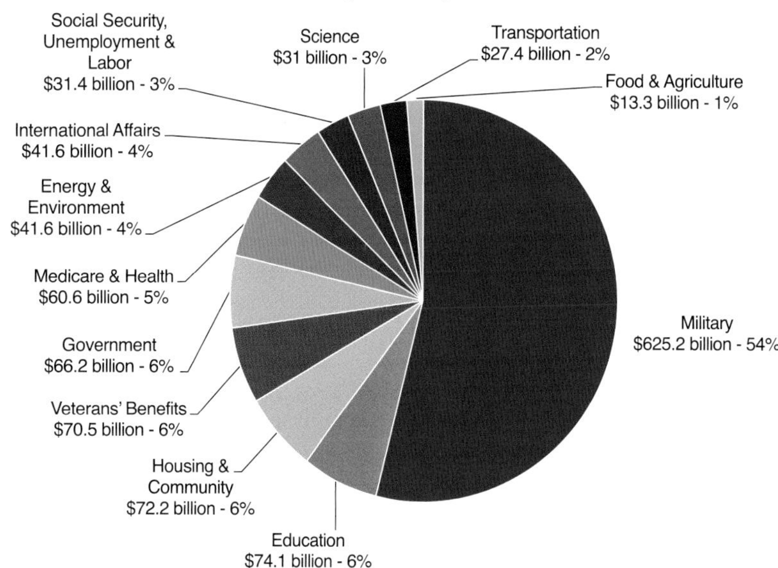

1. Make a note of the first few things you see.

- big blue wedge
- a bunch of little slices
- lots of lines and labels

2. Make a note of the first idea that forms in your mind and then search for more.

- Military is bigger than everything else. That idea came to me almost immediately. Military is bigger than everything else *combined*. That came after looking and thinking for a bit longer. "Everything else" isn't visualized as a singular entity, so I wasn't immediately led in that direction—already I'm thinking about how to make that idea pop more immediately.
- It occurs to me after looking for about 20 seconds that this is only *proposed* discretionary spending. I assumed that this is what the government spends, but that's not right. It's proposed spending, and it's not the entire budget—just the discretionary part. Even though the pie makes it feel like a whole, it's actually part of something bigger.

3. Make notes on likes, dislikes, and wish-I-saws.

Like	Dislike	Wish I saw
Showing dollar values	Labels are too busy for me. Need percentages? Simplify wording?	Non-discretionary spending
The way military dominates and is offset (because I think that's the point?)	All those lines	Categories
Colorful	Colors, order of small slices uses descending value clockwise, but feels random by type of spending	More pointed headline?

Your list may be longer or shorter depending on the complexity and execution of the chart. If the "like" column is long and the "dislike" column short, you're probably looking at a good chart. You could stop the process here and save the chart in a "good charts" folder (with the notes on what you liked) for later reference. The charts that you find yourself picking apart will be ripe for reimagining.

4. Find three things you'd change and briefly say why.

- Group spending by categories so that people can quickly get a sense of proportion for what *type* of spending. Most of the slices are small, and in comparison to military look roughly the same, so categories might be a more useful way to look at differences. I could group everything into one "all other" group, but that seems too simple.
- Somehow add mandatory spending so that people have a sense of the overall government budget. It's one data point that adds a lot of context for what we're talking about in budget debates.
- Try a form other than a pie. I don't like pies with more than a few slices total. Also, if I'm intent on adding mandatory spending, that slice might dominate and make the others even thinner. Possible forms that come to mind are a treemap and proportional bars.

Notice how, even when I'm unsure whether my hypothesis is right, I try to justify why I'd make each change. The goal isn't to assert that I can make a better chart, full stop. I'm just trying to improve, and I may discover through the exercise that I was wrong. That's OK. That's still instructive. Sometimes your changes will come straight from your "wish I saw" list, but not always. You may decide that what you wish you saw doesn't rise to this level of importance.

5. Sketch and/or prototype your own version, and critique yourself. I decided to try a treemap. A website called Raw allows for rapid prototyping of treemaps.[1] Once I'd imported the simple budget data spreadsheet, prototyping took just a few minutes. It was so quick that I tried two versions, one without mandatory spending and one with:

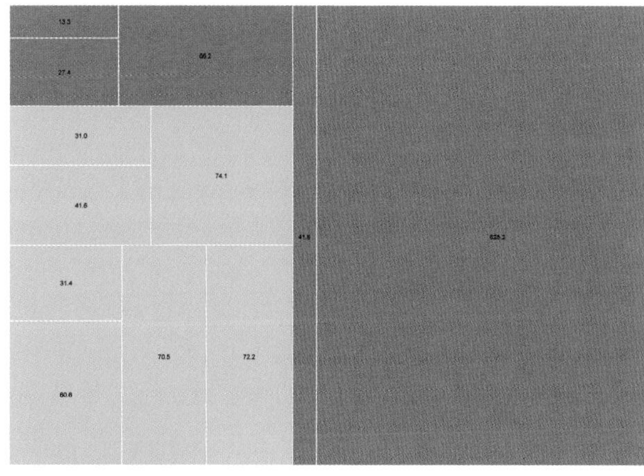

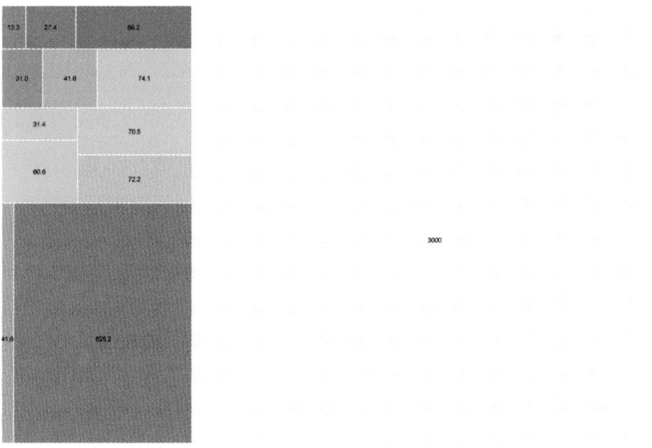

The budget data prototyped, first showing only discretionary spending, and second adding in the mandatory spending in light pink.

Self-critique: I think both could be made more effective than the pie chart. Which of these would I use in a presentation? That depends on context. Seeing how much of the budget is untouchable puts the spending that politicians argue over in perspective, and the military chunk still pops as much larger than everything else. (Making mandatory spending light pink also sends a signal about what to focus on and what is secondary information here.)

But mandatory spending *is* untouchable, so in some ways it doesn't matter to any discussion about spending. In that context, the mandatory piece will distract from that conversation.

In either case, I think the categorization is what most improves the chart for me. What was a bunch of slim, similar pie wedges in a rainbow of colors is now four usefully distinct categories of spending. I've preserved those original distinctions as separate pieces in the same color for anyone who wants to spend more time thinking about more specific allocations, but I've de-emphasized them by not giving each component a unique color.

To test my theory that categorization is what clarifies the visual for me, I made another prototype, color-coded by each piece of the budget, as in the original pie chart:

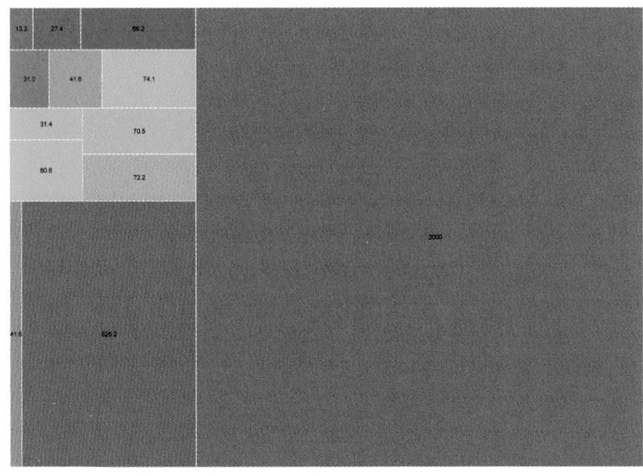

This suffers from the same busyness as the original. Military spending pops, yes, but so many different colors are required that the distinctions aren't easy to use as reference points, and they don't feel meaningful.

Another critique: regardless of color, the treemap creates labeling challenges I haven't fully worked out. Should I use a key? Try to label each piece? But that's as far as I'll take this one. You don't need to produce a final visualization when you practice. You just want to test your ideas until you see that you've made something better—or not.

CRIT 2

Here's one presented without commentary. The original chart:

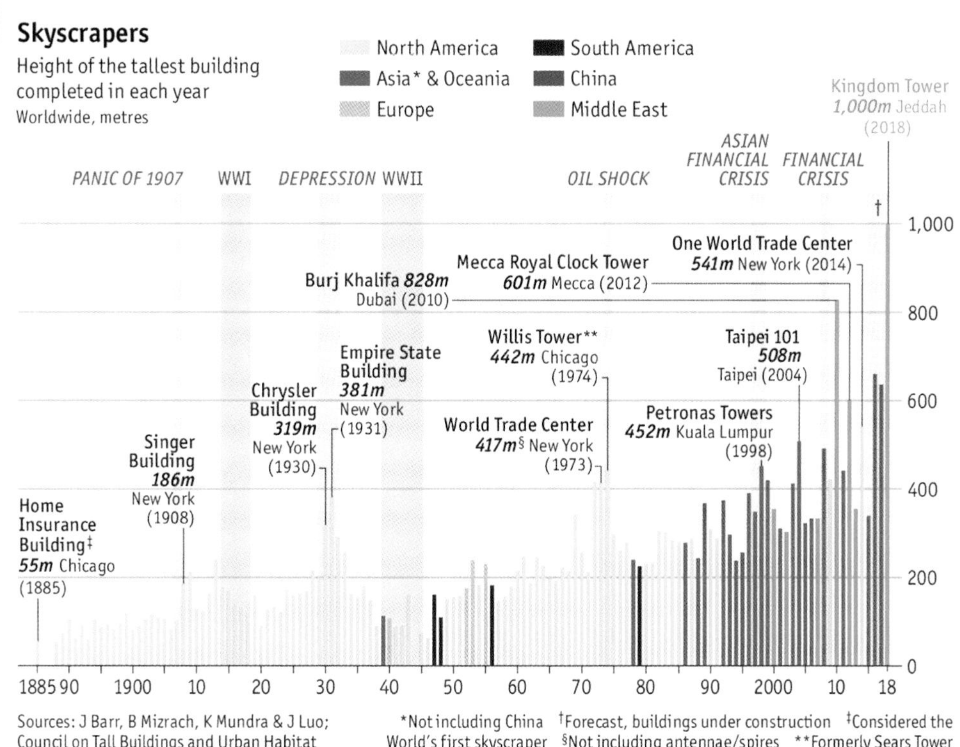

1. Make a note of what you see first.

- Chrysler Building and Empire State Building
- Many stripes, salmon-colored ones especially
- Blue, then lots of colors

2. Make a note of the first idea that forms in your mind and then search for more.

- All the tall buildings used to be in North America, and now they're not. I got that pretty quickly from the color. But if I'm supposed to be able to think about who's building tall buildings now, that's harder to see, because the colors are so various. It reads to me like North America and Everywhere Else unless I work at it.
- There's an amazing surge in the height of the tallest buildings right now. It's hard to pick up, though, because heavy labels and lines and stripes denoting eras drown it out.
- Those stripes denoting important world events may be meant to tell me something about the height of buildings during that time, but the more I look at them, the more random they seem.

3. Make notes on likes, dislikes, and wish-I-saws.

Like	Dislike	Wish I saw
Thin lines, feels like skyscrapers, gives sense of great height	Era demarcations heavy and overpowering	Less stuff overall
Labeling important buildings	Pointers, y-axis grid heavy, labels redundant (year)	Catchier title?
Using color to denote location	Color choice makes it hard to quickly pick location in recent times	Some point of reference for height, hugeness
Y-axis on right for easier reference of tallest buildings	Footnotes and symbols confuse me	

4. Find three things you'd change and briefly say why.

- Eliminate the demarcations for eras. It's not clear what they add, and they definitely make it harder for me to see the progression of tall buildings.
- Work on labels. Make them simpler so that they don't overpower the bars. No elbows in pointers. Make labels less intrusive in the visual field. Lighten the grid lines.
- Color. Find a way to make color more instructive at a glance. Combine China with Asia?

5. Sketch and/or prototype your own version, and critique yourself.

Self-critique: I like how simple my prototype (on the facing page) feels. I don't miss the era demarcations. A key breakthrough was dividing the labels into milestones that run neatly aligned along the bottom and landmarks in the visual field. This helped solve the busyness of so many labels in one space. Also, the labels in the field escalate in an echo of the visual itself. Removing some belt-and-suspenders design with the labels also helped. I haven't addressed the problem that some of these buildings are "projected heights" rather than completed structures. And I don't think I've solved the color puzzle at all. I want to ask a professional designer what she would do to make so many lines that require so many colors render as clearly distinct. Finally, I wish the chart included some point of reference to get a sense of just how astonishingly high 1,000 meters actually reaches. Could it be included without cluttering? I could keep going, but I'll stop this one here.

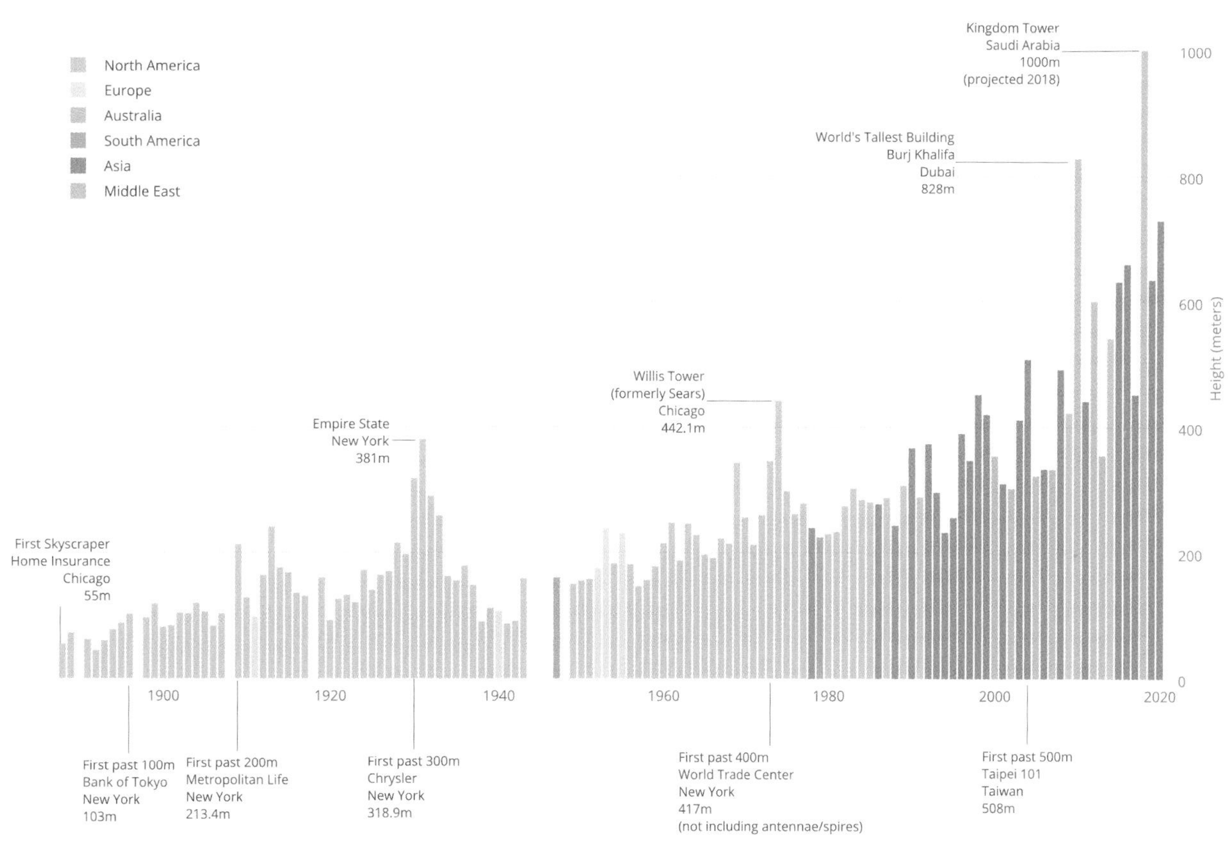

CRIT 3

Another: The original chart was a proposed design for a dashboard that would show the performance of videos on a website.

1. Make a note of what you see first.

- Gradient bars, cold to hot
- "Lollipop" numbers
- Tick marks/labels

2. Make a note of the first idea that forms in your mind and then search for more.

- Right side is good and left side is bad. Performance that's "hot" is what we're looking for. That's a pretty clear metaphor, and the colors are right on for that.
- Percentile ranks mean this is putting video in context of other videos. It's not a raw score or temperature. Conflicting metaphor?
- This video did well. The lollipops are all clearly to the right on the red side, so I'm looking at something that performed well above average on all measures shown. I have to read a bit to know what each comparison is, and on which comparisons it was exceptional versus just just above average, but I get that this is in general a good score or grade.
- What's the overall score? It took me a moment to realize the first score against all other videos served essentially as an overall score, while the others are finer cuts on the analytics. It makes me wonder about the relative value of each ranking. They are presented equally, does that mean I should focus on them as all equally important or valuable rankings?

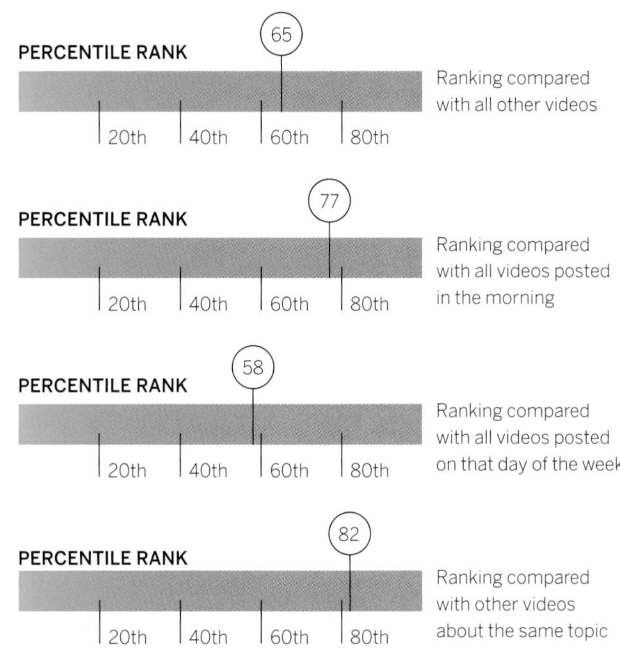

3. Make notes on likes, dislikes, and wish-I-saws.

Like	Dislike	Wish I saw
How quickly I get the idea at a glance	Key info small and not quickly apparent	Maybe overall guidelines, e.g. "average" line or "poor/excellent" performer line, for each or for all
Simple one-axis	Percentile ticks too prominent?	Overall score shown as different, more prominent?
Callout of key figure in lollipop	Repetition draws away from key metrics	
Hot/cold metaphor		

4. Find three things you'd change and briefly say why.

- Make what each category measures much more prominent. I don't have to work to get at each score, but then I have to reference a caption to know what that score refers to.
- Increase the prominence of the lollipop and decrease the prominence of the gradient scale. I like the metaphor, but I wonder if it's necessary. It doesn't add new information; it repeats what horizontal placement of the lollipop already tells us.
- Reduce repetition, volume of labels. When I've seen "percentile rank" once, I think that's enough. Do the scales need to be divided into fifths?

5. Sketch and/or prototype your own version, and critique yourself.

Self-critique. Despite my initial fondness for the gradient "heat" scale, I eliminated it in my prototype (on the following page). Since horizontal position immediately conveys performance level, the gradient, though a nice metaphorical flourish, was redundant and

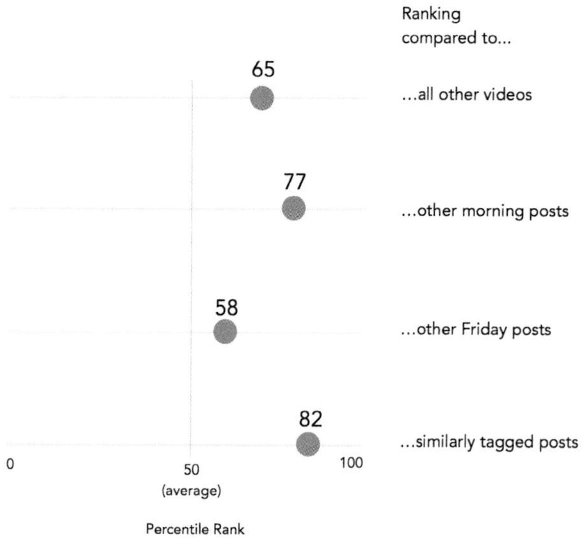

in some ways fought for attention with the more important information: percentile rank. The scale itself seemed to overwhelm the data plotted on the scale, so I reluctantly parted with it.

I'm happy with how much redundancy was eliminated (the quintile marks, individual labels for each plot). This version creates white space such that the eye immediately goes to the four points. I can imagine using other reference points in future iterations, such as a target goal percentile rank, or qualitative ones, such as a line for "excellent" performance.

I haven't distinguished overall performance here; I would take that on in the next pass. I also wonder about looking at many—maybe dozens—of these scales simultaneously as small multiples to compare videos against one another. Would the dots start to run together? Would I stack them vertically, aligned so that you could see their relative rankings more easily? I'm not sure. It's something to consider. But I'm convinced that as a dashboard element for checking on an individual video's performance, this is an improvement on the original.

Some readers may scoff at my revisions to the charts here. I hope they do (politely). I hope readers take it upon themselves to improve my versions with their own. I hope they try different visual forms, change colors, and find elegant ways to reintroduce elements that I removed if they think they're important.

Workshop sessions like this are not unlike the "crit" sessions creative types endure in their schooling and professional work. Designers, notably, gather to evaluate a peer's work, with the peer present, in order to help him improve it. Editing is a formal, institutional type of critical review that writers need to make their work publishable.

Even for professionals who welcome crit because they know that it makes their work appreciably better, the process can be brutally unpleasant.[2] No matter how much we tell ourselves it's not, the criticism often feels deeply, intimately personal.

Like any other creative effort, information visualization has incorporated critique from the start. Willard Brinton was dismissing poor charting techniques in his 1914 book *Graphic Methods for Presenting Facts.* Edward Tufte dared to suggest that bad chart design hid information that might have spurred NASA to cancel the doomed *Challenger* launch. Even today, much of the science devoted to visualization is focused on the *right* and *wrong* ways to visualize.

All this is useful and necessary, but something is happening now that makes it problematic: Visual critiques are broadcast across the web, often on social media. These public displays can feel like shaming rather than learning.

Crit as a practice is usually done in person, in small groups, sometimes one-on-one. What's happening with dataviz now isn't that.

In an excellent, important essay on visualization critique, dataviz pioneers Martin Wattenberg and Fernanda Viégas address how the internet and ubiquitous publishing make viz critique a coarser, more brutal thing:

> All redesigns have the potential to seem adversarial, as if the critic is pointing out flaws in the designer personally, asserting their own superior skill . . . We need more criticism, and redesign is an essential part of visualization criticism. But with so much of it happening on the web—in public, instantly in view of everyone involved, available to the world without context or preparation—it can be a difficult process.[3]

This is a major reason why many nonexperts find the dataviz community intimidating and unwelcoming. There's a real fear of failing publicly. Wattenberg and Viégas accept that public crit won't stop, so they propose some smart, common-sense rules for critiquing charts in the public sphere: document things you see that work well, not just what you think falls short; have a reason for proposing changes; respect one another.

I would add to their list avoid the pejorative. Don't call a chart "ugly" or "a mess"; say, "The colors are distracting" or "I'm not sure where to focus." When I critique, I find myself reflexively adding phrases such as "to me it seems . . ." or "doesn't work for me"—acknowledgments that others won't always agree with me, and my critique won't always be right; it, too, should be open to critique.

Above all, don't approach someone else's chart with the mind-set that you will *fix* it—that you will get *right* what they got *wrong*. Think of it instead as a chance to improve your skills. If you do publish your revised version, do it collegially—and be prepared for a critique of your critique.

And no matter how hard it may sometimes be, remember, as Wattenberg and Viégas say, "none of this is a personal evaluation, but instead a way for the field as a whole to improve."

RECAP

VISUAL CRIT

Just as good writers are great readers, good chart makers are great at mining other people's visualizations for inspiration and instruction. One of the best ways to get better at making charts is to look at and think about a lot of them. Critique, or crit, sessions are a common feature of design, writing, and many other creative jobs.

First pick out some charts to evaluate. Don't pick only ones that you like or you think look cool. Pick all different kinds. Simple ones. Boring ones. Complex, artful ones. Ones on topics you know nothing about. Then follow this simple process for critiquing and workshopping them:

1. Make a note of the first few things you see.
Don't think—react. What stands out? Is it a peak? A color? Lots of words?

2. Make a note of the first idea that forms in your mind and then search for more.
Decide what idea you think is being conveyed. Does it match the chart's seeming intent? Is the chart misleading? Is something missing?

3. Make notes on likes, dislikes, and wish-I-saws.
Don't focus on what you think is *right* or *wrong*. Instead, think about your gut reaction to the visual, the feeling you get. Do you like the use of gray? Do you not like how many labels there are? Do you wish you saw more historical context from previous years?

4. Find three things you'd change and briefly say why.
Limit them to three so that you're forced to prioritize only the most important changes. Saying "why" is key to making sure you focus on effectiveness rather than taste. "Because I don't like blue" is not a good reason to make a change. "Because it's hard to see blue next to yellow" is.

5. Sketch and/or prototype your own version, and critique yourself.
Just as when you sketch and prototype your own dataviz, value speed over precision here. Include both positives and negatives in your self-critique.

CONCLUSION

KEEP GOING

IN SOME WAYS, *data visualization* is a terrible term. It reduces the idea of good charts to a mechanical procedure. It evokes the tools and methodology required to create rather than the creation itself. It's like calling *Moby-Dick* a "word sequentialization" or *Starry Night* a "pigment distribution."

It also reflects an ongoing obsession in the dataviz world with process over outcomes. Even now, most of the energy poured into teaching dataviz focuses on making sure you do it the "right" way or judging you if you do it the "wrong" way; on picking the right form; on when to use what colors. Chart crit is all about technique, how the thing was built, what it looks like.

Enough of all that. Forget right charts and wrong charts. Data is only a middleman between phenomena and your ideas about them.[1] And visualization is merely a procedure, a way of using that middleman to communicate ideas that convey much more than just pictures of statistics. What we do, really, when we make good charts is get at some truth and move people to feel that truth: To see what couldn't be seen before. To change minds. To cause action. It's not data visualization so much as visual rhetoric: the art of graphical discourse.

A common understanding of some basic grammar is necessary to that, of course. We all need to use subjects and verbs in roughly the same way if we're to communicate. But letting them govern our communication would be paralyzing and counter-productive. When you obsess on the minutiae of visualization rules—or, worse, when you judge a chart according to its relative adherence to those rules—you become one of Emerson's little statesmen, adoring foolish consistencies.

Besides, software is beginning to take care of all that for you. Tools are evolving to manage some of the grammar.[2] They're getting their own versions of document templates, spell check, and grammar check to guide formatting decisions and correct common missteps. Decisions about color, labels, grid lines, even what chart type to use—decisions to which entire books and courses have been devoted—are being encoded into visualization software so that the output in its default state is at least pretty good.

Interactivity helps too. The number and type of labels to include in a visualization, for example, is a decision that we're used to making as we construct charts, and it can be difficult. Too many labels create clutter, making it hard to know where to focus; not enough confuse viewers and, likewise, make choosing the proper focus a challenge. But hover states help solve the problem. Toggles manage complexity by showing or hiding variables as needed. A simple Next button can control the pace at which information is added or removed from a visualization.

If you want a peek at the future of data visualization—at least, the mechanical process of it—look at *The Atlas of Economic Complexity*, an interactive site codeveloped by Harvard and MIT and managed by

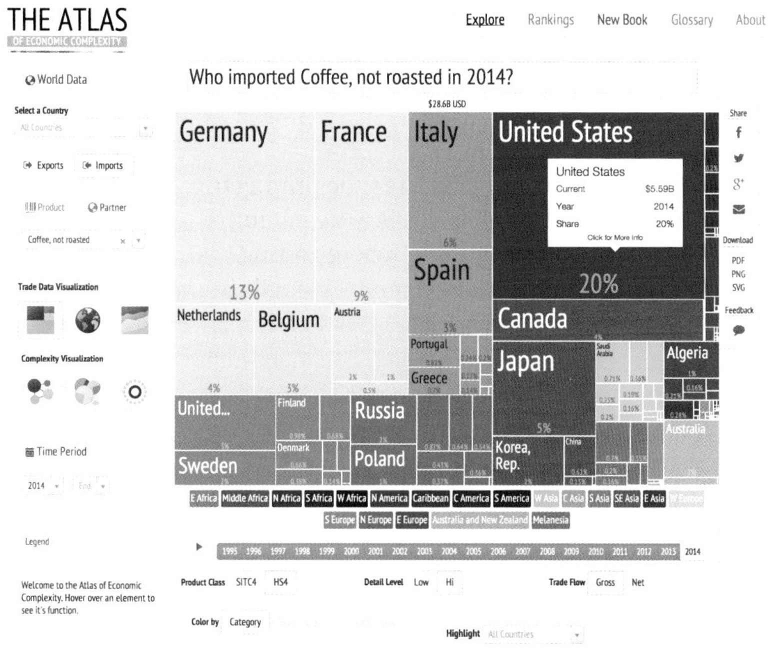

The Atlas of Economic Complexity points to a future in which presentation-worthy visualization becomes inherently collaborative.

Harvard's Center for International Development.[3] Shown above is a tree map generated by the site.

Notice that the color scheme logically groups continents. I didn't have to do that. That's built into the application. Labeling is clear and sized appropriately—again, automatically generated. More detail is available on hover, and I have used multiple toggles to adjust what I see. This is on demand exploratory visualization, and automated declarative visualization. All I have to do is find the idea I want to convey, the story I want to tell, and iterate until I have it.

In short, visualization tools are evolving to make everything *available* but not always *visible*. That cracks things wide open. It changes a visualization's essential nature from *imparted* to *shared*; from a transaction—something you present or hand over—to a collaboration, which you work on and adjust with others.

Visualization is becoming fundamentally more interactive. In the near future we'll take for granted that decisions about what to show or where to focus—decisions you once had to make ahead of time and commit to—can be handled at the moment the dataviz is seen, often by the user. And those decisions will be alterable. Users will control the pace of the storytelling. Depth and complexity will become on-demand services. *Show me more. Show me less. Show me just this. Show me only that.* In a presentation, a manager will display a good chart and then filter and adjust it when the CEO asks, "What does that curve look like if we exclude the younger demographic?" A new good chart will immediately appear on the screen. "Now just show me how women responded." Presentations will become conversations, exploratory dataviz in the boardroom.

Charles Hooper is a dataviz consultant who works mostly with Tableau these days, but he used to work in Excel and remembers using Lotus 1-2-3, Harvard Graphics, and a program called Brio. Before that, he hand-drew his visualizations, transferred them to acetate, and displayed them with an overhead projector. "I'm turning 70 next week," he declares.

"And right now, I'm telling you, this is the most exciting time, because it's getting easy to try things. When it's not easy, people just follow the specs. But you make it easy, put it in the hands of the masses, give it to businesspeople and not just specialists like me, and they come up with really innovative ways of looking at things. I learn something new every day from people trying out visualization."

Software will continue to get better, in the ways we can already see and in ways we can't yet imagine. But what it won't do—what it can't do—is intuit your context. And context, still, is everything.

Visual thinking and visual communication will become no less relevant no matter what features are added to software programs. If anything, the better the software gets, and the less you need to stress over the number of ticks you put on your x-axis, the freer you will be to focus on the ideas you want to communicate. The process of understanding your context, finding your main idea, and visualizing it persuasively—that is, the guts of this book—will be the most critical skills you can develop.

You are here, at the end, which means you've started. Now keep going.

GLOSSARY

2 × 2 matrix: Box bisected horizontally and vertically to create four quadrants. Often used to illustrate a typology based on two variables, such as the Four Types chart presented in this book. (Also called a *matrix*.)

+ Easy-to-use organizing principle for categorizing elements and creating "zones"
- Plotting items within quadrants at different spatial intervals suggests a statistical relationship that likely doesn't exist

Alluvial diagram: Nodes and streams show how values move from one point to another. Often used to show changes over time or details in how values are organized, such as how budget allocations are spent month by month. (Also called a *flow diagram*.)

+ Exposes detail in value changes or exposes detailed breakdowns in broad categories of data
- Many values and changes in flow make for complex, crisscrossed visuals that, while pretty, may be difficult to interpret

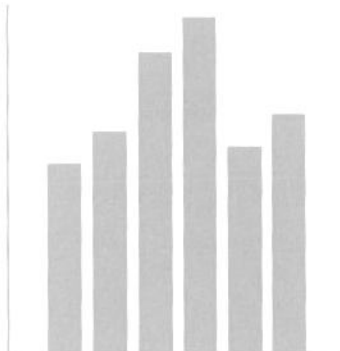

Bar chart: Height or length of bars shows relationship between categories ("categorical data"). Often used to compare discrete groups on the same measure, such as salaries of ten different CEOs. (Also called a *column chart* when bars are vertical.)

+ Familiar form that's universally understood; great for simple comparisons between categories
- Many bars may create the impression of a trend line rather than highlight discrete values; multiple groups of bars may become difficult to parse

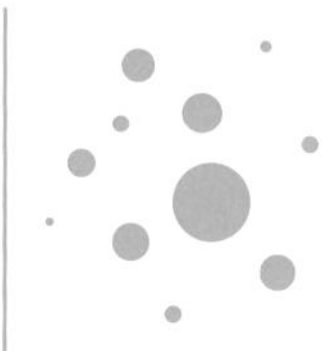

Bubble chart: Dots scattered along two measures that add a third (size of bubble) and sometimes fourth (color of bubble) dimension to the data to show distributions of several variables. Often used to show complex relationships, such as multiple pieces of demographic data plotted by country. (Also called, erroneously, a *scatter plot*, which typically doesn't contain a third or fourth dimension.)

+ One of the simplest ways to incorporate a "z-axis"; bubble sizes can add crucial context to distribution visuals
- Sizing bubbles proportionally is tricky (area is not proportional to radius); by their nature, three- and four-axis charts require more time to parse, so are less ideal for at-a-glance presentation

Bump chart: Lines show change in ordinal rank over time. Often used to show popularity, such as box office rankings week to week. (Also called a *bumps chart*.)

+ Simple way to express popularity, winners, and losers
- Changes aren't statistically significant (values are ordinal, not cardinal); many levels and more change make for eye-catching skeins but may make it difficult to follow rankings

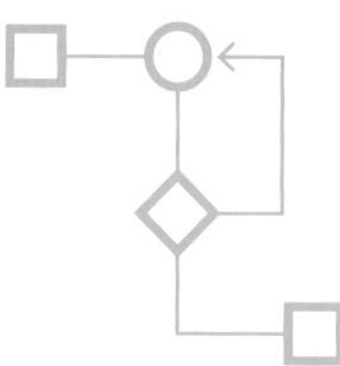

Flow chart: Polygons and arrows arranged to show a process or workflow. Often used to map out decision making, how data moves through a system, or how people interact with systems, such as the process a user goes through to buy a product on a website. (Also called a *decision tree*, which is one type of flow chart.)

+ Formalized system, universally accepted, for representing a process with many decision points
- Must understand established syntax (e.g., diamonds represent decision points; parallelograms represent input/output, etc.)

Geographical chart: Maps used to represent values attributed to locations in the physical world. Often used to compare values between countries or regions, such as a map showing political affiliations. (Also called a *map*.)

+ Familiarity with geography makes it easy to find values and compare them at multiple levels (i.e., comparing data by country and region simultaneously)
- Using the size of places to represent other values can over- or underrepresent the value encoded in those places

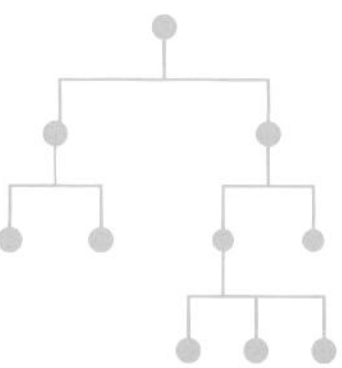

Hierarchical chart: Lines and points used to show the relationship and relative rank of a collection of elements. Often used to show how an organization is structured, such as a family or a company. (Also called an *org chart,* a *family tree,* or a *tree chart,* all of which are types of hierarchies.)

+ Easily understood method for documenting and illustrating relationships and complex structures
- Line-and-box approach limited in the amount of complexity it can show; harder to show less formal relationships such as how people work together outside the bounds of a corporate hierarchy

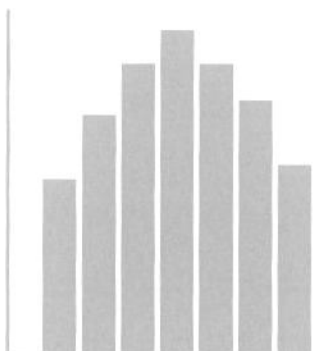

Histogram: Bars show distribution based on the frequency of occurrences for each value in a range. Often used to show probability, such as the results of a risk-analysis simulation. (Also called, erroneously, a *bar chart,* which compares values between categories, whereas a histogram shows the distribution of values for one variable.)

+ A fundamental chart type used to show statistical distribution and probability
- Audiences sometimes mistake a histogram for a bar chart

Line chart: Connected points show how values change, usually over time (continuous data). Often used to compare trends by plotting multiple lines together, such as revenues for several companies. (Also called a *fever chart* or a *trend line.*)

+ Familiar form that's universally understood; great for at-a-glance representation of trends
- Focusing on the trend line makes it harder to see and talk about discrete data points; too many trend lines make it difficult to see any individual line

Metaphorical chart: Arrows, pyramids, circles, and other well-recognized figures used to show a nonstatistical concept. Often used to represent abstract ideas and processes, such as business cycles.

+ Can simplify complex ideas; universal recognition of metaphors makes understanding feel innate
- Easy to mix metaphors, misapply them, or overdesign them

Network diagram: Nodes and lines connected to show the relationship between elements within a group. Often used to show interconnectedness of physical things, such as computers or people.

+ Helps illustrate relationships between nodes that might otherwise be hard to see; highlights clusters and outliers
- Networks tend to get complex quickly. Some network diagrams, while beautiful, can become difficult to interpret

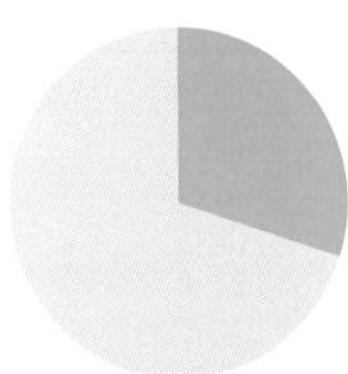

Pie chart: A circle divided into sections that each represent some variable's proportion of the whole value. Often used to show simple breakdowns of totals, such as population demographics. (Also called a *donut chart*, a variation shown as a ring.)

+ Ubiquitous chart type; shows dominant versus nondominant shares well
- People don't estimate the area of pie wedges very well; more than a few slices makes values hard to distinguish and quantify

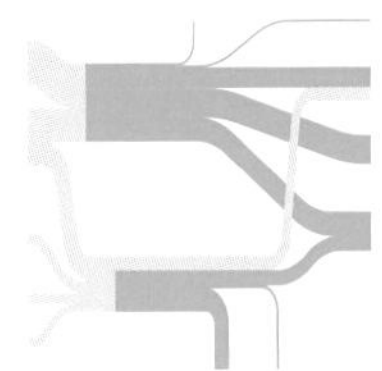

Sankey diagram: Arrows or bars show how values are distributed and transferred. Often used to show the flow of physical quantities, such as energy or people. (Also called a *flow diagram*.)

+ Exposes detail in system flows; helps identify dominant components and inefficiencies
- Complex systems with many components and flow paths make for complex diagrams

Scatter plot: Dots plotted against two variables show the relationship between those two variables for a particular set of data. Often used to detect and show correlation, such as a plot of people's ages against their incomes. (Also called a *scatter diagram*, *scatter chart*, or *scatter*.)

+ A basic chart type that most people are familiar with; spatial approach makes it easy to see correlation, negative correlation, clusters, and outliers
- Shows correlation so well that people may make a causal leap even though correlation doesn't imply causation

Slope chart: Lines show a simple change in values. Often used to show dramatic change or outliers that run counter to most of the slopes, such as revenues falling in one region while rising in all others. (Also called a *line chart*.)

+ Creates a simple before-and-after narrative that's easy to see and grasp either for individual values or as an aggregate trend for many values
- Excludes all detail of what happened to the values between the two states; too many crisscrossing lines may make it hard to see changes in individual values

Small multiples: A series of small charts, usually line charts, that show different categories measured on the same scale. Often used to show simple trends dozens of times over, such as GDP trends by country. (Also called *grid charts* or *trellis charts*.)

+ Makes simple comparisons across multiple, even dozens, of categories more accessible than if all the lines were stacked in one chart
- Without dramatic change or difference, can be hard to find meaning in the comparison; some "events" you'd see in a single chart, such as crossover points between variables, are lost

Stacked area chart: Lines plot a particular variable over time, and the area between lines is filled with color to emphasize volume or cumulative totals. Often used to show multiple values proportionally over time, such as product sales volume for several products over the course of a year. (Also called an *area chart*.)

+ Shows changing proportions over time well; emphasizes a sense of volume or accumulation
- Too many "layers" create slices so thin it's hard to see changes or differences or track values over time

Stacked bar chart: Rectangles divided into sections that each represent some variable's proportion to the whole. Often used to show simple breakdowns of totals, such as sales by region. (Also called a *proportional bar chart*.)

+ Some consider it a superior alternative to a pie chart; shows dominant versus nondominant shares well; may effectively handle more categories than a pie chart; works horizontally and vertically
- Including too many categories or grouping multiple stacked bars together may make it difficult to see differences and changes

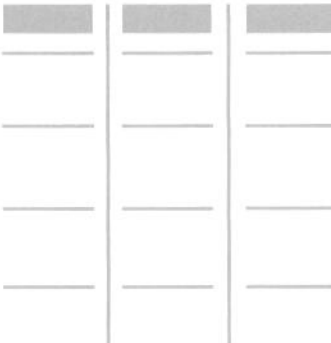

Table: Information arranged in columns and rows. Often used to show individual values over time across multiple categories, such as quarterly financial performance.

+ Makes every individual value available; easier to read and compare values than a prose version of the same information
- Difficult to get an at-a-glance sense of trends or to make quick comparisons between groups of values

Treemap: A rectangle divided into smaller rectangles that each represent some variable's proportion to the whole value. Often used to show hierarchical proportions, such as a budget divided into categories and subcategories.

+ Compact form for showing detailed proportional breakdowns; overcomes some limitations of pie charts with many slices
- Detail-oriented form not optimal for at-a-glance understanding; too many categories makes for a stunning but harder-to-parse visual; usually requires software capable of accurately arranging the squares.

Unit chart: Dots or icons arranged to represent collections of individual values associated with categorical variables. Often used to show tallies of physical items, such as dollars spent or people stricken in an epidemic. (Also called a *dot chart* or *dot plot*.)

+ Represents values in a way that feels more concrete, less abstract than some statistical representations
- Too many unit categories may make it hard to focus on central meaning; strong design skills needed to make arrangement of units most effective

NOTES

Introduction

1. The socialization of marketing and the consumerization of technology, two ideas that can be applied to what's happening to data visualizations, come from the work of Josh Bernoff. See Charlene Li and Josh Bernoff, *Groundswell* (Harvard Business Review Press, 2008, rev. ed. 2011); and Josh Bernoff and Ted Schadler, *Empowered* (Harvard Business Review Press, 2010).

2. See hotshotcharts.com. Basketball analytics are a hotbed of advanced visualization because basketball has become a hotbed of advanced statistics.

3. Edward Tufte's books are considered canonical in terms of data visualization best practices. Stephen Few has published similarly smart textbooks on best practices in charting and information dashboard design. Dona M. Wong's compact, unambiguous *The Wall Street Journal Guide to Information Graphics* (W.W. Norton, 2010) is a rule book for quick reference.

4. Joseph M. Williams, *Style: Toward Clarity and Grace* (University of Chicago Press, 1990), 1.

5. Wong, *The Wall Street Journal Guide to Information Graphics*, 90.

6. See "Terabyte" at http://www.whatsabyte.com/.

7. Mary Bells, "The First Spreadsheet—VisiCalc—Dan Bricklin and Bob Frankston," About.com Inventors, http://inventors.about.com/library/weekly/aa010199.htm.

8. For an excellent summary of the research on visual versus verbal learning styles, listen to the podcast "Visual, verbal, or auditory? The truth behind the myth of learning styles," part of a podcast series called "Learning About Teaching Physics" (http://www.compadre.org/per/items/detail.cfm?ID=11566). In it, Hal Pashler, of the University of California, San Diego, and Richard Mayer, of the University of California, Santa Barbara, review their separate work, all of which points to a muddy picture about inherent learning biases. In a meta-analysis, Pashler couldn't find many studies that were even constructed to test learning styles effectively. Mayer found that people do tend to sense that they prefer to learn one way or the other—and their brains actually respond differently—but also found that whether or not people identified as visual or verbal learners, they found visually oriented information more valuable. The podcast cohost, Michael Fuchs, says: "Our intuition of how we learn sometimes doesn't match how we actually learn." Pashler adds: "We should be very distrustful of our casual intuition about what works best for us . . . without having evidence of it." Ultimately, Mayer concludes that

"multimedia" information that combines pictures and words is what leads to "deeper understanding."

9. For the smartest discussion of the state of visualization and critique, see Fernanda Viégas and Martin Wattenberg, "Design and Redesign in Data Visualization," https://medium.com/@hint_fm/design-and-redesign-4ab77206cf9.

Chapter 1

1. Though it's popularly reported that more than 80% of brain activity is devoted to what we see, the Harvard visual perception scientist George Alvarez says the number is probably closer to 55%—still far more than for any other perceptual activity.

2. Willard C. Brinton, *Graphic Methods for Presenting Facts,* (1914) 61, 82, https://archive.org/details/graphicmethods foo0brinrich.

3. Naveen Srivatsav, "Insights for Visualizations—Jacques Bertin & Jock Mackinlay," hastac.org blog post, February 16, 2014, https://www.hastac.org/blogs/nsrivatsav/2014/02/16/insights-visualizations-jacques-bertin-jock-mackinlay.

4. Jock Mackinlay, "Automating the Design of Graphical Presentations of Relational Information," *ACM Transactions on Graphics* 5 (1986), http://dl.acm.org/citation.cfm?id=22950.

5. One computer scientist and visualization expert, who asked not to be named, has described Tufte as "basically a Bauhaus designer with an understanding of statistics."

6. William S. Cleveland and Robert McGill, "Graphical Perception: Theory, Experimentation, and Application to the Development of Graphical Methods," *Journal of the American Statistical Association* 79 (1984); "Graphical Perception and Graphical Methods for Analyzing Scientific Data," *Science* 229 (1985); and William S. Cleveland, Charles S. Harris, and Robert McGill, "Experiments on Quantitative Judgments of Graphs and Maps," *Bell System Technical Journal* 62 (1983).

7. In order to get through this history quickly so that we can move on to the practical lessons, I'm skimming right over important researchers such as Stephen Kosslyn and Barbara Tversky, among others. Suffice to say that dozens of important people and papers were influential during this time.

8. For better or worse, pie charts became anathema, while treemaps and other new procedures gained purchase.

9. I'm also speeding past the development of visualization software. It started in the 1970s, but in the past ten years the number of tools has exploded, and their ease of use is one of their core selling points. Strangely, Excel, among business's core data tools, remains in the estimation of many frustratingly behind the curve in its visualization capabilities and default settings. Most visualization software mitigates this disconnect by allowing easy imports of data from the Excel spreadsheets that businesses will no doubt continue to use.

10. See davidmccandless.com and Carey Dunne, "How Designers Turn Data into Beautiful Infographics," *Fast Company Design*, January 6, 2015, http://www.fastcodesign.com/3040415/how-designers-turn-data-into-beautiful-infographics.

11. See Manuel Lima's website, visualcomplexity.com.

12. An excellent example is "A Visual Guide to Machine Learning," R2D3, http://www.r2d3.us/visual-intro-to-machine-learning-part-1/.

13. See Alex Lundry, "Chart Wars: The Political Power of Data Visualization," YouTube video, April 28, 2015, https://www.youtube.com/watch?v=tZl-1OHw9MM.

14. M. A. Borkin, et al., "What Makes a Visualization Memorable?," *IEEE Transactions on Visualization and Computer Graphics* (Proceedings of InfoVis 2013). This research is still highly controversial. Memorability is a useful quality in a chart, but the research doesn't test the effectiveness of communicating the idea in the data, or whether the chartjunk skews attitudes toward it. Still, that the authors merely call into question the long-held belief that chartjunk is verboten indicates the provocative tenor of the new generation of research, which doesn't assume anything about tenets that *feel* true.

15. The research also suggests that pies work well when proportions are recognizable, such as 25% or 75%. J. G. Hollands and Ian Spence, "Judging Proportion with Graphs: The Summation Model," *Applied Cognitive Psychology* 12 (1998); and Ian Spence, "No Humble Pie: The Origins and Usage of a Statistical Chart," *Journal of Educational and Behavioral Statistics* 30 (2005).

16. Alvitta Ottley, Huahai Yang, and Remco Chang, "Personality as a Predictor of User Strategy: How Locus of Control Affects Search Strategies on Tree Visualizations," *Proceedings of the 33rd Annual ACM Conference on Human Factors in Computing Systems,* 2015; Caroline Ziemkiewicz, Alvitta Ottley, R. Jordan Crouser, Ashley Rye Yauilla, Sara L. Su, William Ribarsky, and Remco Chang, "How Visualization Layout Relates to Locus of Control and Other Personality Factors," *IEEE Transactions on Visualization & Computer Graphics* 19 (2013); Evan M. Peck, Beste F. Yuksel, Lane Harrison, Alvitta Ottley, and Remco Chang, "Towards a 3-Dimensional Model of Individual Cognitive Differences," *Proceedings of the 2012 BELIV Workshop: Beyond Time and Errors—Novel Evaluation Methods for Visualization* (2012).

17. Anshul Vikram Pandey et al., "The Persuasive Power of Data Visualization," *New York University Public Law and Legal Theory Working Papers*, paper 474 (2014), http://lsr.nellco.org/cgi/viewcontent.cgi?article=1476&context=nyu_plltwp.

18. Brendan Nyhan and Jason Reifler, "The Roles of Information Deficits and Identity Threat in the Prevalence of Misperceptions," June 22, 2015, http://www.dartmouth.edu/~nyhan/opening-political-mind.pdf.

19. Jeremy Boy, Ronald A. Rensink, Enrico Bertini, and Jean-Daniel Fekete, "A Principled Way of Assessing Visualization Literacy," *IEEE Transactions on Visualization and Computer Graphics* 20 (2014).

20. Michael Greicher et al., "Perception of Average Value in Multiclass Scatterplots," http://viscog.psych.northwestern.edu/publications/GleicherCorellNothelferFranconeri_inpress.pdf; Michael Correll et al., "Comparing Averages in Time Series Data," http://viscog.psych.northwestern.edu/publications/CorrellAlbersFranconeriGleicher2012.pdf.

21. *Encyclopedia Britannica Online*, s.v. "Weber's law," http://www.britannica.com/science/Webers-law.

22. Ronald A. Rensink and Gideon Baldridge, "The Perception of Correlation in Scatterplots," *Computer Graphics Forum* 29 (2010).

23. In statistics, correlation is referred to with "r" where r = -1 is negative correlation, r = 0 is no correlation, and r = 1 is correlation.

24. Lane Harrison, Fumeng Yang, Steven Franconeri, and Remco Chang, "Ranking Visualizations of Correlation Using Weber's Law," *IEEE Transactions on Visualization and Computer Graphics* 20 (2014); Matthew Kay and Jeffrey Heer, "Beyond Weber's Law: A Second Look at Ranking Visualizations of Correlation," *IEEE Transactions on Visualization and Computer Graphics* 22 (2016).

Chapter 2

1. Gestalt psychology principles are often used to describe how we see charts. For example, the law of similarity suggests that like objects, such as data categories, should share values, such as color. Throughout this chapter and in others, I offer principles that borrow from Gestalt psychology but also go beyond it to other science.

2. See "Writing Direction Index," Omniglot.com, http://www.omniglot.com/writing/direction.htm#ltr.

3. Dereck Toker, Cristina Conati, Ben Steichen, and Giuseppe Carenini, "Individual User Characteristics and Information Visualization: Connecting the Dots through Eye Tracking," *Proceedings of the SIGCHI Conference on Human Factors in Computing Systems* (2013); Dereck Toker and Cristina Conati, "Eye Tracking to Understand User Differences in Visualization Processing with Highlighting Interventions," *Proceedings of UMAP 2014, the 22nd International Conference on User Modeling, Adaptation, and Personalization* (2014).

4. No magic number exists as the threshold for the number of variables we can handle before they become "too much." I chose eight colors as a maximum on the basis of a conversation with the visualization researcher and author Tamara Munzer, who said, "There are fewer distinguishable categorical colors than you'd like. You don't get more than eight."

5. Display media limits this visualization as well. We can't zoom in to discrete points here, but all the data points are plotted, and the creator of this chart, Alex "Sandy" Pentland of MIT, had a version from which he could zoom into subsets to see all the points.

6. Researcher Steven Franconeri used this term to distinguish how we process information at two levels. The "blurry level" is fast, almost subconscious and helps us quickly pick out patterns. More deliberate parsing, which evaluates single values and compares values, is a slower process. Franconeri's point was that the blurry level, which is often disregarded when talking about making good charts, shouldn't be. He said: "Heat maps are disparaged because it's hard to pick out a single value from them. But take a year's worth of sales data, typically shown as a line graph, then imagine it as a heat map. It's hard in the heat map to read off absolute values, but ask someone what is the month with highest average sales and it turns out that the heat map is way better because you're not obsessed with the peaks and shape recognition as you would be with a line chart." George Alvarez of Harvard University

described perception similarly as happening on a "low road" and a "high road."

7. Viola S. Störmer and George A. Alvarez, "Feature-Based Attention Elicits Surround Suppression in Feature Space," *Current Biology* 24 (2014); and Steven B. Most, Brian Scholl, Erin R. Clifford, and Daniel J. Simons, "What You See Is What You Set: Sustained Inattentional Blindness and the Capture of Awareness," *Psychological Review* 112 (2005).

8. Jon Lieff, "How Does Expectation Affect Perception," Searching for the Mind blog, April 12, 2015, http://jonlieffmd.com/blog/how-does-expectation-affect-perception.

9. Scott Berinato, "In Marketing, South Beats North," *Harvard Business Review*, June 22, 2010, https://hbr.org/2010/06/in-marketing-south-beats-north/.

10. I've changed the title, subject, and data points to protect the innocent, but the structure and conventions they used remain the same.

11. Daniel M. Oppenheimer and Michael C. Frank, "A Rose in Any Other Font Wouldn't Smell as Sweet: Effects of Perceptual Fluency on Categorization," *Cognition* 106 (2008).

Chapter 3

1. For thoughtful and entertaining examinations of "crap circles," see Gardiner Morse, "Crap Circles," *Harvard Business Review*, November 2005, https://hbr.org/2005/11/crap-circles; and Gardiner Morse, "It's Time to Retire 'Crap Circles,'" *Harvard Business Review*, March 19, 2013, https://hbr.org/2013/03/its-time-to-retire-crap-circle.

2. An idea pioneered by Eric von Hippel, as cited in Marion Poetz and Reinhard Prügl, "Find the Right Expert for Any Problem, *Harvard Business Review*, June 2015, https://hbr.org/2014/12/find-the-right-expert-for-any-problem.

3. The process described here is inspired by the process used by a data analysis company called Quid. The network diagram is inspired by one of Quid's examples. See Sean Gourley, "Vision Statement: Locating Your Next Strategic Opportunity," *Harvard Business Review*, March 2011, https://hbr.org/2011/03/vision-statement-locating-your-next-strategic-opportunity.

Chapter 4

1. Clayton M. Christensen and Derek van Bever, "The Capitalist's Dilemma," *Harvard Business Review*, June 2014, https://hbr.org/2014/06/the-capitalists-dilemma.

2. Clayton M. Christensen and Derek van Bever, "A New Approach to Research," *Harvard Business Review*, June 2014, https://hbr.org/web/infographic/2014/06/a-new-approach-to-research.

3. Abela's best-known book is *Advanced Presentations by Design: Creating Communication That Drives Action*, 2nd ed. (Wiley, 2013).

4. The sketches in this book look neat and reasonably orderly. A highly skilled designer created them to be readable. You should not expect or aim to sketch as neatly

as what appears here. It's only necessary that you can interpret your sketches. Value speed over aesthetics.

5. Andrew Wade and Roger Nicholson, "Improving Airplane Safety: Tableau and Bird Strikes," http://de2010.cpsc.ucalgary.ca/uploads/Entries/Wade_2010_InfoVisDE_final.pdf.

6. See Richard Arias-Hernandez, Linda T. Kaastra, Tera M. Green, and Brian Fisher, "Pair Analytics: Capturing Reasoning Processes in Collaborative Analytics," *Proceedings of Hawai'i International Conference on System Sciences 44*, International Conference on System Sciences 44, January 2011, Kauai, Hawai'i.

7. Michael Lewis, *Flash Boys* (W.W. Norton, 2014), 222.

8. Roger Nicholson and Andrew Wade, "A Cognitive and Visual Analytic Assessment of Pilot Response to a Bird Strike," International Bird Strike Committee Annual Meeting, 2009, http://www.int-birdstrike.org/Cairns%20 2010%20Presentations/IBSC%202010%20Presentation%20-%20R%20Nicholson.pdf.

9. David McCandless, "If Twitter Was 100 People . . ." information is beautiful, July 10, 2009, http://www.informationisbeautiful.net/2009/if-twitter-was-100-people/.

Chapter 5

1. Williams, *Style*, 17.

2. Sometimes a title more like the former is not only okay but desirable. If you're striving for total objectivity, a literal transfer of facts and a straight description of the chart's structure may work fine as a headline. By using more-descriptive supporting elements, you may be shaping the audience's thinking.

3. Like Twain, Einstein is too often cited as the source of quotations. As Quote Investigator shows, we can't be sure that he said this first, but he seems to have said something like it. http://quoteinvestigator.com/2011/05/13/einstein-simple/.

4. Edward Tufte, *The Visual Display of Quantitative Information,* 2nd ed. (Graphic Press, 2001).

5. Remember, though, that the medium of presentation matters. Some grays that appear "quiet" but readable on a page disappear when projected on a large screen or in a light room. Light colors, too, may fade or disappear, or their fidelity may be low; oranges may become indistinguishable from reds. Know your equipment and choose colors that work with it.

6. The web is full of sites that help create color schemes. My favorite is paletton.com, which lets you switch easily between complementary and contrasting color schemes.

Chapter 6

1. Most recently, Steve J. Martin, Noah J. Goldstein, and Robert B. Cialdini, *The Small Big: Small Changes That Spark Big Influence* (Grand Central Publishing, 2014), about how small persuasions can lead to massive change. Cialdini is the author of several seminal works on persuasion science.

2. Steve J. Martin, from the April 2015 issue of *High Life*, the British Airways in-flight magazine.

3. Noah J. Goldstein, Steve J. Martin, and Robert B. Cialdini, *Yes!: 50 Scientifically Proven Ways to Be Persuasive* (Free Press, 2008).

4. Koert van Ittersum and Brian Wansink, "Plate Size and Color Suggestibility: The Delboeuf Illusion's Bias on Serving and Eating Behavior," *Journal of Consumer Research* 39 (2012).

5. "U.S. Budget Boosts Funding for Weapons, Research, in New Areas," Reuters, February 2, 2015, http://www.reuters.com/article/2015/02/02/us-usa-budget-arms-idUSKBN0L625Q20150202.

6. Martha McSally, "Saving a Plane That Saves Lives," *New York Times*, April 20, 2015, http://www.nytimes.com/2015/04/20/opinion/saving-a-plane-that-saves-lives.html.

7. I recognize that in the modern, blogging world, this line has smudged to near imperceptibility, a trend some rue. The point stands that reporters report, don't insert opinion without evidence, and present both sides of an argument, whereas editorials are well-structured arguments that proffer a point of view.

8. Daniel Kahneman and Richard Thaler, "Anomalies: Utility Maximization and Experienced Utility," *Journal of Economic Perspectives* 20 (2006); Amos Tversky and Daniel Kahneman, "Availability: A Heuristic for Judging Frequency and Probability, *Cognitive Psychology* 5 (1973).

9. Petia K. Petrova and Robert B. Cialdini, "Evoking the Imagination as a Strategy of Influence," *Handbook of Consumer Psychology* (Routledge, 2008), 505–524.

10. We tend to react more viscerally to the unit chart than to a statistically driven chart. This is related to a phenomenon known as *imaging the numerator.* In a notable study that demonstrates this effect, experienced psychiatrists were given the responsibility of deciding whether or not to discharge a psychiatric patient. All the doctors were given an expert analysis, but some were told by the expert that *20%* of patients like this one were likely to commit an act of violence upon release. Other doctors were told that *20 out of every 100* patients like this one were likely to commit an act of violence.

In the group that was told "20%," about 80% of the doctors decided to release the patient. In the group that was told "20 out of every 100," only about 60% suggested releasing him. The likelihood of recidivism was the same for both groups, so why the great disparity? The latter group was imaging the numerator. In the minds of those doctors, 20 out of 100 turned into 20 people committing acts of violence. The former group didn't react the same way because percentages don't commit acts of violence.

This phenomenon occurs because the experiential part of the brain—the part that relies on metaphor and narrative to create feelings—quickly and powerfully overrides the rational part that analyzes statistics. Unit charts take advantage of this. See Veronica Denes-Raj and Seymour Epstein, "Conflict Between Intuitive and Rational

Processing: When People Behave against Their Better Judgment," *Journal of Personality and Social Psychology* 66 (1994); and Paul Slovic, John Monahan, and Donald G. MacGregor, "Violence Risk Assessment and Risk Communication: The Effects of Using Actual Cases, Providing Instruction, and Employing Probability Versus Frequency Formats," *Law and Human Behavior* 24 (2000), 271–296.

11. I should note that imaging the numerator in evaluating risk is considered a negative phenomenon. For example, in the original study Denes-Raj and Epstein showed that when people were offered a chance to win money by picking red beans from a jar, they chose to pick from a jar that had more red beans even if red beans were proportionally fewer in that jar. Thus they were picking from a jar in which their odds of getting a red bean were lower. Imaging the numerator can also make us inflate risks. Paul Slovic noted in one study that when trying to communicate how infinitesimal parts per billion were, researchers told people to imagine one crouton in a 1,000-ton salad. Unfortunately, although the numerator (the crouton) was an easily understood concept, the massive salad was not. People ended up thinking that risks stated in parts per billion were more significant than they actually are. So although unit charts can persuasively convey individuality and help connect us to values by making statistics less abstract, they can also backfire or artificially exaggerate the data.

12. I kept the design and the data but changed the subject.

13. Suzanne B. Shu and Kurt A. Carlson, "When Three Charms but Four Alarms: Identifying the Optimal Number of Claims in Persuasion Settings, *Journal of Marketing* 78 (2014).

Chapter 7

1. A term coined by Matthew Zeitlin as part of a discussion with my former colleague Justin Fox, who had the temerity to tweet positively about a chart with a truncated y-axis. Read the entertaining and thoughtful account here: Justin Fox, "The Rise of the Y-Axis-Zero Fundamentalists," byjustinfox.com, December 14, 2014, http://byjustinfox.com/2014/12/14/the-rise-of-the-y-axis-zero-fundamentalists/.

2. It's hard to imagine an executive's being duped by a cumulative revenue bar chart; I include it here to be instructive. But political campaigns, cable news shows, and sometimes marketing campaigns use our lack of knowledge about topics and the briefest glimpses of dataviz to try to pass off such efforts. As this book was nearing completion, a chart that used different y-axes to show a crossover where none existed was presented in the US Congress. The chart had been constructed to suggest the number of abortions being performed had surpassed the number of cancer screenings at Planned Parenthood, when in fact screenings outnumber abortions threefold. It created a firestorm of controversy. Timothy B. Lee, "Whatever you think of Planned Parenthood, this is a terrible and dishonest chart," Vox, September 29, 2015, http://www.vox.com/2015/9/29/9417845/planned-parenthood-terrible-chart.

3. This was the case Tufte cited when arguing for truncation. You might suspect he'd be a y-axis-zero fundamentalist, but in fact he was open to the idea of truncation and cited its common use in scientific and academic circles as support for his view. "The scientists want to show their data, not zero." See the bulletin board conversation

"Baseline for Amount Scale" at http://www.edwardtufte.com/bboard/q-and-a-fetch-msg?msg_id=00003q.

4. Hannah Groch-Begley and David Shere, "A History of Dishonest Fox Charts," *Media Matters*, October 1, 2012, http://mediamatters.org/research/2012/10/01/a-history-of-dishonest-fox-charts/190225.

5. Berinato, "In Marketing, South Beats North."

6. This comes from tylervigen.com, whose owner, Tyler Vigen, is a JD student at Harvard Law School. He wrote a script that finds statistical correlations in unrelated data sets and then charted them. Vigen's examples are usually silly; he has collected them in an entertaining book, *Spurious Correlations* (Hachette Books, 2015).

7. Ioannidis was writing about data, not visualizations—specifically, how research into the effects of nutrients on the human body is notoriously dodgy: "Almost every single nutrient imaginable has peer reviewed publications associating it with almost any outcome." We can apply what he says about big data sets to the visualization of such sets. John P. A. Ioannidis, "Implausible Results in Human Nutrition Research," *BMJ*, November 14, 2013, http://www.bmj.com/content/347/bmj.f6698.

8. For an excellent discussion of this trend, see Nathan Yau, "The Great Grid Map Debate of 2015," FlowingData, May 12, 2015, https://flowingdata.com/2015/05/12/the-great-grid-map-debate-of-2015/; and Danny DeBelius, "Let's Tesselate: Hexagons for Tile Grid Maps," NPR Visuals Team, May 11, 2015, http://blog.apps.npr.org/2015/05/11/hex-tile-maps.html.

Chapter 8

1. I recommend Nancy Duarte, *HBR Guide to Persuasive Presentations* (Harvard Business Review Press, 2012); Duarte's work at Duarte.com; and Andrew Abela, *Advanced Presentations by Design: Creating Communication That Drives Action* (Wiley, 2013).

2. Mary Budd Rowe is generally considered the inventor of this educational technique, and multiple studies have confirmed its positive effects. See Mary Budd Rowe, "Wait Time: Slowing Down May Be a Way of Speeding Up!" *Journal of Teacher Education* 37 (January–February 1986), http://www.sagepub.com/eis2study/articles/Budd%20Rowe.pdf.

3. You might suggest that this presenter change the title of the chart to something that reflects the idea, such as "Money Doesn't Buy Comfort in Air Travel (Unless You Spend a Lot)."

4. Some may take exception to connecting discrete categorical data like this. For example, if I rolled this radial chart out flat, it would essentially be a line chart whose area was filled in with color. And connecting would make categorical data look like a continuous trend line, which is one of the few absolute no-nos in charting, because there is no inherent connection between categories of sales skills rankings, but a trend would suggest that they are connected. That's a fair argument, and I'd understand if you chose to forgo using radar charts because of it. But I still believe they're useful, because connecting the points radially doesn't spark the trend line convention in our minds. Instead, it makes us see a shape to which we can assign meaning.

5. Two of my favorites: Gregor Aisch et al., "Where We Came From and Where We Went, State by State," *New York Times* Upshot, August 14, 2014, http://www.nytimes.com/interactive/2014/08/13/upshot/where-people-in-each-state-were-born.html; and Timothy B. Lee, "40 Maps That Explain the Roman Empire," Vox, August 19, 2014, http://www.vox.com/2014/8/19/5942585/40-maps-that-explain-the-roman-empire.

6. Ho Ming Chow, Raymond A. Mar, Yisheng Xu, Siyuan Liu, Suraji Wagage, and Allen R. Braun, "Personal Experience with Narrated Events Modulates Functional Connectivity within Visual and Motor Systems During Story Comprehension," *Human Brain Mapping* 36 (2015).

7. Robyn M. Dawes, "A Message from Psychologists to Economists," *Journal of Economic Behavior & Organization* 39 (May 1999), http://www.sciencedirect.com/science/article/pii/S0167268199000244.

8. Ingraham's story was an online article, not a live presentation. Smartly, he broke up the page so that the visualizations were separated by enough text that the audience could see only one at a time, as if they were presentation slides. This maximizes the effect of the final reveal. Each block of text that follows its visualization could actually serve as a smart script for a live presentation, because it adds context and understanding about the amount of water we're looking at and doesn't simply repeat what we see. Christopher Ingraham, "Visualized: How the Insane Amount of Rain in Texas Could Turn Rhode Island into a Lake," Washington Post Wonkblog, May 27, 2015, http://www.washingtonpost.com/blogs/wonkblog/wp/2015/05/27/the-insane-amount-of-rain-thats-fallen-in-texas-visualized/.

9. See "Bait and Switch," changingminds.org, http://changingminds.org/techniques/general/sequential/bait_switch.html; and Robert V. Joule, Fabienne Gouilloux, and Florent Weber, "The Lure: A New Compliance Procedure," *Journal of Social Psychology* 129 (1989). This work refers more to people's commitment to a menial task when they thought they'd be doing a fun one, but the mechanism is similar: if you get someone to commit to one way of seeing things, the inconsistency upon reveal of a new way of seeing things creates tension that the person feels compelled to resolve. The greater the inconsistency, the more they will feel compelled to understand and resolve the dissonance.

10. See "Consistency," changingminds.org, http://changingminds.org/principles/consistency.htm.

11. Dietrich Braess, Anna Nagurney, and Tina Wakolbinger, "On a Paradox of Traffic Planning," *Transportation Science* 39 (November 2005), http://homepage.rub.de/Dietrich.Braess/Paradox-BNW.pdf.

12. Moran Cerf and Samuel Barnett, "Engaged Minds Think Alike: Measures of Neural Similarity Predict Content Engagement," *Journal of Consumer Research,* in review.

13. writzter, comment on "The Fallen of World War II," http://www.fallen.io/ww2/#comment-2044710701.

Chapter 9

1. Raw's URL is raw.densitydesign.org.

2. Submitting a 5,000-word feature article to 12 peers and then sitting in a circle with them as they offered an hour of critique is one of my more intense and visceral memories from graduate school.

3. Viégas and Wattenberg, "Design and Redesign in Data Visualization."

Conclusion

1. This sentence is paraphrased from Kirk Goldsberry.

2. Some visualization pros marvel at Microsoft's missed opportunity with charts and graphs in Excel, where a lot of corporate data sits. Excel wasn't originally terrible at generating charts, says Leland Wilkinson, a dataviz veteran and the author of *The Grammar of Graphics* (Springer, 2nd ed., 2005), who recently joined Tableau. "Its first charts were rather nice," he said to me. "Then they got nervous because people were out there doing chartjunk"—3-D charts and gradient fills; cones instead of flat bars; exploded pies. There's a certain look to Excel charts from the 1990s and the early 2000s that is closely identified with the prototypical business presentation: gray background, heavy horizontal grid lines, blue line with large square dots as data points. "Bad software leads people to do bad graphics," Wilkinson says. "I'm delighted by PowerPoint. If you use it right, it's wonderful. I think almost the opposite of charting in Excel." At any rate, other software and online services have filled the void left by Excel, and the ease of importing and exporting spreadsheet data has obviated the need for good charting in the spreadsheet program itself.

3. See http://atlas.cid.harvard.edu, which is also a book: http://atlas.cid.harvard.edu/book/. Also, recently launched and similarly impressive is DataViva, a site devoted to the economics of Brazil (http://en.dataviva.info/).

Illustration Credits

All sketches by James de Vries

Page number 3 (top left) Sportvision Inc.

3 (top right) Bloomberg Business

13 Catalin Ciobanu, CWT

19 (all) Wikimedia Commons

20 (both) Internet Archive

25 (top left) Martin Krzywinski, BC Cancer Research Centre

25 (top right) Poppy Field is the result of a collaboration between D'Efilippo Valentina and Nicolas Pigelet. The project is a reflection on human life lost in war, and it was launched on Commemoration Day of 2014, which marked the Centenary of the Great War. It was a war without parallel—its scale of destruction eclipsed all previous wars. Sadly, the sacrifice of lives did not end with "The war to end all wars." D'Efilippo Valentina, www.valentinadefilippo.

co.uk. Nicolas Pigelet, http://cargocollective.com/nicopigelet.

25 (bottom right) Quartz

25 (bottom left) David McCandless

28 Lane Harrison

29 (left) Lane Harrison

39 Alex "Sandy" Pentland, MIT

40 (bottom left) James de Vries

42 (top) Wikimedia Commons

55 (top left) HBR.org Visual Library

55 (top right) Created in Plot.ly

55 (bottom right) Direct Capital, a Division of CIT Bank, N.A.

55 (bottom left) Jeremykemp at English Wikipedia

59 (left) HBR.org

62 (top right) Carlson Wagonlit Travel (CWT) Solutions Group, Travel Stress Index research (2013)

65 David Sparks

66 (left) Sean Gourley, Quid Inc.

81 (top) Tom Hulme/IDEO

81 (bottom) HBR.org

93 (all charts) Created in Datawrapper.de

96 (both charts) Produced using the IN-SPIRE™ software developed at the Pacific Northwest National Laboratory, operated by Battelle for the U.S. Department of Energy, and Tableau Software

97 (all charts) Produced using the IN-SPIRE™ software developed at the Pacific Northwest National Laboratory, operated by Battelle for the U.S. Department of Energy, and Tableau Software

112 (left) "The Modi Bounce," Pew Research Center, Washington, DC (September, 2015) http://www.pewglobal.org/2015/09/17/the-modi-bounce/

112 (center) HBR.org

112 (right) Peter Dunn

117 (left) From *The New England Journal of Medicine*, Willem G. van Panhuis, M.D., Ph.D., John Grefenstette, Ph.D., Su Yon Jung, Ph.D., Nian Shong Chok, M.Sc., Anne Cross, M.L.I.S., Heather Eng, B.A., Bruce Y. Lee, M.D., Vladimir Zadorozhny, Ph.D., Shawn Brown, Ph.D., Derek Cummings, Ph.D., M.P.H., and Donald S. Burke, M.D., Contagious Diseases in the United States from 1888 to the Present, 369, 2152–2158, Copyright © (2013) Massachusetts Medical Society. Reprinted with permission from Massachusetts Medical Society.

117 (right) Republished with permission of Dow Jones Inc., from WSJ.com, "Battling Infectious Diseases in the 20th Century: The Impact of Vaccines" by Tynan DeBold and

Dov Friedman; permission conveyed through Copyright Clearance Center, Inc.

118 Max Woolf

119 Getty Images/Mark Wilson

121 (top right) Matt Parrilla

124 Jessica Hagy

125 (both) Jessica Hagy

144 (bottom) USDA/Economic Research Service, www.ers.usda.gov, Feb. 1, 2011

157 Mark Jackson

163 (top left) Scott Berinato

165 (bottom right) Tyler Vigen, tylervigen.com.

170 (right) Wikimedia Commons

171 (top) NPR

171 (bottom) J. Emory Parker

179 Bonnie Scranton

180 Carlson Wagonlit Travel (CWT) Solutions Group, Travel Stress Index research (2013)

183 (all) Methodology courtesy of Lynette Ryals, Iain Davies

184 (all) Methodology courtesy of Lynette Ryals, Iain Davies

192 (both) Christopher Ingraham, *Washington Post*

193 (both) Christopher Ingraham, *Washington Post*

198 (all) Neil Halloran, *fallen.io*

213 (both) Created with Raw

214 Created with Raw

215 © The Economist Newspaper Limited, London (4.24.15)

225 "The Atlas of Economic Complexity," Center for International Development at Harvard University, http://www.atlas.cid.harvard.edu

INDEX

ACKNOWLEDGMENTS

Publishing a book is no small thing. Publishing a book on its side, in color, with a few hundred charts is no sane thing. Fortunately, I'm surrounded by smart, energetic people who are willing to embrace a little insanity.

Principally, I need to thank **Jeff Kehoe**, my editor, whose steadfast enthusiasm for this project was eclipsed only by his patience with the author. Getting to work with someone as skilled at crafting books as Jeff is winning the editorial lottery for a first-timer like me.

Also, if you are impressed with the charts in this book—and you should be—it's because of the elite information design skills of **Bonnie Scranton**. Bonnie was given scratched-out sketches, messy data sets, rough prototypes, and sometimes just a description on the phone. With that raw material, she created the effective and elegant charts that give this book its meaning.

The compelling structure and deluxe design of what you're holding is a testament to **James de Vries**, who brings sophistication and a sense of play to everything he touches. He also masterfully penned all of the freehand sketches in this book, most of them in one go. Most of what I know about the role of design in visualization, and in life, comes from my friend James.

I'm also indebted to HBR's leadership, especially **Tim Sullivan** and **Adi Ignatius**, who championed this project; and to my HBR colleagues, including **Martha Spaulding**, who makes average prose exceptional; **Erica Truxler**, who managed innumerable and mind-numbing details; and **Allison Peter**, **Dave Lievens**, and **Ralph Fowler**, who expertly managed the construction of the book. Special thanks, too, to dataviz researcher **Lane Harrison** of Tufts University, who was beyond generous with his time and knowledge.

Thank you also to the many colleagues and friends who listened to me, read for me, and ultimately endured me, especially **Amy Bernstein**, **Stephani Finks**, **Susan Francis**, **Walter Frick**, and **Marta Kusztra**.

To these people and to anyone I've accidentally omitted, thank you for your time, knowledge, and support: Andrew Abela, Kate Adams, George Alvarez, Alison Beard, Katherine Bell, Jeremy Boy, Remco Chang, Catalin Ciobanu, #dataviz on Slack, Julie Devoll, Lindsey Dietrich, Nancy Duarte, Kevin Evers, Steven Franconeri, Kaiser Fung, Jeffrey Heer, Eric Hellweg, David Kasik, Robert Kosara, Josh Macht, Jock Mackinlay, Steve J. Martin, the Magazine Team, Sarah McConville, Dan McGinn, Maggy McGloin, Greg Mroczek, Tamara Munzer, Nina Nocciolino, Karen Palmer, Matt Perry, Keith Pfeffer, Ronald Rensink, Raquel Rosenbloom, Michael Segalla, Romain Vuillemot, Adam Waytz, the Web Team, Leland Wilkinson, and Jim Wilson.

Finally, thank you to my entire family—Sara, Emily, Molly; Vin, Paula, my siblings, and my extended family—many of whom endured a grueling night of shouting and insults over truncated y-axes.

ABOUT THE AUTHOR

Scott Berinato, senior editor at *Harvard Business Review*, is an award-winning writer, editor, content architect, and self-described "dataviz geek" who relishes the challenge of finding visual solutions to communication problems. At HBR he has championed the use of visual communication and storytelling and has launched successful visual formats, including popular narrated infographics, on HBR.org. Before joining HBR, Scott was an executive editor at CXO Media, where he pioneered the use of visual features in several of the company's publications. In addition to his work on visualization, he also enjoys writing and thinking about technology, business, science, and the future of publishing. He has a master's degree in journalism from the Medill School at Northwestern University.